Englisch in Wirtschaft und Handel

NEUE AUSGABE

Herbert Geisen ■ Dieter Hamblock
John Poziemski ■ Dieter Wessels

Cornelsen

Verfasser:	Dr. Herbert Geisen Dr. Dieter Hamblock John Poziemski Dr. Dieter Wessels
Berater/in:	Susan Lau, Pinneberg William Proctor, Essen
Verlagsredaktion:	Susanne Schütz
Außenredaktion:	Christine House
Redaktionelle Mitarbeit:	Jill Kitchen
Design / Herstellung:	Oxford Designers & Illustrators
Bildredaktion:	Uta Hübner

Erhältlich sind auch:
Audio-CD ISBN 978-3-8109-2675-3
Answer Key ISBN 978-3-8109-2676-0

www.cornelsen.de

1. Auflage, 4. Druck 2007

Alle Drucke dieser Auflage sind inhaltlich unverändert und können im Unterricht nebeneinander verwendet werden.

Druck: CS-Druck CornelsenStürtz, Berlin

ISBN 978-3-8109-2674-6

Inhalt gedruckt auf säurefreiem Papier aus nachhaltiger Forstwirtschaft.

Table of contents

Vorwort

Wie der gleichnamige Vorgänger wendet sich **Englisch in Wirtschaft und Handel** an alle, die Wirtschaftsenglisch auf einem thematisch und sprachlich anspruchsvollen Niveau lernen – in berufsbildenden Schulen, Sprachenschulen, an Fachhochschulen und Universitäten sowie an Institutionen der Erwachsenen- und Weiterbildung oder in Firmenkursen. Neben relevanten Lehrplänen wurden insbesondere die Rahmenstoffpläne der Deutschen Industrie- und Handelskammer (DIHK) berücksichtigt. Deshalb eignet sich dieses Lehrwerk zur Vorbereitung auf anerkannte Prüfungen wie die Fremdsprachenprüfungen der Industrie- und Handelskammern.

In einer stetigen Lernprogression vermittelt dieses Lehrwerk folgende Fähigkeiten:

- Die rezeptiven Kompetenzen Leseverstehen und Hörverstehen werden gezielt eingeübt. Die Lernenden sollen in die Lage versetzt werden, zumeist authentische Texte und mündlich (auf CD) vorgetragene Sequenzen unterschiedlicher Art und Länge sowohl in ihrer Gesamtheit als auch in allen Details in Verbindung mit Texterschließungsaufgaben richtig zu verstehen.
- Die produktiven Kompetenzen Sprechen und Schreiben werden ebenfalls in einer nach sprachlichen und inhaltlichen Kriterien gestuften Abfolge eingeübt. Von einfachen Meinungsäußerungen über Diskussionen und Rollenspiele bis hin zu Präsentationen sollen die Lernenden in die Lage versetzt werden, sich über wirtschaftliche Zusammenhänge in angemessener Weise zu äußern. Kompositorische Fertigkeiten werden in einer ähnlichen Stufung eingeübt – ausgehend von Satz- und Textergänzungsaufgaben, der Versprachlichung von Statistiken und Diagrammen bis hin zu Langformen (Essay). Englische Handelskorrespondenz ist kein eigener Schwerpunkt des Lehrwerks, wird jedoch ebenfalls berücksichtigt.
- Das Übersetzen – eine im internationalen Wirtschaftsleben wichtige Form der Kommunikation, die nicht ohne Grund in den Prüfungsordnungen der Industrie- und Handelskammern eine wichtige Stellung einnimmt – wird systematisch eingeübt. Diese Fertigkeit soll mit Hilfe gestufter Übungen durch Hinübersetzung (Deutsch – Englisch) und Herübersetzung (Englisch – Deutsch) entwickelt und verfestigt werden. Zudem sind im Anhang jeweils acht Übersetzungsaufgaben im Schwierigkeitsgrad der IHK-Fremdsprachenkorrespondentenprüfung enthalten.

Außerdem wird das Internet als zeitgemäßes Mittel der Kommunikation in diesem Lehrwerk in angemessener Weise berücksichtigt – als Wirtschaftsfaktor, als eigenständiges Thema, als Textquelle und als Arbeitsmittel – für die Bewältigung bestimmter Aufgaben.

Englisch in Wirtschaft und Handel will nicht zuletzt Sachkenntnisse vermitteln. Eine kommunikative Kompetenz im Bereich Wirtschaftsenglisch kann nur dann glaubhaft erworben werden, wenn die Lernenden über das notwendige Hintergrundwissen verfügen. Somit eignet sich das Lehrwerk auch zur gezielten Vorbereitung auf mündliche Prüfungen, in denen neben der Sprachkompetenz auch Sachkenntnisse nachzuweisen sind.

Die Autoren

Trade and industry: past and present

1

How have trade and industry developed over the years?

The evolution of business

Before the introduction of trade, most small social groups like families and tribes produced only as much as was necessary to cover their own basic needs. These small, isolated groups were self-sufficient in every respect. However, when these social groups became larger, more complex economic activities emerged. Since people had different skills, they concentrated on what they were best at and this division of labour led to a system of exchange known as barter.

As barter became increasingly problematic, money was introduced as a medium of exchange and markets enabled people to conduct their business transactions more efficiently. Economic activities were divided into three sectors: primary (the extraction of raw materials), secondary (the conversion of raw materials into finished products) and tertiary (the distribution of goods).

In many developing countries, the secondary or manufacturing sector will soon become the predominant industry as it did in Europe during the nineteenth century, when it created industrial cities like Manchester and Essen. The resulting concentration of production in a few locations meant that the necessary infrastructure had to be developed to make goods available wherever and whenever they were needed. This led to the expansion of businesses in the tertiary sector such as transport, banking and insurance.

In the last thirty years, there has been a dramatic shift away from manufacturing to services. In most industrialized countries, the tertiary sector has overtaken the secondary sector, so much so that many of these countries now earn 70 per cent or more of their national income from services. Health care, entertainment and tourism are the growth industries of today. New forms of working, like teleworking, are increasingly replacing traditional jobs, while modern forms of communication are likely to shift the emphasis even further in the direction of services.

The past 250 years have seen unprecedented changes in economic activity. From an agrarian society, the western world has progressed through several stages of industrialization before becoming a largely service-oriented society, while many developing countries are continuously expanding their industrial base; and who would dare predict what will happen in the future?

1 Answer the following questions on text A.

1 Why did early societies not trade with each other?
2 What is barter?
3 What are the main drawbacks of barter? (You may wish to refer to the cartoon.)
4 What are the traditional economic sectors?
5 How does the rise of the manufacturing sector affect the development of a country?
6 What has replaced the secondary sector as the major source of employment in industrialized countries and to what extent?
7 Give examples of the industries providing most employment today.
8 In your opinion, why will there be further changes in the relative importance of the three sectors?

2 Use these conjunctions to complete the following sentences.

as • because • before • but also • if • unless • until • while

1 Considerable changes will have to be made ... African countries become less dependent on the primary sector.
2 The division of labour was not introduced ... societies became larger.
3 Money was introduced ... barter had severe drawbacks.
4 The primary sector does not only include agriculture ... fishing and mining.
5 Quite a few tertiary sector jobs are concerned with trade, ... other fields like health care are also becoming more important.
6 Russia will have to invest heavily in its infrastructure ... it is to achieve a satisfactory distribution of its products.
7 The tertiary sector became highly complex ... new forms of work and innovations in the field of information technology were introduced.
8 The economic situation in many African countries will not improve ... their governments try to develop their secondary and tertiary sectors.

3 Answer the following questions on the three industrial sectors.

1 Which of the industrial sectors do these companies belong to?

2 Explain what the following people do, and say which sector they work in.

assembly-line worker • baker • bricklayer • coal miner • farmer • insurance agent • nurse • police officer • software programmer • TV presenter

3 Put the following into the correct categories below.

agriculture • chemicals • domestic trade • education • electricity • entertainment • foreign trade • forestry • insurance • mining • nursing • pharmaceuticals • retailing • roadbuilding • shipbuilding • transport • wholesaling

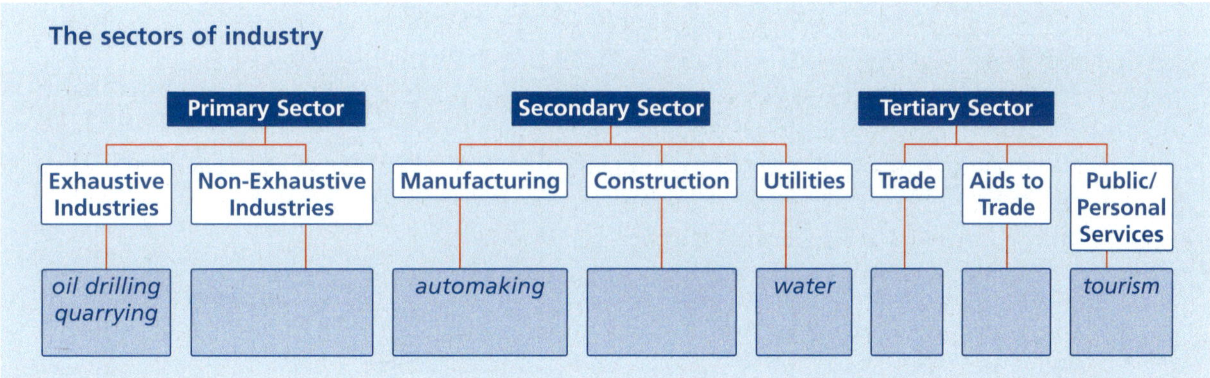

INFORMATION

Types of economic systems

- family economy: complementary skills; self-sufficient; no trade; no money
- planned economy: state sets production targets and prices; no competition; limited function of money; no private ownership of means of production and distribution; identical pay for everybody; cheap staple foods
- free-market economy: motivated by individuals' desire to accumulate wealth; prices and availability of goods determined by supply and demand; no state interference; competition as driving force; constant innovation

4 Answer the following questions on economic systems.

1 Why is it correct to say that competition leads to innovations?
2 Why are rents and staple foods so cheap in planned economies?
3 How would you describe the economic system in your own country?

TEXT B 03

Barter's latest comeback

SAN FRANCISCO

Most people know barter only from the playground where they traded baseball or soccer cards for sweets. But some American start-ups are trying to turn swapping into big business on the internet.

Barter is still alive and well – and not just in countries with chronically weak currencies. In America, it has even made something of a comeback: in 1998, roughly $10 billion in goods and services were bartered, either offline or on the internet. One reason for this revival is that barter can be attractive for small businesses keen to save money. A printing shop, for instance, can finance the purchase of goods and services it needs by printing brochures in return.

There are more than 400 regional barter exchanges in America, many of them with only a few hundred clients. Using the internet, the start-ups now want to scale barter to new levels, and hope eventually to create global exchanges. Their models are firms which have used technology to revolutionize auctions. They make bartering almost as easy as online bidding. Users sign up, have their credit checked and can then start trading goods and services. Barter firms charge both sides a transaction fee of up to 4% of the amount traded.

Making barter accessible is the easy part, however. The real challenge is attracting a critical mass of customers. Here, the two leading players have different strategies. Bigvine works closely with American Express, which is marketing this new service to its own small-business customers. By contrast, BarterTrust is acquiring old barter exchanges and bringing them online: in the past year, it has bought several offline exchanges in the United States and Canada. It hopes to create an international barter network.

Both companies are still far from reaching big numbers. BarterTrust, for instance, admits that it has about 30,000 clients, who trade a combined $1m worth of goods and services a day. The list of traded products is quite varied, however, ranging from books and services such as tax advice to airline tickets and advertising space.

It already seems clear that online barter exchanges are unlikely to grow fast. This is because, even with new technology, barter is still a tricky concept, and therefore a hard sell. Also, many businesses are reluctant to lock up value in the special trading currencies that barter exchanges use, such as 'trade dollars', rather than in cash. Moreover, online-only barter sites do not seem to work.

If these reservations can be overcome, online barter could become a trend to watch. Yet regulators might become interested in this new form of business, not least since the trading currency used by a huge barter exchange could become a rival to many weaker national currencies. And as 'trade dollars' and the like are not convertible, a successful global swapping site might even find itself in the same situation as a country with exchange controls: fighting a black market in its own currency.

(adapted from *The Economist*)

5 Explain the following words from text B.

1 currency (line 8)
2 exchange (line 19)
3 scale (line 21)
4 bidding (line 26)
5 fee (line 30)
6 acquire (line 40)
7 tax advice (line 51)
8 advertising space (line 52)
9 regulator (line 65)
10 black market (line 74)

6 Complete the sentences using these words from text B.

start-up (line 4) • offline (line 11) • revival (line 12) • accessible (line 32) • site (line 61) • reservation (line 63)

1 Of course, you cannot use internet bartering if you stay ... .
2 The term ... refers to a business that is entirely new on the market.
3 Products will only be bought if they are easily ... .
4 Barter was long regarded as extremely old-fashioned, but it appears to have experienced a ... .
5 I agree wholeheartedly – I do not have the slightest ... about this new form of business.
6 Rather than exchange goods at a market, you can now also swap them using an internet ... .

7 Answer the following questions on text B.

1 What do you usually associate with bartering arrangements?
2 How can a small business profit from bartering?
3 What is the relationship between barter firms and auction firms?
4 In what way do barter firms profit from barter transactions?
5 What different approaches do Bigvine and BarterTrust pursue?
6 How many clients does BarterTrust have and how much trade do they generate?
7 Why are many businesses reluctant to trade by barter?
8 What is the difference between 'trade dollars' and countries' currencies?

8 LETS stands for Local Exchange Trading System and is a form of community bartering. Go to the LETS homepage www.gmlets.u-net.com to find out how the system works.

9 Consider this view of the internet and discuss its global impact. Work in groups.

Revolution? What revolution?

THE INTERNET has made little difference to the lives of ordinary people. The internet is primarily an information medium, and the plain fact is that our lives are not very information-intensive.

GRAMMAR

Singular and plural nouns

- Some words ending in *-s* have no plurals:
  economics, news, acoustics
  – The good **news is** that I've got a new job.
- Other nouns without a plural are:
  advice, information, knowledge, merchandise, progress, work
  – This **information is** important.
- Words like *hundred, thousand* and *million* do not take a plural *-s* if preceded by a number:
  – Our labour costs amounted to some **two million** euros last year.
  – This item will cost **thousands** of dollars.
- Latin and Greek words usually retain their original plural form:
  analysis ➔ analyses, criterion ➔ criteria, medium ➔ media
- The following nouns, which can be singular or plural in German, are plural words in English:
  clothes, goods, premises, savings, surroundings
- Nouns denoting a group of people rather than the institution are followed by the plural form of the verb:
  – The board **are** of the opinion ...
  – The board **consists** of 21 members.
  – The police **believe** that ...
  – The Metropolitan Police **was** founded in 1829.
  – England **sweep** to victory ...
  – England **is** one of four countries which make up the UK.
  – The majority of applicants **are** ...
  – The government's majority **has been** reduced to a mere three.

10 Choose the correct forms of the verb *to be* to complete these sentences.

1 Politics ... fascinating for some people.
2 The media ... dependent on advertising.
3 Our premises ... in Maid Marian Way, Nottingham.
4 The family ... one of the oldest social institutions.
5 All my family ... insured against accidents.
6 The goods ... in almost perfect condition.
7 The news ... disappointing.
8 The necessary information ... missing.

11 Translate the following sentences.

1 Viele Berufe im Primärsektor verlieren zunehmend an Bedeutung.
2 Früher versorgten sich kleine soziale Gruppen selbst.
3 Rohstoffe wurden ursprünglich gegen Fertigerzeugnisse getauscht.
4 Die Ware ist heute angekommen.
5 In einem kapitalistischen System werden Preise durch Angebot und Nachfrage bestimmt.
6 Ohne Konkurrenz kann es keine Marktwirtschaft geben.
7 Verschiedene Analysen haben gezeigt, dass Millionen von Menschen kein Interesse an Politik haben.
8 Wir können die Frage erst beantworten, wenn wir alle erforderlichen Informationen haben.
9 Die moderne Form des Tauschhandels wird nur erfolgreich sein, wenn alle wichtigen Kriterien erfüllt sind.
10 Wirtschaftskrisen hat es immer gegeben.
11 In unserer Firma sind gute Englischkenntnisse unbedingt erforderlich.
12 Im Laufe der Jahrhunderte hat die menschliche Zivilisation große Fortschritte gemacht.

The UK and the USA: facts and figures

2

Choose the correct answer.

1 Fifty stars but how many stripes in the US flag?
- a eleven
- b twelve
- c thirteen

2 Not part of Great Britain?
- a Scotland
- b Wales
- c Northern Ireland

3 Location of Manchester?
- a North West England
- b Midlands
- c East Anglia

4 US state with the largest population?
- a California
- b Florida
- c Texas

5 Time difference between New York and Los Angeles?
- a three hours
- b four hours
- c five hours

6 Centre of the US computer industry?
- a Death Valley
- b Monument Valley
- c Silicon Valley

7 UK oil capital?
- a Aberdeen
- b Bristol
- c Liverpool

8 Centre of the US motor industry?
- a Chicago
- b Detroit
- c Pittsburgh

9 American industrialist?
- a John Ford
- b Henry Ford
- c Gerald Ford

10 Centre of UK finance?
- a The City
- b The Docklands
- c The West End

TEXT A 04

The United Kingdom

The United Kingdom has a population of approximately 60 million (more than France or Italy, less than Germany) and a surface area of 243,000 km^2 (less than France, Germany or Italy). It is one of the most urbanized countries in the world.

The British economy is based on services, international trade and manufacturing. In the 1980s and 1990s, the production of coal, steel and ships, the utilities (i.e. the production and distribution of water, gas and electricity), British Rail and British Airways were privatized. Although Britain's gross national product (GNP*) is growing faster than the population, its GNP per capita lags behind that of many other western European countries.

Agriculture accounts for 2% of GNP and employs some 2% of the workforce. But despite high production levels in grain farming and also in livestock farming (cattle, sheep, pigs and poultry), areas in which the UK is almost self-sufficient, Britain has to import fruit and vegetables on a large scale to cover its food requirements.

Mining, oil and gas contribute approximately 6% to GNP with less than 1% of the country's workforce. The exploitation of oil and gas from the North Sea fields has enabled the UK to become self-sufficient with regard to fuels.

With 22% of the labour force, manufacturing industries contribute 24% to GNP. Small companies predominate. The major manufacturers include motor vehicles, aerospace equipment, information technology (IT) and telecommunications equipment, metal products, precision instruments, pharmaceuticals and chemicals. Since the early 1980s, massive cutbacks have hit the traditional smokestack industries like steel, shipbuilding and textiles. The cleaner high-tech industries have not been able to offset job losses in the old industrial centres in the Midlands and the North, especially since many new firms prefer locations in the South. The so-called M4 corridor between London and Bristol has been the centre of this development. "Silicon Glen" between Glasgow and Edinburgh is also a notable exception in that a number of Japanese and US computer firms have located factories there.

The service industries continue to grow. They now account for over two thirds of GNP and, at the same time, are the only sectors creating new jobs. About three quarters of the working population in the UK are employed in the service sector, with financial services, tourism, trade and transport being among the fastest growing industries. Again, the South has benefited most from this development.

* GNP = gross national product: total value of goods and services produced by a country in a year, including net income from abroad. Today also the following term is used: GNI: gross national income.

1 Find words in text A to match the following definitions.

1 having the character and infrastructure of a town
2 make up a particular amount of something
3 transferred from state to private ownership
4 able to produce everything necessary without needing to import goods
5 discovery, removal and processing of raw materials
6 be most important or most frequent
7 reductions in production and workforce
8 balance out
9 particular place or position
10 profited

2 Provide the correct figures on the UK from text A.

1 agriculture's contribution to GNP
2 contribution of mining, oil and gas to GNP
3 manufacturing sector's share of GNP
4 percentage of the labour force in the manufacturing sector
5 percentage of the UK workforce employed in the service industries
6 service sector's approximate share of GNP
7 surface area of the UK
8 UK population

INFORMATION

Discussing statistics

- first make a general statement indicating what the whole set of figures is about
- proceed from the general to the specific
- point to striking developments and also state what has not changed
- use figures or percentages to indicate trends
- end with a comment to sum up your observations

3 Describe the development of these UK employment figures. Use the outline below.

UK employment figures between 1980 and 2000.
in 000s employed

Sector	1980	1990	2000
Primary sector	**1,099**	**771**	**471**
Secondary sector	**8,180**	**6,295**	**4,945**
Tertiary sector	**13,712**	**15,679**	**17,225**
Total	**22,991**	**22,745**	**22,641**

(source: *Britain 2001 – The Official Yearbook of the United Kingdom*)

The table shows the development of employment figures ...
While in 1980 the primary sector still employed ...
While both the primary ..., these job losses were only partly offset by ...
To sum up, total employment in the UK between ... saw ...

TEXT B

05

Southern Nevada

Southern Nevada has arrived. Countless surveys and news stories praise the Las Vegas Valley as the fastest growing state, the new business hub of the West, economically strong, having the lowest taxes, one of the best places in America to live; and the list goes on.

Less than a decade ago, analysts were predicting Southern Nevada's population would reach 1,000,000 by the year 2000. Surpassing even the most ambitious predictions, our area topped the million mark in 1994. As experts examine the future of the Las Vegas Valley, the latest predictions indicate the area's population will double by the year 2005.

It comes as no surprise that the housing market is among the nation's fastest growing. So far, we seem to be on track for another record year in new home sales. The cost of living in Southern Nevada is substantially lower than in most western urban areas. As an example, the average price of a home in the Las Vegas Valley is about $50,000 less than the same home would cost in Los Angeles and $75,000 less than in San Diego.

Aside from its pro-business attitude, the area offers a favorable tax structure, a talented labor force, reasonably priced commercial land and low utility and transportation costs.

Consequently, there is a consolidated effort to make Southern Nevada an attractive destination for companies seeking to relocate or expand. For example, the City of Las Vegas is the developer/owner of three mixed-use business parks. Last year, the Nevada Development Authority assisted over 34 non-gaming companies to relocate here, creating more than 3,000 new jobs. The vast majority of these companies arrived from California, with manufacturing representing the largest type of industry. As Southern Nevada continues to prosper, all indicators point to an increasing number of businesses relocating here in the future.

One of the fastest growing industries in Southern Nevada is retail. The number of new retail stores opening far outpaces all expectations. Many of these shops can now be found in mega resorts, such as the Forum Shops at Caesars Palace. Sixty percent of the gross revenue generated at Treasure Island is non-gaming. That is revolutionary!

Today, the tourism industry, with over 32 million visitors last year, continues to be the lifeblood of the Las Vegas Valley. The gaming industry, which contributes about one-third of the state's tax revenue, has never been healthier. A number of resorts are currently under construction, or nearing completion, and will add over 27,000 new rooms to our inventory, which is already the largest in the nation, bringing our room total to over 118,600!

Regardless of where you look in Southern Nevada, you'll see a dynamic community that's on the move – a community that made quality of life a way of life. Regardless of how the community is measured, one thing is clear, Southern Nevada has arrived!

4 Explain the following terms from text B.

1 business hub (line 4)
2 prediction (line 12)
3 be on track (line 19)
4 commercial land (line 32)
5 business park (line 40)
6 relocate (line 42)
7 outpace expectations (lines 53–54)
8 gross revenue (line 58)
9 resort (line 67)
10 on the move (line 75)

5 What do the following figures from text B refer to?

1 1,000,000
2 2005
3 $75,000
4 three
5 3,000
6 32 million
7 one-third
8 118,600

6 Ask ten questions on text B using these question words.

why • what • how many • where • when

EXAMPLE *Why is Southern Nevada such an attractive location?*

7 Ask and answer your questions from exercise 6. Work in pairs.

EXAMPLE *... because its economy is doing well, taxes are low and people like living there.*

INFORMATION

Facts and figures on US employment and trade (2000)

Employment

agriculture	2.6%
industry	23.9%
services	73.5%

Contribution to GDP*

agriculture	1.6%
industry	25.2%
services	73.2%

Exports

engineering products & transport equipment	45%
industrial raw materials	22%
consumer goods	12%
vehicles & parts	11%
food	7%

Imports

consumer goods	23%
industrial raw materials	22%
capital goods	22%
vehicles & parts	16%
computers & related equipment	7%
crude oil & oil products	6%
food	4%

Export destinations

Canada	23%
Mexico	12%
Japan	9%
Britain	6%
Germany	4%
Taiwan	3%

Countries of origin

Canada	19%
Japan	13%
Mexico	10%
China	8%
Germany	5%
Britain	4%
Taiwan	4%

* GDP = gross domestic product: total value of all goods and services produced by a country in a year, less the net income from abroad (see GNP page 14)

8 Complete this text with some of the facts and figures on page 17.

Engineering products and transport equipment account for 45% of US exports, followed by industrial raw materials and ...[1] with ...[2] and 12% respectively. The share of vehicles and parts in US exports is ...[3], while ...[4] products make up 7% of the export total. It is interesting to observe that the range of goods imported is similar to the range of goods exported. The US is a major importer of ...[5], which make up 23% of total imports. The percentage figures for imports and exports of ...[6] are identical. In percentage terms, the US imports more ...[7] than it exports (16% and 11% respectively). Despite the huge reserves of petroleum, ...[8] make up no less than 6% of total US imports. Only a small number of countries account for close to 60% of US foreign trade in volume terms. The neighbouring countries, Canada and Mexico, are the most important ...[9], taking up a total of 35% of US exports. Japan accounts for ...[10] of US exports, followed by Britain and ...[11] with 6% and 4% respectively. With 19% Canada also heads the list of the ...[12] of US imports, followed by ...[13] and ...[14] with 13% and 10% respectively, while the People's Republic of China accounts for no less than 8% of US imports.

9 Match the English and German terms and then translate the sentences.

1 account for	a ähnlich wie; annähernd gleich hoch wie
2 respectively	b ausmachen; entfallen auf
3 similar to	c beziehungsweise
4 range of goods	d in Prozent ausgedrückt
5 in percentage terms	e mengenmäßig
6 in volume terms	f Produktpalette

1 US exports to Mexico and Japan amount to 12% and 9% respectively.
2 In volume terms, almost a fifth of US foreign trade is with Canada.
3 The employment level in the service industry is similar to that industry's contribution to GDP.
4 The range of goods imported covers everything from food to crude oil.
5 In percentage terms, the US exports more food than it imports.
6 Engineering products account for 45% of US exports.

GRAMMAR

Adjectives: comparatives and superlatives

- Adjectives with one syllable take *-er* and *-est: high, higher, highest.*
- Adjectives with two syllables usually take *more* and *most: more/most modern.*
- However, if they are stressed on the second syllable or have one of the following endings: *-y, -er, -ow, -le*, they can also take *-er* and *-est: remote, remoter, remotest; wealthy, wealthier, wealthiest.*
- Adjectives with three or more syllables take *more* and *most: more/most profitable.*
- Some frequently used adjectives have irregular comparatives and superlatives: *good, better, best; bad, worse, worst; little, less, least.*

NOTE Comparative adjectives are followed by *than*, not *as*:
– The cost of living in Southern Nevada is lower **than** in most western urban areas.

10 Make complete sentences using the comparative or superlative.

EXAMPLE M25 / busy / motorway / Britain
The M25 is the busiest motorway in Britain.

1 UK / urbanized / countries / world
2 Scotland / densely populated / England
3 job losses / bad / smokestack industries
4 tourism industry / healthy / today / ten years ago
5 taxes / Southern Nevada / low / other states
6 housing / fast growing / industry / US
7 manufacturing / large / industries / Nevada
8 agricultural output / US / little / two per cent / GDP
9 Canada / important / trading partner / US
10 service sector / big / employer / UK / US

11 Translate the following sentences.

1 Auf Grund der niedrigen Lebenshaltungskosten sind Immobilien in Süd-Nevada stark gefragt.
2 Immobilienpreise in Nevada liegen deutlich unter denen von Los Angeles.
3 Fremdenverkehr und Glücksspiel sind Nevadas Haupteinnahmequellen.
4 In Prozentzahlen führen die USA genauso viele Industrierohstoffe ein, wie sie ausführen.
5 Sowohl in Großbritannien als auch in den USA trägt der Dienstleistungssektor erheblich mehr als 65 Prozent zum Bruttosozialprodukt bei.
6 Flächenmäßig ist Großbritannien kleiner als beispielsweise Frankreich oder Deutschland.
7 Das Pro-Kopf-Bruttosozialprodukt Großbritanniens wächst zurzeit schneller als seine Bevölkerung.
8 Der Norden Englands hat weniger von der Entwicklung im Tourismus profitiert als der Süden.
9 Die USA, Frankreich, Deutschland und die Niederlande gehören zu den wichtigsten Handelspartnern Großbritanniens.
10 Im Jahre 2000 wurden im Primärsektor deutlich weniger Menschen beschäftigt als zehn Jahre zuvor.
11 Die Zahl der Beschäftigten in der herstellenden Industrie macht weniger als ein Drittel der Gesamtbeschäftigtenzahl aus.
12 Mehr als 30% der amerikanischen Exporte entfallen auf die beiden Nachbarländer Kanada und Mexiko.

3 Tourism and business travel

What do the people in the photos need or expect when they travel?

TEXT A 06

CHAOS ON THE COSTAS

Hot, noisy and uncomfortable. The beaches of Benidorm are going to be packed this summer and flying tempers could be the name of the game in overcrowded resorts as Brits and Germans fight for a poolside sunbed or a patch of sand.

Chaos on the Costas is a very real prospect, but it is also a good description of what is going on among the big package companies in the European holiday industry. In the struggle for market domination, experts predict a big shake-up. As the summer booking period reaches its peak, all eyes are on the two new German corporate names – Preussag (TUI) and Condor Neckermann Touristik (C&N), who are expected to dominate the tourist market in Europe over the next couple of years.

UK market leader Thomson and high street chain Thomas Cook are in fact already owned by the Germans. Ironically, one of the main forces which is believed to be driving consolidation is a shortage of accommodation in the mass tourism resorts of Spain. After years of diversification away from the Mediterranean beach package into long haul and cruising, the package in Majorca is back in vogue and players are fighting over limited hotel capacity.

BUCKET AND SPADE BRIGADE: EUROPE'S TOP SIX

Tour operator	Package holidays	Agencies	Planes	Ships	Hotels
TUI	13.5m	3,469	60	4	164
Airtours	9.0m	940	47	11	26
Thomson	7.0m	862	41	4	13
C&N	6.0m	1,200	39	0	51
Kuoni	4.0m	150	3	0	2
First Choice	3.2m	300	25	1	0

Martin Brackenbury, a director of Airtours and president of the International Federation of Tour Operators, says: "In the eighties there were more and more new destinations – small Greek islands, Kenya, Goa in India, the Far East, Florida and the Caribbean. But new package travel regulations made it more difficult to expand into developing countries. So instead of going to more new destinations, the big companies in the UK and on the Continent flocked back to the Med. Mediterranean resorts are under extreme pressure, with planning restrictions preventing expansion. So big UK and German tour operators are falling over themselves to sign long-term contracts with Spanish hoteliers."

The irony about current developments in the European tourist industry is that, for most of the nineties, UK operators were trying to buy up their German counterparts, rather than the other way round. But complicated German ownership structures, often involving state-owned banks, made takeovers difficult if not impossible.

At the start of the twenty-first century, it is the Germans who have woken up first and placed their towel on the UK corporate sunbed. Will the Brits be forced into the shade?

(adapted from *The Observer*)

1 Explain the following words and phrases from text A.

1 package company (line 11)
2 market domination (line 13)
3 shake-up (line 14)
4 booking period (lines 14–15)
5 accommodation (line 26)
6 diversification (line 28)
7 tour operator (lines 35–36)
8 planning restriction (lines 47–48)
9 ownership structure (line 58)
10 takeover (line 59)

2 Answer the following questions on text A.

1 What impression of a Mediterranean holiday does the article convey?
2 What is happening in the European holiday industry?
3 What is the main problem operators are facing in Spanish resorts?
4 Why have tour operators shifted away from developing countries?
5 How are tour operators reacting to planning restrictions?
6 Why did UK operators have problems taking over German companies?
7 What does the idea of the towel on the sunbed refer to?

3 **Which expressions in text A do these cartoons illustrate? Explain them in your own words.**

1

2

3

4

4 **Replace the verbs in brackets with suitable phrasal verbs.**

1 Last year's increase in the number of overseas visitors to this country is (attributed to) … the advertising efforts of the British Tourist Authority.
2 All you have to do is to (save) … a certain amount each month for your Swiss skiing holiday.
3 We won't (accept) … second-rate accommodation at that price.
4 Going to the Antarctic seems a rather strange proposal to (make) … .
5 Italy's tourist earnings this year are (thought to be) … €34bn.
6 As we are somewhat short of money, we may have to (postpone) … our trip to LA.
7 The government has (passed) … new legislation to protect holidaymakers.
8 You'll have to (do) … a lot of overtime to get a few more days off.

put aside reserve money for a particular purpose
put at calculate or estimate
put down to consider sth the result of sth
put forward suggest
put in devote time
put off delay
put through proceed with and complete successfully
put up with tolerate or bear

TEXT B 07

CLICK TO GO

BY THE TIME IT TAKES you to read this article, several thousand airline reservations and several hundred hotel rooms will probably have been booked on the worldwide web by internet users from around the globe. But given the explosive growth of online activity worldwide, even this estimate – and nobody really knows the true figures – may be far too conservative.

Online travel booking has become a reality; more money, in fact, is spent on travel e-commerce in the US than on all the other consumer e-commerce sectors, such as books, music and even computer equipment.

Travel is an ideal product for selling over the internet. Already all the airlines and much of the hotel availability is included on databases, the so-called global distribution or computer reservations systems. From here it is only one short step to offering flights or hotel rooms via the internet. Moreover, unlike other forms of e-commerce, travel carries no problems (or costs) with getting the goods to the consumer; in fact, it is the traveller who goes to the product, be it airline or hotel. And with the development of electronic ticketing for airlines, there is less and less need for any paper transaction to be carried out in advance.

Times are changing in the way that the distribution of airline seats and hotel rooms are sold. Hotel reservations specialist Utell International, for example, reports that online reservations are increasing at a rate of 35 per cent a month, which it says confirms the internet as the company's fastest growing distribution channel. Heather Barnaby, European managing director, says, "The internet will be the biggest challenge of the next decade for the travel sector."

For companies, these developments provide an opportunity to take more control over their travel spending strategy, utilizing the power of new technology to capture and control data as never before. For suppliers, including airlines, hotels and car rental companies, new technology poses a threat to the way they do business, but also an opportunity to secure new sales.

But should business travellers continue to use a specialist business travel agency to make their bookings? After all, if you can book direct via the internet, why choose an agent?

"The death of the travel agent has been predicted many times," says Richard Lovell, European vice-president for business travel agency Carlson Travel. "But it seems to me that the major agents are getting stronger at playing their role in distributing rooms and seats to corporates than ever before."

He notes, for example, that at the start of the 1990s, only about 10 per cent of hotel rooms were being sold to companies through travel agents such as Carlson. Now that figure is at least 30 per cent or more.

Certainly the travel growth on the web this year has mainly been directed towards leisure travellers. But such is the power of the web's growth that it is clearly going to have a major impact on business travel in the years ahead.

What next? The age of the electronic traveller is virtually upon us as a result of the web: executives will, in a few years, be able to use a palmtop computer to book a flight, download an electronic ticket, look up flight schedules and even check in by beaming a hand-held computer at a receiver at the gate. Business travel will never be the same again.

(adapted from *Business Life*)

5 Match the terms below with those from text B.

cost of business trip • increasing volume of travel • issue of travel documents • large company • non-electronic business activity • rapid increase • room vacancies • route of goods to customers

1 explosive growth (line 7)
2 hotel availability (lines 19–20)
3 ticketing (line 31)
4 paper transaction (lines 32–33)
5 distribution channel (line 43)
6 travel spending (line 50)
7 corporate (line 70)
8 travel growth (line 78)

6 True or false? Correct these statements on text B where necessary.

1 Travel booking on the internet is the most successful of all e-commerce sectors.
2 Tourism lends itself quite naturally to online transactions.
3 Online reservations are currently increasing by 35 per cent annually.
4 Companies are very sceptical about the increase in online booking.
5 Online booking poses a serious threat to travel agents.
6 Businesses are increasingly relying on the services of travel agents.
7 Since 1990 the number of hotel rooms booked online has more than trebled.
8 Online booking will make travelling even easier than it is today.

7 Complete the sentences using the information in text B.

1 When you have finished reading this article, …
2 More money is spent on travel e-commerce than on …
3 Travel e-commerce is so convenient for the suppliers of tourist services because …
4 Of all Utell's distribution channels, …
5 In addition to hotels, suppliers include …
6 Even today, the vast majority of hotel rooms …
7 Online booking is still primarily designed for …
8 In the not-too-distant future, hand-held computers will …

08

8 Booking hotel accommodation: listen to the phone call and complete the booking form.

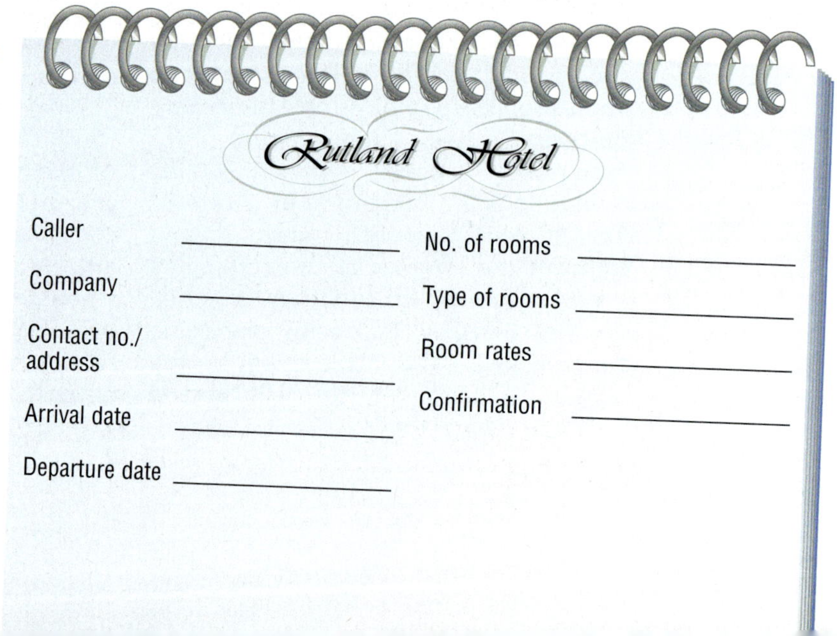
Rutland Hotel

Caller ____________
Company ____________
Contact no./ address ____________
Arrival date ____________
Departure date ____________
No. of rooms ____________
Type of rooms ____________
Room rates ____________
Confirmation ____________

9 Use the role card below to make a hotel booking by telephone. The reservations manager's role card is on page 134.

Julia Schmidt of Kaufstadt AG rings up the Mackintosh Hotel in Glasgow, on behalf of her boss, to book accommodation for a conference.

Caller

- *sales managers' conference 18/8*
- *arrival: 17/8, departure: 19/8*
- *requirements:*
  - *double room for two nights*
  - *quiet room*
  - *conference room and refreshments for 8 persons: 18/8 (usual equipment)*
- *check rates*
- *ask for confirmation*
- *email: kaufstadt@t-online.de*

09

Now listen to the model answer.

GRAMMAR

The simple present and present continuous

The simple present is primarily used for:

- regular occurrences:
  - Planes from Europe usually **land** at JFK Airport or Newark, NJ.
- habits and customs:
  - Many of our guests **come** here on business.
- timetables:
  - The ferry **departs** every 15 minutes.

NOTE As a rule, certain verbs only take the simple present, e.g. *believe, belong, hear, include, know, like, matter, mean, own, resemble, understand.*

The present continuous is primarily used for:

- actions in progress at the present time:
  - **I'm trying** to find accommodation in London.
- future arrangements:
  - **I'm flying** to Edinburgh next month.
- present-time actions with increasing or decreasing momentum:
  - New York **is becoming** more and more expensive.

10 Complete the sentences using the simple present or present continuous.

1 Although most people (own) … cars, car rental companies are very successful.
2 The consumer (become) … very good at shopping around for bargain holidays.
3 Thousands of small hotels (increasingly post) … their details on the internet.
4 Short city breaks (be) … more popular than ever.
5 From charming to elegant, we (have) … the locations to suit you.
6 Experts (believe) … that tourist spending in Britain will reach £24.3bn.
7 Access is limited as our hotel (undergo) … major refurbishment.
8 Increasingly, young people (turn) … their backs on cheap package tours.
9 The internet, experts say, (drive) … independent travel rapidly forward.
10 Announcement: dinner (now be served) … in the restaurant on B Deck.

11 Translate the following sentences.

1 Nächste Woche fahren wir zur Modemesse nach Mailand.
2 Die Nachfrage nach Hotelunterkünften in spanischen Urlaubsorten wird immer größer.
3 Der Reiseveranstalter haftet für alle Handlungen des Hoteliers.
4 In vielen Fällen ist die örtliche Bevölkerung nicht mehr bereit, sich mit dem Verhalten mancher Touristen abzufinden.
5 Viele Reiseveranstalter besitzen heutzutage sogar Hotels und Schiffe.
6 Nordeuropäische Reiseveranstalter verhandeln zurzeit mit spanischen Hotelbesitzern.
7 Unternehmen verlassen sich weitgehend auf Reisebüros, wenn sie Geschäftsreisen planen.
8 Heutzutage werden 70 Prozent aller Hotelbuchungen per Internet vorgenommen.
9 Junge Leute buchen nicht mehr so häufig Pauschalreisen wie früher.
10 Unser Verkaufsleiter reist in der nächsten Woche nach Cardiff.
11 Unser Flugzeug kommt morgen früh um 7.30 in Detroit an.
12 Wir werden zurzeit von Anfragen nach billigen Busreisen überschwemmt.

4

Personal banking

Do you have a bank account? What do you use it for?

TEXT A 10

BANKING SERVICES IN THE UK

Banking with us helps you control your money. A current account offers you – the account holder – everything you need to make your day-to-day banking easier:

- A debit card for a quick and easy way to pay for whatever you buy
- Instant access to your account from any of our cashpoints – free of charge
- Free direct debits providing an easy way to pay bills
- A convenient way to manage your account by phone, at times that suit you
- An overdraft facility as a safety net for emergency spending
- Free cheques, deposits and transfers
- Regular account statements so that you can see payments into and out of your account

It all adds up to a convenient way to control your money.

→

YOU CAN PAY in cash or cheques, free of charge, at any of our branches. Many have machines where you can pay in money automatically. We can arrange for money you receive regularly to be credited direct to your account.

Whatever you buy day-to-day, our debit card makes paying for it quick and easy. You can use your debit card at supermarkets, shops and DIY stores, plus thousands of smaller shops, restaurants and hotels. Our cards are welcome at over 300,000 places in the UK. Your debit card gives you access to your account, and withdrawals of up to £200 from any of our cashpoints are free of charge.

The easiest way for you to pay bills of varying amounts is by direct debit and regular bills of fixed amounts is by standing order. They are easy to set up – just ask your branch for details. We'll also give you a cheque book for those bills that you prefer to pay by cheque.

To help you keep track of your money, we'll send you regular statements. You can also keep track of your money by using your card to check how much money is in your account and print out a statement.

If you sign up for our telephone banking service, you can also manage your account by phone – 24 hours a day and 365 days a year. You can use it to check the balance of your account, order a statement and transfer money between your savings and current accounts. Of course, you may prefer to use our electronic banking facility for your transactions.

Sometimes you may find you need to spend more money than you have in your account. If you think this is going to happen, you only have to talk to us about applying for an overdraft or a personal loan. Once we've approved your application, you'll have an arrangement that allows you to borrow up to an agreed amount. If you use £10 or less of your overdraft, we'll waive the interest. If you use your agreed overdraft, you'll be charged a £5 monthly fee on the amount you use. And you'll have no charges at all when you are in credit.

You'll find it easy to open your account with us. And if you are moving your account to us, we'll help you make the transfer as smooth as possible. We'll also give you a welcome pack to help you get the most from your account.

1 Match the definitions with the terms below.

account statement • balance • cashpoint • direct debiting • interest • overdraft facility • personal loan • savings account • standing order • transfer

1 amount of money paid by the bank for the money in your savings account
2 difference between the amounts paid into and withdrawn from an account
3 "hole-in-the-wall" machine for withdrawing money around the clock
4 list showing amounts paid in and taken out of a bank account
5 authorizing an organization to transfer money from your account
6 amount of money borrowed from the bank
7 movement of money from one account to another
8 order to the bank to pay the same amount regularly
9 agreement allowing you to withdraw money in excess of your balance
10 type of account where the money paid in earns interest

2 Answer the following questions on text A.

1 What is a debit card?
2 Why is it a good idea to have a debit card?
3 How can you pay your bills?
4 Why is it useful to get regular statements?
5 How can you pay money into your account?
6 Why might some customers want to use the telephone banking facility?
7 What should you do if you wish to spend more than you have in your account?
8 What is the level of charges you have to pay for banking services?

3 Write a short text explaining what a current account is useful for.

4 Which banks offer the most and the least favourable terms for students?

	Abbey National	HSBC	Lloyds TSB	Royal Bank of Scotland
Contact	0800 731 777	0800 130 130	0845 3000 184	0808 1000148
Max. daily cashpoint withdrawal	**£500**	**£500**	**£200**	**£250**
Number of free cash-points	**25,000+**	**7,000**	**9,800**	**27,000+**
Interest earned with account in credit	**0.1%**	**0.19%**	**Nil**	**3.05%**
Max. free overdraft	Year 1: **£1,000** Year 2: **£1,250** Year 3: **£1,500**	Year 1: **£750** Year 2: **£1,000** Year 3: **£1,250**	Year 1-3: **£1,500**	Year 1: **£1,000** Year 2: **£1,300** Year 3: **£1,600**
Special offers	free WAP phone and 33% off bills or £40 cash	£50 cash or four-year Young Persons Railcard	£40 for existing customers or their children	20% off books, CDs, DVDs and computer software, 25% off concert tickets and travel insurance

(adapted from *The Independent*)

INFORMATION

Cheques

Even today, a large number of bills in Britain and the USA are still paid by cheque, which is a written instruction to an account holder's bank to pay a specified amount to a person named or to the person presenting it (open cheque) or into someone's account (crossed cheque). Here is a typical crossed cheque provided by the Royal Bank of Scotland to its personal customers.

5 Find the following information on the cheque above.

1 account number
2 amount
3 cheque counterfoil
4 cheque crossing
5 cheque number (2×)
6 date
7 name of account holder
8 name of payee
9 name of bank
10 sort code

6 Discuss the pros and cons of cheques. Work in groups.

11

7 Telephone banking: listen to the dialogue and answer the questions.

1 What is the name of the caller's bank?
2 Who is the caller?
3 What is her account number?
4 What is the account holder's balance?
5 Who is the remittance to be made to?
6 What is the payee's bank branch?
7 What is the payee's address?
8 What is the payee's account number?
9 What is the sort code?
10 How much is to be remitted?

TEXT B 12

BANKING IN AMERICA

IN 1987 THERE WERE 13,723 commercial banks in the US. By 1999 there were just 9,143. In the early months of 2000 alone, there were 117 mergers, mostly small. The speed of consolidation has led to many complaints from customers that they can't keep track of their bank's name. If you opened an account with Centerre Bank in Missouri, you will have seen your bank change ownership and names four times in twenty years.

The US has a tradition, dating back to the nineteenth century, of community banks with a few branches in one town. In some states, such as Illinois, it was illegal for banks – however much business they did – to have more than one branch. Almost all state governments prevented their banks from operating outside state borders.

The system was designed to prevent small communities being pushed around by monopolistic banks. But it has resulted in an industry that is extremely fragmented, with consequences that many Europeans consider pre-historic if not comical. Many Americans cannot use their cheque books or any cashpoint machines if they cross the state border. It can often be difficult or expensive to send money to people in other states.

That system is now coming to an end. "It's been an evolution rather than a revolution," says David Berry, head of research at a renowned financial analyst. "States have been cutting back the regulations restricting the way their banks operate, allowing them to offer other services and operate in other regions. Federal law was changed a couple of years ago, simply recognizing what had already happened at state level."

But most analysts reckon that the deals made in June 2000 represent a change in the process. BankAmerica and Nations Bank will have 8 per cent of all bank deposits in the country with 29 million customers in 22 states. Banc One and First Chicago NBD will do business across 14 states with 4 per cent of bank deposits. David Coulter, who will be president of the enlarged BankAmerica says, "We've taken a giant, even historic step."

These deals are seen as first attempts to create truly national banks, operating from all areas, with brand names as readily recognized as Coca-Cola. Customers will be able to use the banks' cash machines and branches thousands of miles from home.

But there is widespread doubt about how much services will really improve. Not just hard-to-satisfy consumers, but even the Fed, the US central bank, has concerns. In a report to Congress last year, it said that large banks have higher fees than small ones that operate in just one state. On average, they charge 21 per cent more for processing or bouncing a cheque, and a 16 per cent higher monthly fee for simply keeping an account.

(adapted from *The Observer*)

8 Find words or phrases in text B to match the following definitions.

1 combining of commercial companies into one (paragraph 1)
2 reduction in number with resulting increase in competitiveness (paragraph 1)
3 local office or shop belonging to a large organization (paragraph 2)
4 reduce legal restrictions (paragraph 4)
5 do business (paragraph 4)
6 sum of money paid into a bank (paragraph 5)
7 head of a bank or business in the US (paragraph 5)
8 financial institution with branches throughout the country (paragraph 6)
9 amount of money paid for professional services (paragraph 7)
10 form of financial transaction (paragraph 7)

9 Choose the correct option.

1 Between 1987 and 1999, the number of banks in the US went down by
a some 5,000. b some 4,500. c some 4,000.

2 Illinois used to be … in which banks were not allowed to have more than one outlet.
a the only state
b one of a large number of states
c one of several states

3 The state of the American banking system is … by Europeans.
a generally admired
b not regarded as particularly progressive
c hardly known

4 Remitting amounts to people in another federal state is
a out of the question.
b neither simple nor cheap.
c as easy as in Europe.

5 The recent restructuring of American banks
a is restricted to some states.
b is supported by federal legislation.
c only applies to state banks.

6 Together, the four banks mentioned in the text
a have 12 per cent of bank deposits in the US.
b operate in 22 states.
c have 29 million customers.

7 The main aim of the latest deals is to
a reduce the number of national banks operating in the US.
b comply with current legislation.
c create banks as well known as some famous brand products.

8 Recent developments in the banking industry in the US
a are generally welcomed.
b are regarded with some scepticism by the US central bank and other groups.
c will lead to improved services.

GRAMMAR

The present perfect simple and present perfect continuous

The present perfect simple

- refers to an action which is over but still relevant at the time of speaking or writing:
  – We **have approved** your loan application and the agreed amount will be transferred immediately.
- is used with time adverbials that have a link to the present:
  – America's banking system **has changed** dramatically in the last ten years.

The present perfect continuous

- is used to describe actions which started in the past and continue at the time of speaking or writing:
  – For several years / Since 1990, states **have been cutting back** banking regulations.

10 Complete the text using the present perfect simple or continuous.

Banking in the US (always be) …[1] rather inconvenient. Yet a significant change (affect) …[2] the country for some time. The government (reduce) …[3] the number of obstacles in the way of customers who for one reason or another (become) …[4] dissatisfied with their bank's services. Until now, federal legislation (hinder) …[5] the banking world. However, more and more states (put through) …[6] new acts to modernize banking. The trend towards a more efficient system (gather momentum) …[7] in recent years. This will bring the US into line with European banks, which (always be) …[8] much more flexible and consumer-friendly. European tourists now profit from this development as well. Many large American banks (adapt) …[9] their ATMs so that now tourists can withdraw money by using their bank card and their PIN. Yet the US banks (not fully introduce) …[10] all the major changes that (become) …[11] possible as a result of computers and IT.

11 Translate the text above into German.

INFORMATION

Points to remember when listing details of a recorded message

- first listen for the "story"
- then listen for detail and make notes
- be brief
- state who phoned? when? what about?
- state details of the message
- mention action to be taken, if any

13

12 Answerphone message from a bank: listen to the message and list the main points.

13 Translate the following sentences.

1 Ich habe gerade meine Kreditkarte abgeholt. Damit kann ich auch Bargeld am Automaten abheben.
2 Ich habe den Kontoauszug geprüft und festgestellt, dass eine Überweisung nicht ausgeführt worden ist.
3 Wir haben Ihrem Konto den Betrag von £265 gutgeschrieben. Das Guthaben beträgt jetzt £456,37.
4 Sie haben mir geraten, ein Sparkonto zu eröffnen. Wie hoch ist der Zinssatz für Sparguthaben?
5 In letzter Zeit geht die Zahl der kleinen Banken in den USA ständig zurück.
6 Ich habe seit Anfang August einen Überziehungskredit, habe ihn aber noch nicht genutzt.
7 Das Bankensystem befindet sich seit den frühen Neunzigern in einem rasanten Konzentrationsprozess.
8 Einige amerikanische Bundesstaaten deregulieren seit einigen Jahren ihr Bankensystem.
9 Ein Verrechnungsscheck ist auf jeden Fall sicherer als ein Barscheck.
10 Solange Ihr Konto ein Guthaben aufweist, zahlen Sie keine Bankgebühren.
11 Die Überweisung können Sie auch telefonisch erledigen. Dafür benötigen Sie eine besondere Geheimnummer.
12 Schecks werden in den USA noch oft verwendet.

Recruitment

W	N	E	W	S	P	A	P	E	R	V	D	E	Q
O	C	S	T	H	I	K	R	V	E	W	S	T	A
R	O	Y	X	C	V	B	N	J	K	J	T	M	D
K	X	T	E	L	E	V	I	S	I	O	N	H	V
P	W	K	L	P	M	L	N	D	X	B	W	Y	E
L	R	E	Z	R	A	F	T	N	B	C	C	D	R
A	Z	T	T	U	G	P	E	E	D	E	R	B	T
C	B	R	F	D	E	J	R	K	L	N	Y	E	I
E	G	A	C	S	N	K	N	K	L	T	F	W	S
M	V	D	B	N	C	M	E	T	P	R	F	M	E
E	D	E	W	B	Y	N	T	M	K	E	E	K	M
N	G	F	B	N	O	O	M	R	T	W	B	N	E
T	R	A	D	E	J	O	U	R	N	A	L	V	N
W	T	I	H	J	L	U	L	F	S	F	V	C	T
C	A	R	E	E	R	S	O	F	F	I	C	E	M

Find ten job sources in the puzzle and complete the sentences below.

1 Occasionally, commercials on … advertise job opportunities.

2 Job advertisements are printed in a special section of the … .

3 Did you see the call centre job … in the Saturday edition of *The Herald*?

4 Why not surf the … for useful recruitment websites?

5 You may have to approach a commercial recruitment … to help you find employment.

6 Joe Bloggs paid a visit to the … in the high street to see what jobs were on offer.

7 Pete Newboy did an eight-week … at Hallam Engineering in Sheffield this summer.

8 A … like CEBIT is also a good place to meet prospective employers.

9 The spring issue of *Forging Ahead*, the steel industry's …, was published yesterday.

10 Expert advice on job opportunities can be had at any army … .

TEXT A 14

The right person for the right job

When small and medium-sized enterprises (SMEs) grow or need to replace staff, managers often have to take on new roles such as searching for, interviewing and selecting staff. And they find it difficult because few are trained to do this. Finding the right person from a pile of CVs*, a couple of short interviews and two cautious references is not easy. Sometimes it comes down to guesswork. Recruitment would therefore seem an obvious task to outsource, especially for SMEs.

Many of these companies start the recruitment process with either over-optimistic or ill-judged ideas about the type of person that will fit into their team. Whatever the candidates' qualifications, their personal attributes are as important, since they are going to have to integrate with existing staff. This is where, the recruitment industry argues, professionals come into their own.

Ken Dixon, a human resources (HR) manager, says, "The professional recruiter can go off and ask candidates all sorts of questions you don't like to ask and then present you with a very short list of people who not only have the skills, but who are likely to fit in with your company's way of doing things. Most essentially, they will check the references of the person you choose."

The interview can only present a snapshot of abilities and personality. But narrowing the field means companies can at least spend more than the standard ten minutes finding out about the applicant.

Nicola Rowe and her colleagues at a Surrey-based recruitment agency have been looking for a method of reducing the time spent on candidate selection. They believe that "screen-to-client" technology provides the solution. "Our objective is to provide management with live interviews from a shortlist of candidates on a PC screen using state-of-the-art IT," says Rowe. "The system not only significantly reduces the amount of time managers spend on recruitment assignments, but also ensures a high rate of success in identifying and selecting the right candidate."

Together with the client, the recruitment consultant develops a list of critical criteria for the position on offer. The five or six candidates on the shortlist go through filmed interviews which are recorded on CD and sent to the client, who then decides who gets a face-to-face interview.

"But the CV will continue to play a vital role in recruitment," says Rowe. "The issue for us as recruitment consultants is to provide a system that will improve the recruitment process, both for management and candidates."

*CV = curriculum vitae

1 Explain the following words from text A.

1 CV (line 4)
2 interview (line 4)
3 reference (line 5)
4 outsource (line 6)
5 professional (line 11)
6 human resources manager (line 12)
7 applicant (line 19)
8 shortlist (line 23)
9 assignment (line 25)
10 consultant (line 32)

2 Answer the following questions on text A.

1 Why do some companies consider recruitment an obvious task to outsource?
2 What problems are some companies faced with when they start recruiting?
3 Why can it be useful to involve a professional recruiter?
4 How can the time spent on candidate selection be reduced?
5 What happens to the filmed interview?
6 Do you agree with the statement that CVs will continue to play an important role in the recruitment process? (Give reasons for or against.)

3 Complete the flow chart below using these terms.

agency interviews • candidate profile • company magazine • in-house • internet • noticeboard • personnel department • selection • shortlisting (2x)

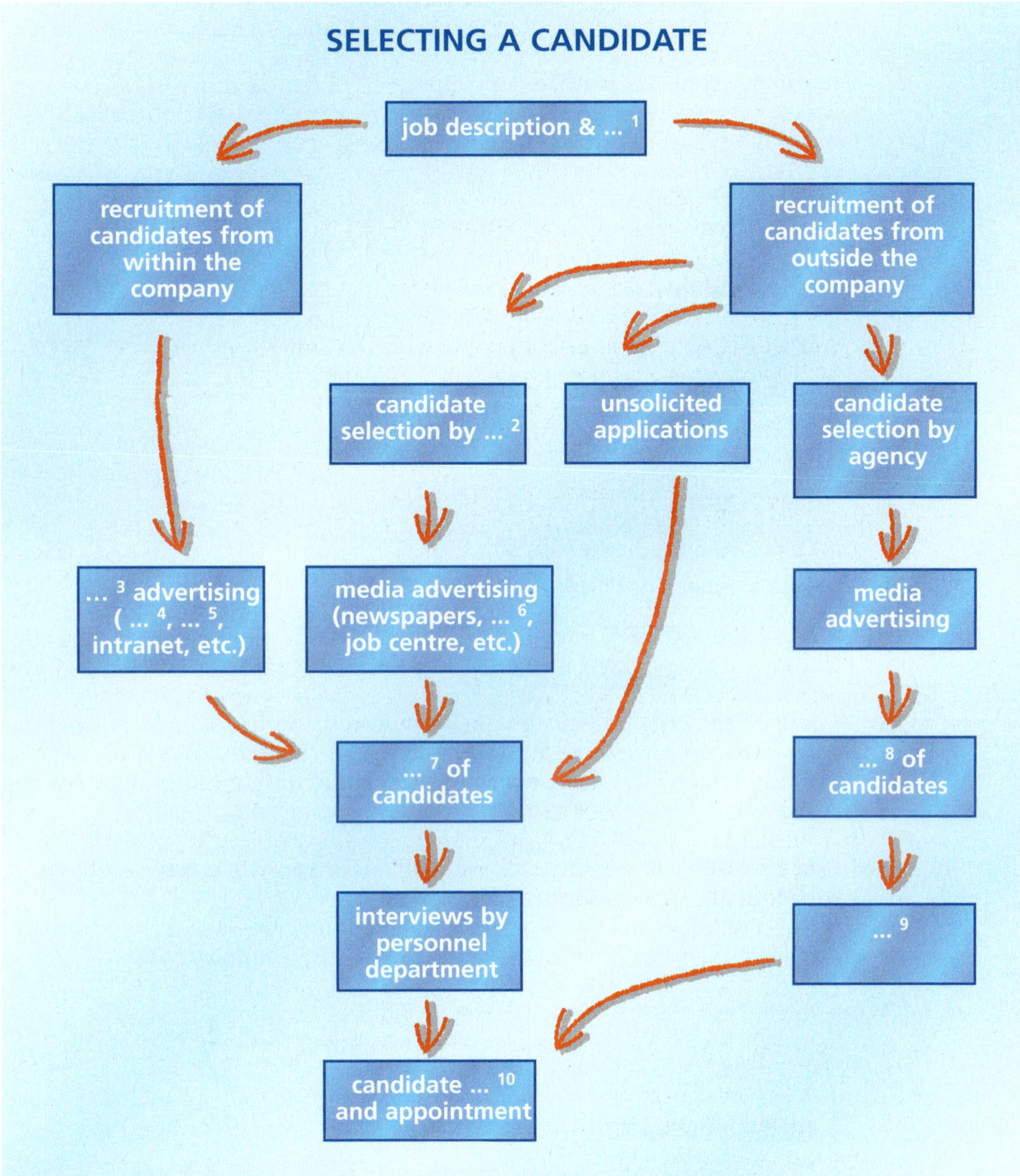

4 Explain the process of candidate selection using the flow chart. Work in groups.

5 What information is required if you apply for a job online? Compare at least two company sites.

Suggested sites:
www.hp.com (Hewlett-Packard)
www.bbc.co.uk/jobs (British Broadcasting Corporation)

TEXT B

An example of a CV

KAREN RUTH FOSTER

01482 348275
07968 029352 (mobile)
email karfoster@freemail.com

16 COLLEGE STREET
KINGSTON-UPON-HULL
HU5 7AP

Personal profile	well-organized, reliable team player with ability to take charge in pressure situations
Date of birth	23 March 1980

EDUCATION

1998 – 2002	University of Hull: BA in Economics • Economics (with Politics and French) • staff-student representative (1999–2000)
2000 – 2001	Université de Marne La Vallée, France • doing research on marketing methods
1991 – 1998	Newcastle Royal Grammar School • A-levels: Economics, Social Sciences, French

WORK EXPERIENCE

July – Sept 2001	Assistant courier with Airtours in Benidorm, Spain • coordinating travel arrangements • supervising accommodation matters • promoting entertainment programmes
July – Aug 2000	Accounts department at Fenwick's, Newcastle (department store) • providing support in five-person team • in charge of day-to-day administration
July – Sept 1999	Goods-in department at Fenwick's, Newcastle • responsible for keeping records of deliveries • reviewing stock levels

OTHER SKILLS AND QUALIFICATIONS

- Competence in MS Office, Lotus Notes
- Languages: French – fluent; Spanish – fair

INTERESTS	• Parachuting, travelling, water polo
REFEREES	• References available upon request

6 **Study the above CV and write your own.**

7 Put the sentences in this cover letter in the right order.

KAREN RUTH FOSTER

01482 348275
07968 029352 (mobile)
email karfoster@freemail.com

16 COLLEGE STREET
KINGSTON-UPON-HULL
HU5 7AP

James Mann
Recruitment Manager
Fortune Bank plc
Bank Building
8–14 Chiswell Street
London EC1Y 1UQ

25 April 2002

Dear Mr Mann

<u>Graduate trainee programme</u>

1. As you will see from my CV, I will be completing my four-year course in Economics in June this year and hope to obtain a good honours degree.
2. During my training I hope to get to know as many departments as possible.
3. I am sure that my degree and my international experience will qualify me for a place on your graduate programme.
4. I would very much like to apply for one of these places.
5. I would be pleased to be invited for an interview and look forward to hearing from you.
6. In my final year I have been specializing in finance and risk management.
7. In the April issue of *The Banker* you advertised traineeships on your graduate trainee programme for next year.
8. Therefore, I would very much like to start my career in a bank such as yours.

Yours sincerely

Karen R Foster

Karen R Foster

Encl.

7, 4, ~~2~~, 1, 6, 3, 8, 2, 5

8 Select the most appropriate answers to complete these sentences.

1 I wish to apply for the post of HR assistant, as ... in yesterday's *Evening News*.
a announced b publicized c advertised

2 In my present job, I am responsible for ... after-sales complaints.
a checking b controlling c proving

3 I ... an eight-week work placement in Birmingham over the summer.
a made b did c had

4 I was human resources officer at Atlantic Chemicals ... five years.
a during b since c for

5 Thank you for your ... for the post of sales executive.
a application b request c demand

6 You will be ... by our senior personnel officer.
a questioned b interrogated c interviewed

7 Further to our recent ..., I am pleased to offer you the post of personnel officer.
a meeting b rendezvous c date

8 The successful applicant will be able to gain ... in different departments.
a information b popularity c experience

9 Rephrase the following sentences using the verbs in brackets and, if necessary, add a preposition.

EXAMPLE I saw your advertisement in *The Irish Times*. (refer)
I refer to your advertisement in 'The Irish Times'.

1 At present, I am working at Dillons & Co on a part-time basis. (be employed)
2 Since leaving university I have done some temporary work. (graduate)
3 I can work with software programs like Word and Excel. (be experienced)
4 To improve my keyboarding skills I went to evening classes. (attend)
5 In order to get an insight into the full range of activities I would like to work for a small company. (gain)
6 I shall be pleased to send you copies of my certificates. (provide)
7 I hope you will look at my application. (consider)
8 I hope to hear from you soon. (look forward)

10 Write an application letter for one of these jobs.

PERSONAL ASSISTANT

TO EXPORT MANAGER WITH FRENCH/GERMAN – £18K + BENEFITS

American e-commerce company in W. London requires a very dynamic PA. Excellent prospects. Start ASAP.

Forward CV to fax +44 (0) 20 7287 0467 or email ray.crooter@jobpeople.com

GRADUATES LOOKING FOR A PEOPLE-BASED CAREER

Competitive package (£25,000 p.a.). You are used to dealing with people in the business world, taking responsibility, beating deadlines and making things happen. At Middleton International we are looking for a junior recruitment officer. Please reply with CV and cover letter to Teresa Green, 360 Kensington High Street, London W14 7NS, fax no. 020 7689 8817.

TELESALES MARKETING

We are market leaders in our field with a current customer database in excess of 2,000 companies. We are looking for experienced telesales people with a proven track record to work full time 9.30 a.m. to 5 p.m. If you also have good communicative skills and are computer-literate, send your CV with salary details to *Pam Lawrenson, 16 Bromells Road, Guildford, Surrey GU3 4UQ.*

15

11 Invitation to an interview: listen to the dialogue and note down the details.

"This is your first interview, I take it?"

12 Prepare a list of interview questions with a partner. Refer to the topics below.

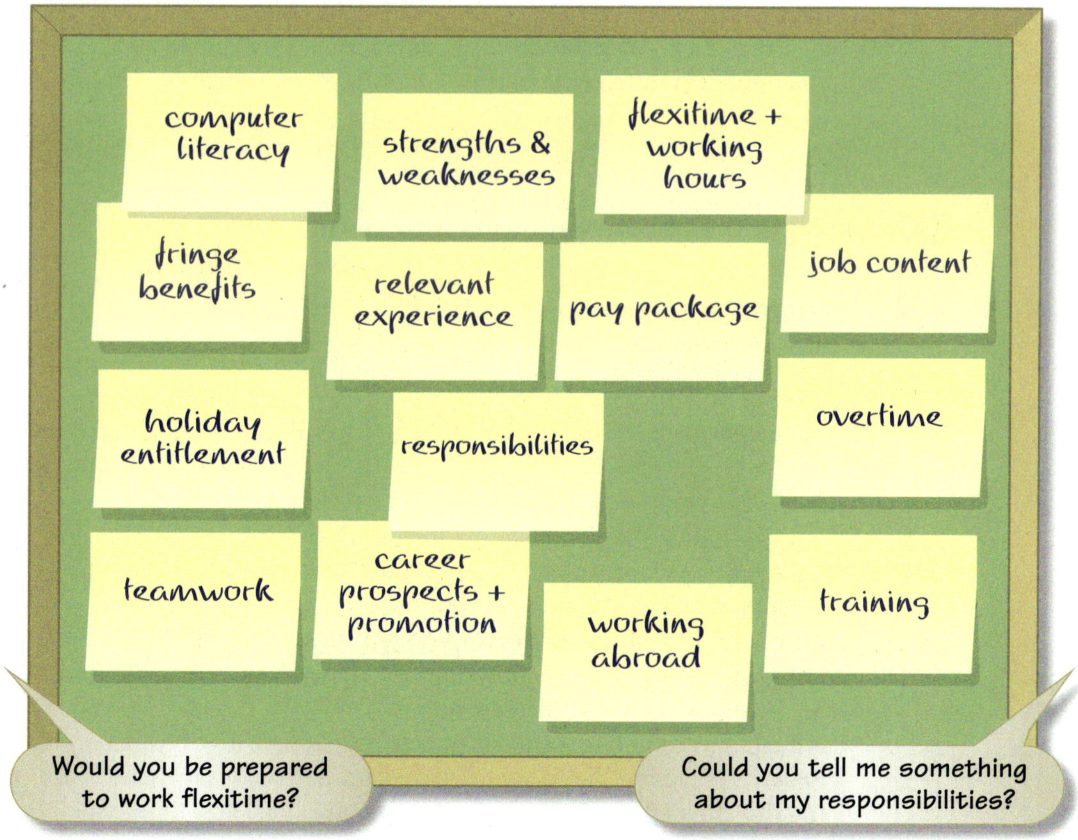

13 Conduct a job interview for one of the jobs in exercise 10 using some of the questions from exercise 12. Work in pairs.

GRAMMAR

The present perfect and simple past

Both the present perfect and the simple past are used to refer to actions and events in the past.

The present perfect is used

- for actions and events which are still relevant at the present time.
  - We **have received** your letter (i.e. we are dealing with it now).
- to introduce past actions and events.
  - One of the applicants **has had** an accident. His car collided with a bus last night.
- for actions and events which have happened (repeatedly) up to now and may happen again.
  - **I've applied** for 25 jobs so far.

The simple past is used with adverbials of definite past time (*a week ago, last month, during the interview*) and/or if the context suggests that the action or event took place at a definite time in the past.

- I **did** a course in statistics last year.
- (While I was at university) I also **attended** lectures on business management.

14 Complete the sentences using the present perfect or simple past.

1 I (decide) ... to apply for this position as I am looking for work near Cologne.
2 After secondary school, I (study) ... economics at the University of Tübingen.
3 While at university I (complete) ... several internships with companies in the chemical and pharmaceutical industries.
4 During that time I (get to know) ... the marketing and PR departments.
5 Since then I (be interested) ... in publications by firms in this sector.
6 I (spend) ... my fifth semester at Johns Hopkins University, Baltimore.
7 I (graduate) ... last month with a diploma in business administration.
8 Since beginning my studies I (attend) ... two courses in Business English.

15 Translate the above sentences into German.

16 Translate the following sentences.

1 Ich beziehe mich auf Ihre Anzeige in der *New York Times* vom 27. Juli und möchte mich um die Stelle als Marketing-Assistent bewerben.
2 Während meines Studiums habe ich ein Praktikum bei einer Bank gemacht.
3 Vor zwei Jahren habe ich einen Programmierkurs besucht und mit einer Prüfung abgeschlossen.
4 Ich beschäftige mich seit drei Jahren mit der Erstellung von PC-Programmen.
5 Sollten Sie weitere Informationen benötigen, so können Sie mich jederzeit unter folgender Telefonnummer erreichen.
6 Über eine Einladung zu einem Vorstellungsgespräch würde ich mich freuen.
7 Mittelständische Unternehmen übertragen oft Personalberatungsfirmen die Suche nach neuen Mitarbeitern.
8 Mitarbeiter dieser Agenturen haben es leichter, den Bewerbern schwierige Fragen zu stellen, denn sie müssen nachher nicht mit ihnen zusammenarbeiten.
9 Bei der Einstellung ist es nicht nur wichtig, dass die Bewerber die erforderlichen Fertigkeiten haben. Sie müssen auch in das Unternehmen passen.
10 Es ist ratsam, bei der Besetzung einer freien Stelle auch Bewerbungen aus dem Unternehmen zu berücksichtigen.

Modern forms of work 6

TEXT A 16

Which of these offices would you like to work in and why?

Teleworking on trial

Teleworking, or telecommuting, is on the increase, and it's no longer just piece workers and freelancers who are doing it. Senior managers are at it too. Take Nick Shelness, chief technology officer at software giant Lotus.

Shelness is a prime example of an employee who managed to negotiate himself into a position where he could work away from the office – around 3,500 miles away, in fact. Nine years ago, he was living in the US and rising through the ranks of Lotus (now owned by IBM). His Scottish wife, who had been ill for a number of years, was advised by her doctor to pursue a more restful lifestyle. Shelness informed his bosses that he was moving back to Scotland and that it was a non-negotiable condition if he was to remain with the company. Not only did they agree but he went on to become chief technology officer. Shelness is living proof that you do not have to turn up at the office every day to become a senior executive in a major corporation. When he is not travelling, he works from home in his 17th century corn mill in Strathmere, 60 miles north of Edinburgh.

By 2020, 10 per cent of the top 100 British companies will have no head-quarters, says Graeme Leach, chief economist at the Institute of Directors. "The traditional office will have come to be seen by many companies as an outdated concept that has been held on to for too long," he predicted recently. "A quarter of us will work from home, employed by hundreds of thousands of virtual corporations."

According to the Spring 2000 Government Labour Force Survey, around 1.5 million people, or 5.5 per cent of the workforce, already work from home at least one day per week by using a computer and a telephone link to their employer or client. This is still a relatively small figure, but significantly, it is 19 per cent higher than the previous year. Several large UK employers, including the BBC, BT, the AA and Lloyds TSB, already allow staff to work from home.

Whether teleworking will one day render the traditional office obsolete is still a debatable point. For this to happen in the UK, there would need to be a significant change in our corporate culture. Added to this are the very real practical problems of teleworking, such as staff supervision and on-the-job training, security of sensitive data leaving the office and coping with data flow volumes coming into the company's systems from off-site teleworkers.

Shelness agrees that teleworking in the UK still has some way to go and has his doubts about whether he could have persuaded a British employer to be so flexible. "It's so deep in our psyche in the UK that it's difficult to get someone to understand that you can become a senior executive in an organization like IBM and never manage a single person."

Despite being so senior a teleworker, Shelness always makes sure that he conscientiously writes up a report of what he has achieved each week, as much for his own benefit as to keep his boss informed. "I've come to the conclusion that it's an absolutely necessary discipline for anyone working from home, because you could easily fall into the trap of not believing that you are producing anything. When you write a report you often feel, 'Yeah, I achieved quite a lot last week'."

(adapted from *Business 2.0*)

1 Choose the correct definition or synonym for these terms from text A.

1 piece worker (lines 2–3)
- a person in charge of a piece of equipment
- b person paid by the number of items produced
- c person paid by the number of hours worked

2 freelancer (line 3)
- a person who works on a contract basis for several companies
- b person who runs his or her own shop
- c person who is employed on a part-time basis by a company

3 rise through the ranks (lines 12–13)
- a be immediately promoted to a top position
- b have to work hard to achieve promotion
- c advance steadily from a junior to a senior position

4 non-negotiable (line 19)
- a unalterable
- b inflexible
- c inevitable

5 outdated (line 35)
- a ultra-modern
- b ancient
- c old-fashioned

6 corporate culture (lines 56–57)
- a company behaviour and attitude
- b company arts programme
- c company advertising

7 off-site (line 63)
- a far from home
- b away from the main office
- c near a building site

8 conscientiously (line 75)
- a carefully and consistently
- b self-consciously
- c confidentially

2 Answer the following questions on text A.

1 What sections of today's workforce are involved in teleworking?
2 How did Shelness persuade his employers to allow him to work from home?
3 What role will the traditional office play in the not-too-distant future?
4 How widespread is teleworking in the British economy?
5 What attitude prevents teleworking from expanding more rapidly?
6 Why does Shelness write a weekly report of things he has achieved?

3 Complete the sentences and then add the words to the puzzle. The highlighted column gives you another term for 'teleworker'.

1 Telecommuters tend to experience less … due to working in a more relaxed environment.
2 One of the main employee … is a flexible working environment.
3 A … is the main item of equipment for a teleworker.
4 A teleworker is more … than an employee stuck in a traditional office.
5 One of the main problems facing teleworkers is that of … .
6 Nearly everyone who ..., i.e. works from home, has a computer and email.
7 A … is someone who works away from the main office with computer technology.
8 Many say working from … rather than at the office increases productivity.
9 Not having to commute to work can also help reduce … jams.
10 Time management is a major teleworking drawback: teleworkers could end up working round the … .
11 A mobile worker has to be more … than those with traditional nine-to-five jobs.
12 The virtual office may be the office of the … .

			1 s					s					
		2			e			t					
			3			p							
				4 m					e				
5	s							n					
		6 t								u			s

	7	e						k					
				8		m							
				9						c			
	10		o										
			11			x							
	12 f				r								

4 **Decide which of the following activities could be done by teleworkers.**

hairdressing
bookkeeping
dealing with customer enquiries
managing events
nursing
performing a medical operation
repairing a washing machine
selling cars
teaching
translating
writing software programs

5 **List the pros and cons of teleworking for employers and employees. Work in groups.**

✔ Pros for employers

Companies can retain valued employees who move away
...

✘ Cons for employers

Fewer people available to pass on company knowledge to trainees
...

✔ Pros for employees

Less time wasted in traffic jams
...

✘ Cons for employees

Can't keep home life separate from work
...

"I don't mind you bringing your work home but not your entire office."

TEXT B 17

CALL CENTERS: YOUR CALL IS IMPORTANT

COMPAQ TAKES good care of Rosa Esposito. Not only can she tell the computer maker's European customers how to fix their machines, she can do it in Italian, her native tongue. So, like the rest of the tech-support staff at Compaq's Dublin call center, Esposito enjoys perks an executive could envy. There's a cybercafé, a sauna, a gym and even a split-level canteen with panoramic views of Dublin and the sea. Sometimes there's a show marking the national day of one of the 17 nations represented on the center's 750-name payroll (last week: Irish dancers for St. Patrick's Day). No wonder, Esposito – now promoted to section leader and studying for a Compaq-sponsored business degree – loves Ireland.

This is pampering with a purpose. In the last four years more than 60 multinationals, from American Airlines to Xerox, have chosen Ireland as the site for call centers covering the European time zone. The number of call center employees in the country climbed from near zero to 7,000 and looks set to hit 10,000 this year. Book a Lufthansa flight or a Hertz car anywhere in Europe and most likely the call will be routed through Ireland. Many of the jobs require not just high-tech skills but a perfect command of another language. That means tough competition to staff the desks. Ireland alone can't hope to meet the demand, even though the government is now sponsoring special training courses. Employers must trawl Europe with generous offers – salaries begin at about €16,600 – to land the right recruits.

Ireland's charms for overseas investors are well known. Low costs, an efficient telecom system and a steady stream of 'computer-savvy' graduates have lured scores of U.S. firms. And for foreign recruits, most of whom are single twenty-somethings, hyperhip Dublin is a huge draw. Even so, the demand for labor is outstripping supply. "We're recruiting like crazy," says Aidan Donnelly of Xerox, who's looking to fill more than 500 new call-center posts near Dublin by the end of the year. "No matter what your skills are, we have something for you here."

Prosperity does have its costs. Traffic clogs the streets and the price of housing has soared in line with an economy that grew 10 percent last year. That's one reason companies are looking again at alternative sites. Britain is one rival. The country already has more jobs in call centers than in coal mining, steel- and carmaking combined, although the huge majority are serving only the British market. More promising are the Low Countries, an area with criss-crossing linguistic and national frontiers, where a mastery of three or four languages is commonplace. Says Stephen Morrell, who has studied the call-center industry: "If you have ever spoken to a Dutchman, you'll know that their English is better than ours." OK, there isn't the same lifestyle draw; but what about the savings on recruitment? Even in call centers, money talks.

(adapted from *Newsweek*)

6 Answer the following questions on text B.

1. How is Rosa Esposito looked after by her employer?
2. What managerial capacity does Rosa Esposito work in?
3. Which companies have established call centres in Ireland?
4. What special skills must call centre staff have?
5. What is being done to solve the problem of recruiting new call centre staff?
6. Why has Ireland become an attractive location for call centres?
7. What are the drawbacks of an attractive location?
8. Companies are looking at alternative sites for their call centres. What are the advantages and disadvantages of the Low Countries?

7 What do the following figures from text B refer to?

1 17
2 750
3 60
4 7,000
5 10,000
6 16,600
7 500
8 10

8 Find terms in the list that come closest to those from text B.

benefits • economies • exceed • fill the vacancies • finance • hiring • location • maintenance engineers • mechanics • rise steeply • senior manager • trainees • workforce

1 tech-support staff (line 6)
2 perks (line 7)
3 executive (line 8)
4 payroll (line 14)
5 sponsor (line 18)
6 outstrip (line 49)
7 soar (line 57)
8 site (line 60)
9 savings (line 74)
10 recruitment (line 75)

9 Translate the following sentences into German.

1 She enjoys perks.
2 She has been promoted section leader.
3 She is studying for a degree in business administration.
4 The calls are routed through Ireland.
5 Ireland cannot meet the demand for suitably qualified staff.
6 Xerox are trying to fill more than 500 posts.
7 Prices have soared in line with economic growth.
8 Some companies are looking at alternative sites for their call centres.

10 Use the role card below to phone the personnel department of a major call centre in Sheffield to discuss a vacancy advertised on a recruitment website. The personnel manager's role card is on page 134.

Caller

- *refer to vacancy*
- *enquire about duties, hours*
- *give details of call centre experience + language skills*
- *request more details of call centre operation*
- *say when you are available*
- *ask for more information about terms of contract, benefits, overtime, flexitime, holidays*

18

Now listen to the model answer.

GRAMMAR

Reported speech

- The tenses used in reported speech depend on the tense of the reporting verb.
- If the reporting verb is in the present, the tense in reported speech does not change.
  – Nick Shelness says, "When I am not travelling, I work from home."
  – Nick Shelness says that when he **is** not **travelling**, he **works** from home.
- If the reporting verb is in the past, the tense in reported speech is normally 'backshifted'.
  – Aidan Donnelly said, "We're recruiting like crazy."
  – Aidan Donnelly said they **were recruiting** like crazy.

11 Convert the following statements into reported speech.

1 "I've been teleworking for over a year." (She said ...)
2 "This sort of job requires a perfect command of Japanese." (My colleague says ...)
3 "I'm studying for a business degree." (Rosa Esposito told me ...)
4 "Your call will be routed through Dublin." (I should have known ...)
5 "No matter what your skills are, we have something for you here." (I've been told ...)
6 "You can be senior manager in no time." (They promised her ...)
7 "I have my doubts about whether my new employers will be as flexible." (He admitted ...)
8 "It will be difficult to find the right person for the job." (The agency points out ...)
9 "Teleworking in the UK still has some way to go." (The report stressed ...)
10 "I don't want to work in Dublin." (She said ...)

12 Translate the following sentences.

1 Graeme Leach sagte, dass in 15 Jahren jedes zehnte britische Unternehmen keine Hauptverwaltung mehr habe.
2 Er war der Meinung, dass 25 Prozent der Bevölkerung ihre Arbeit von zu Hause aus erledigen werde.
3 Deshalb müsse sich im Denken der Unternehmen einiges ändern.
4 Laut Shelness muss ein Telearbeiter ein hohes Maß an Selbstdisziplin haben.
5 Rosa Esposito glaubte, sie bekomme mehr freiwillige Sozialleistungen als viele leitende Angestellte.
6 *Newsweek* zufolge leiten Lufthansa und Hertz die meisten Anrufe über Irland.
7 Aidan Donnelly äußerte gegenüber *Newsweek*, dass sein Unternehmen im laufenden Jahr eine große Anzahl neuer Stellen zu besetzen habe.
8 Es wurde auch deutlich, dass Bewerber mit Kenntnissen in mehreren Fremdsprachen gute Chancen hätten, als Call-Center-Mitarbeiter eingestellt zu werden.

7 Retailing

Would you like to shop here? Why? Why not?

TEXT A 19

Mall of America

In 1982, Minnesota's professional baseball and football teams, the Twins and the Vikings, moved from Met Stadium in Bloomington to the Metrodome in downtown Minneapolis. This gave Bloomington 78 acres of land in a highly accessible location. The stadium was located only a mile and a half from the airport, there were four major highways intersecting the property. Three years later, Bloomington Port Authority purchased the site and decided to develop a huge retail and entertainment center.

At that time, the Twin Cities of Minneapolis and St. Paul were 'under-retailed'. Research showed that the Twin Cities had 13 square feet of retail space per person compared to a national average of 18 square feet. In August of 1992, when Mall of America opened its doors, the face of the Twin Cities had changed forever. The Mall was 71 percent leased with 330 brand-new stores for business, including four nationally recognized department stores – Bloomingdale's, Macy's, Nordstrom and Sears – together under one roof, for the first time. It was also the first day of work for over 10,000 employees.

Since its grand opening, Mall of America has added many more stores and now has a total of over 520.

- It employs more than 12,000 people and is over 98 percent leased.
- Total traffic has been between 35 to 42 million visits yearly.
- Visitors spend an average of three hours in the Mall, which is three times the national average for shopping malls.
- Mall of America attracts more visitors annually than Disney World, Graceland and the Grand Canyon combined.
- And finally, the Mall has helped retailers and the local economy in a variety of ways.

First of all, by bringing three new department stores and a seven-acre amusement park to the market, Mall of America has actually expanded the retail pie.

Secondly, tourism accounts for four out of every ten visits. Research shows that for every dollar spent at Mall of America another five dollars is spent outside the Mall on gas, lodging, food, transportation, and other attractions, equaling more than $1.2 billion in economic impact on the state of Minnesota.

There are many reasons for the success of Mall of America.

- Location, location, location! Mall of America is situated close to Twin Cities International Airport.
- Daytime drive market. 28 million people live within a day's drive to Mall of America.
- Hotel space. There are more than 7,000 hotel rooms in close proximity.
- Climate. An enclosed shopping center like Mall of America thrives in bad weather – whether too cold or too hot, and Minnesota is not known for 365 days of sunny warm weather – much more famous for its extremes in temperature.

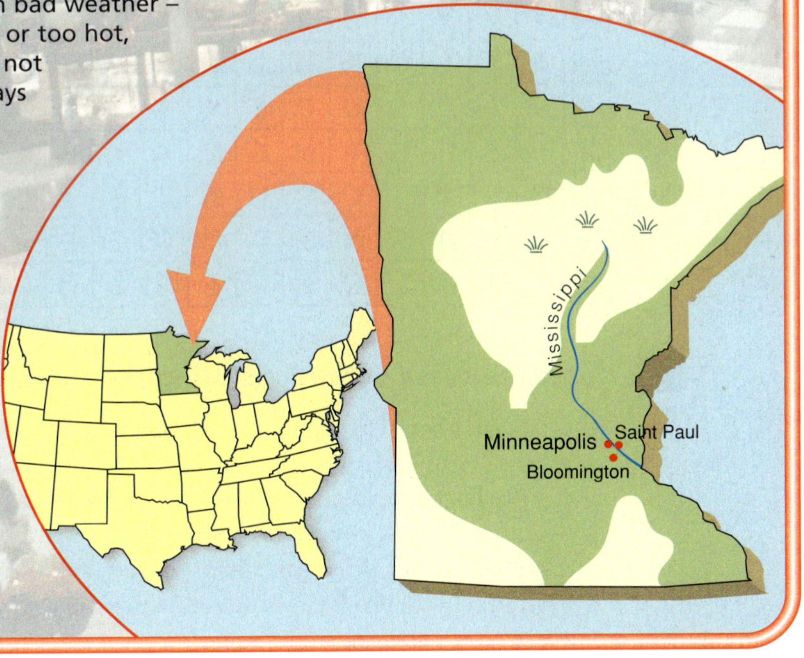

(www.mallofamerica.com)

1 Find words or phrases in text A with a similar meaning to the following.

1 central
2 easily reached
3 bought
4 rented
5 shopkeepers
6 accommodation
7 nearby
8 does well

2 Form sentences corresponding to what is said in text A.

EXAMPLE former stadium / attractive site / development / retail centre
A former stadium in Minnesota proved to be an attractive site for the development of a huge retail centre.

1 location / major roads / airport nearby / ideal for development
2 Twin Cities / scarcity of retail space / national average
3 department stores / other retail outlets / over 12,000 people
4 more time / customers / Mall of America / other malls
5 Mall of America / visitors / well-known tourist destinations
6 the Mall / expansion / retail trade / area
7 Mall of America / densely populated area / 28m people
8 adverse weather conditions / negative impact / financial success

3 Find the retail outlets in the puzzle below.

X	Z	B	C	G	D	E	P	A	R	T	M	E	N	T	S	T	O	R	E	M	B
Z	J	A	N	L	C	M	M	A	R	K	E	T	S	T	A	L	L	F	L	X	G
N	F	J	H	K	E	P	S	K	S	G	P	C	O	R	N	E	R	S	H	O	P
Y	V	M	C	K	A	C	O	N	V	E	N	I	E	N	C	E	S	T	O	R	E
R	E	D	Y	X	C	M	H	M	C	O	O	P	E	R	A	T	I	V	E	V	B
N	T	X	Y	S	U	P	E	R	M	A	R	K	E	T	A	S	D	C	F	Q	M
M	A	I	L	O	R	D	E	R	H	O	U	S	E	F	G	H	C	A	F	K	M
I	M	L	P	S	U	P	E	R	S	T	O	R	E	J	K	L	Y	H	K	L	V
T	V	E	N	D	I	N	G	M	A	C	H	I	N	E	K	L	P	Q	J	S	D
G	Q	D	I	S	C	O	U	N	T	S	T	O	R	E	Q	W	E	B	Q	C	H
S	C	H	A	I	N	S	T	O	R	E	B	X	T	E	D	L	M	C	T	A	Z
C	A	T	A	L	O	G	U	E	S	W	O	H	L	T	X	U	I	O	Q	P	U

4 Complete these definitions using the terms found above.

1 A … is a shop with branches all over the country.
2 A retail outlet owned by its customers is usually referred to as a … .
3 A very large supermarket – often located on the edge of a town – is called a … .
4 A company that advertises its goods in a catalogue is called a … .
5 Tea, coffee and soft drinks can be bought from a … .
6 People buying products online or by ordering them on the phone often like to see them in special … .
7 Traders without a shop sell their goods outside from a … .
8 A … is usually open all day seven days a week.
9 A … is a retail outlet comprising several departments under one roof.
10 Most people do their everyday shopping in their local … .
11 The traditional … is rapidly disappearing due to competition from supermarkets.
12 A … is characterized by its simple shop furnishings and low prices.

5 Discuss these statements. Work in groups.

6 Translate the following text into German.

Store layout

Supermarkets are laid out in such a way that customers are encouraged to spend more money. On average, customers in supermarkets spend twice as much as they intend on each visit. This means that 50% of their purchases are impulse buys, prompted by seeing something on the shelf.

The products that are placed in 'hot spots' – for example, at eye level in the middle of each shelf – will sell best, and most supermarkets tend to place their own brands there, since they have the highest profit margins. Other places where products sell well are on the shelves at the end of each aisle. High-profit goods such as batteries and camera film tend to be placed here.

Supermarkets are also designed to lead you round all the aisles. Essential goods such as tea, bread and sugar are spaced out around the shop so that you have to view all areas, passing as much shelf space as possible.

(adapted from *Food File*, Channel Four Television)

A typical store layout

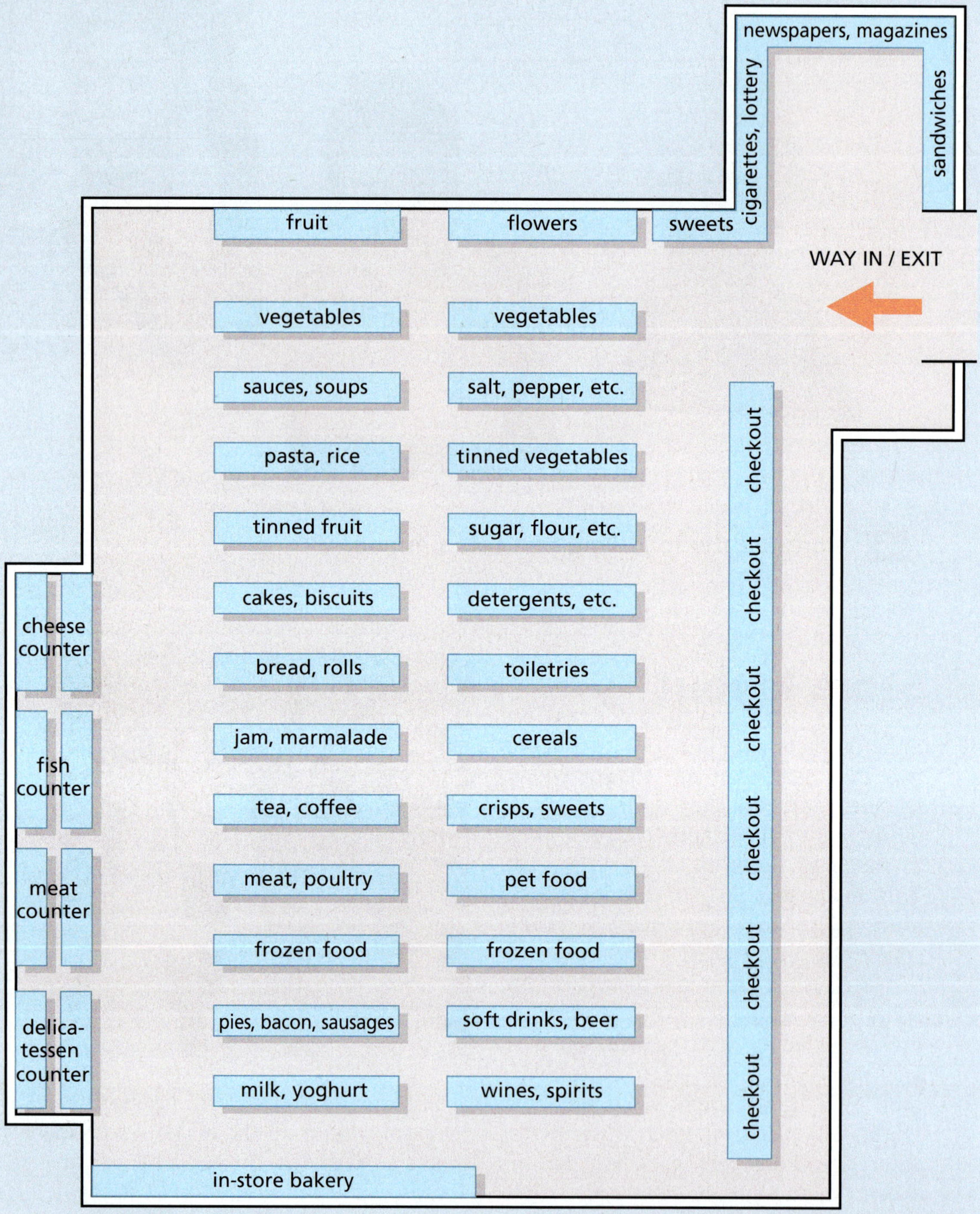

7 **Study the store layout above and give reasons for the positioning of the various product ranges.**

TEXT B

20

SHARP RISE IN ONLINE SHOPPING FORECAST

Online shopping in Britain will be a £12.5bn market within five years, representing 5 per cent of total retail sales, according to a study released today.

Verdict, the retail consultancy, says the growth will be fuelled by the grocery market – with more supermarket shoppers switching to the internet – as well as by interactive digital television shopping services and the growth of mobile telephones.

The figures predicted by Verdict represent a big increase. Last year, British shoppers spent £581m online – or 0.3 per cent of all retail sales.

However, the consultancy has a warning for retailers. It says that by far the largest part of the predicted turnover – 94 per cent – will be cannibalized from existing store and catalogue sales. Just 6 per cent will be new growth.

In the past six months, 26 more of the top 100 UK retailers have launched websites, taking the total represented online to 86, 36 of which can actually be used for shopping. The study also predicts that as 'bricks and mortar' retailers have moved online, pure internet players will open physical presences to make their brands better known and to reach more customers. "This will then lead to consolidation in the market," says Verdict.

"Many businesses will fail as there is a clear 'flight to quality'. Mergers and acquisitions will be rife – including those between dotcoms and established retailers. Winners will grow in scale, muscle, excellence and service, brand differentiation, consumer trust and loyalty."

The study is based on consumer research which showed that the number of UK online shoppers grew by 71 per cent to 3.2m in the six months to April. Of those, the number of women shoppers doubled to 1.1m.

(adapted from the *Financial Times*)

8 Find expressions in text B to match the following.

1 published
2 forecast
3 mail-order purchases
4 with real buildings
5 reduction in the number of suppliers
6 tendency to buy upmarket goods
7 forming one company out of two or more companies
8 enterprise doing business on the internet
9 keeping different makes of products separate and distinct
10 buyers' tendency to buy from the same shop

9 True or false? Correct these statements on text B where necessary.

1 Online shopping is predicted to yield a profit of £12.5bn in the near future.
2 Sales volumes are expected to rise by 5%.
3 Increased use of mobiles will boost retailing.
4 In purely statistical terms, online retail sales have not been of great significance so far.
5 Retailers will not be seriously affected if they do not go online.
6 The majority of retailers with their own websites sell their goods on the internet.
7 In future, most retailers will offer their products online and in shops.
8 Research shows that by April 2000 the number of women shoppers on the internet had grown by 71 per cent.

10 Read the article and discuss the pros and cons of online shopping. Work in groups.

The Wheelton Gazette, 21 December 2001

Online shopping – here to stay

What would life be like in our village without computers and online shopping? The nearest supermarket in Chorley is miles away, getting to the nearest department store in Preston takes more than an hour, not to mention speciality shops, for which you would have to travel as far as Manchester. Only ten years ago, people used to spend whole days away from home only to buy the most basic goods.

When the first e-commerce enterprises were established, critics predicted the wholesale collapse of most of them.

Reality has proved them wrong. How would we be able to do our Christmas shopping without e-commerce? Nothing could be simpler. You need a turkey for your Christmas dinner? Well, find the right website, follow the simple steps on the screen, and your turkey will be delivered to your home in next to no time. Books, computer games, concert tickets as Christmas presents – the same procedure. They are all delivered to your door – just like your daily pint of milk!

Thus, shopping is no longer one of your daily chores, it has become something to be enjoyed – a real, though virtual experience.

11 Send an email to the editor in reply to this article on behalf of your grandmother, who is very sceptical about online shopping.

21

12 Ordering a gift hamper by phone: listen to the answerphone message and list the main points.

GRAMMAR

Ways of expressing the future

- **will + infinitive** is used for predictions and for spontaneous decisions.
  - According to the experts, e-commerce **will be** even more important in years to come.
  - "I can't log onto the internet." – "Don't worry. **I'll see** if I can help."
- **going to + infinitive** refers to the speaker's intentions.
  - I've just bought a new computer. That's why **I'm going to do** most of my shopping on the internet.
- The **present continuous** refers to plans and arrangements concerning the near future.
  - I'm afraid I can't make it tomorrow morning because **I'm seeing** the marketing manager at 9 a.m.
- **will + be + -ing** is used for events and actions taken for granted or in progress at a given future moment.
  - You can give me that letter. **I'll be going** to the post office anyway.
  - This time tomorrow **I'll be sitting** in another meeting.
- The **simple present** is used for scheduled future events and actions.
  - This year, Christmas Day **falls** on a Monday.
  - The next bus **leaves** at 8 a.m.

13 Complete the following sentences using the appropriate future forms.

1 According to retailing experts, the importance of the wholesale trade (decrease) … considerably in the next ten years.
2 Don't bother to go to the bank. I (go) … there anyway.
3 It's official now: our new store at Wigan (open) … on 1 June.
4 What (you do) … about our window decoration?
5 "I've just discovered that we've run out of coffee." – "OK, I (buy) … some at lunch time."
6 I'm afraid I can't make it tonight, I (attend) … a sales seminar at 8 p.m.
7 This time next week we (shop) … at Mall of America.
8 "I could do with a pint." – "OK, I (get) … you one."

14 Translate the following sentences.

1 Amerikas größtes überdachtes Einkaufszentrum wird sich den Experten zufolge auch in der Zukunft als großer Erfolg erweisen.
2 Es gibt Befürchtungen, dass ein riesiges Einkaufszentrum den Einzelhandel der Nachbarstädte ruinieren wird.
3 Sowohl Minneapolis als auch St. Paul werden von diesem Zentrum erheblich profitieren.
4 Die Mall of America feiert im Jahre 2012 ihr zwanzigjähriges Bestehen.
5 Einige der Touristen, die morgen aus Japan einfliegen, besuchen die Mall nur, um dort zu heiraten.

6 An den Delikatessen- und Fischtheken gibt es morgen wegen der Personalknappheit vermutlich lange Schlangen.
7 Wir werden die Molkereiprodukte an der Außenwand platzieren, weil die Regale dort leicht aufgefüllt werden können.
8 Viele der Interneteinzelhandelsunternehmen, die in den letzten Jahren gegründet wurden, werden in Kürze aufgeben.
9 Während ursprünglich nur CDs und Bücher per Internet vertrieben wurden, werden nun sogar Häuser auf diesem Wege verkauft.
10 Was wir auch tun – einige unserer Kunden werden sich ohnehin beschweren.

What target groups are these adverts aimed at?
What kinds of advertising are you most influenced by?

TEXT A 22

What is marketing?

A market is any set of arrangements that allows buyers and sellers to exchange goods and services. It can be anything from a street market in a small town to a large international market. According to the Institute of Marketing, "marketing is the management process involved in identifying, anticipating and satisfying consumer requirements profitably."

- Marketing must be aimed at finding out what consumers' needs are and making sure that products meet them. Market research is often used for this purpose. Managers, however, also place stress on having a "feel" for the market. This could be very important in a market with changing trends, such as fashion or home decoration products.
- Marketing is an ongoing process without a start or an end. Businesses must be prepared to respond to changes. For example, a company marketing its own range of office furniture would be unwise to decide on a strategy without taking consumers' reactions into account. If the business sold modern designs, but sales were poor, a better strategy might be to change the range and target businesses that want a more traditional look for their offices.
- Marketing is a business philosophy – a way of thinking about how to satisfy consumers' needs. A business selling good quality products cheaply may be unsuccessful in its marketing if it has dirty, badly organized or poorly lit facilities. Retailers such as IKEA have large superstores with restaurants and play areas for children.
- Marketing affects all aspects of a business. A production department is unlikely to continue making a product that does not satisfy the needs of the consumers at whom it is aimed. In the same way, pricing decisions cannot be made without knowing how much consumers are prepared to pay. Yet selling is only one part of the marketing process. Before selling their products, businesses carry out a range of activities which take consumer preferences into account.

Advertising is just one of a number of tactics used by marketing departments. Other marketing methods include promotions, such as free gifts, competitions and sponsorships. Even when profit is not the main objective, marketing has a vital role to play. Charities, like Oxfam*, and public-sector organizations, like colleges and hospitals, adapt and change the marketing of their services to satisfy the needs of their target groups and as an image-building exercise.

* Ox(ford Committee for) Fam(ine Relief) – a British charity founded in Oxford in 1942.

(adapted from *Principles of Marketing*)

1 Match the definitions with the terms below.

market research (line 11) • pricing (line 40) • consumer preference (lines 45–46) • advertising (line 47) • promotion (line 49) • free gift (line 49) • sponsorship (line 50) • target group (line 55)

1 describing a product or service publicly to persuade people to buy or use it market research
2 careful investigation of the sales potential of a product or service advertising
3 special marketing activity like a quiz promotion
4 calculating the value of goods or services for sale pricing
5 product given away to attract customers free gift
6 set of people a particular product or service is intended for target group
7 part-financing of TV programmes, films, sports or cultural events in order to attract public attention sponsorship
8 particular interest in or liking for a product or service consumer preference

2 Answer the following questions on text A.

1 How important is market research in marketing a product or service?
2 Why is marketing not just a one-off activity?
3 Why do excellent products not always guarantee sound profits?
4 Why is it not enough to fix the value of the material of a product as its selling price?
5 What is the basic difference between business enterprises and Oxfam?
6 What is marketing? Explain in your own words.

3 Complete the text with the correct prepositions.

Marketing is often confused …[1] sales or advertising, but it is much more. It is …[2] finding …[3] what the customer wants by collecting data …[4] both the customer and the market …[5] market research; and it is also …[6] transporting the product …[7] the customer.

This so-called marketing mix is made … …[8] the four "P"s (product, price, promotion, place): – deciding …[9] the right product …[10] the right price; – persuading customers to buy a product …[11] means of attractive advertising and packaging; – and by making it available …[12] the customer …[13] the right channels.

If companies are to be successful, they must take a close look …[14] the customer and the market before opting …[15] a new product.

4 Complete the text by using the appropriate form of each verb.

AA: NEW MARKETING STRATEGY

Although many motorists realize that there is a risk that their car (break down) …[1], it is all too easy for them to think that it (not happen) …[2], which is why they don't bother to join a rescue organization. Just recently, a hard-hitting advertising campaign, the *4th Emergency Service*, (be used) …[3] to cut through motorists' apathy and to communicate the benefits of AA membership simply but memorably.

The advertisement also (bring home) …[4] to motorists the importance of breakdown cover by creating a little fear, and it (lead) …[5] to consumer action: AA membership (increase) …[6] by 1.8 million immediately after the campaign's launch. Incredibly, 97 per cent of people who (claim) …[7] to have seen the advertisement (believe) …[8] that the AA (be) …[9] the 4th 'real' emergency service together with police, fire and ambulance. Creating such a belief, even if it is somewhat mistaken, (give) …[10] the AA a clear competitive edge over its rivals and (make) …[11] it more likely that the AA (be) …[12] the first choice of that 97 per cent when they (seek) …[13] breakdown cover.

(adapted from *Principles of Marketing*)

5 **Choose the most suitable ways to promote one of the products below. Work in groups.**

billboards · brochures · catalogues · cinema advertising · showrooms · demonstrations · flyers · internet · leaflets · newspaper ads · packaging · personal selling · mailshots · point of sale advertising · samples · posters · press releases · product placement · telephone sales · trade fairs · sponsorship · TV commercials · trade journals · word of mouth

USEFUL PHRASES

Giving presentations

Greetings
I'd like to thank you for inviting me to …
Right then, let's make a start, shall we?

Dealing with questions
I'll be pleased to answer any questions at the end of the presentation.
Please interrupt me if you have any questions.

Introduction
The subject of my presentation is …
I shall be speaking today about …

Length of presentation
I don't intend to speak for longer than ten minutes.
I have a lot to cover in the next ten minutes, so I'd better make a start.

Rephrasing
Let me put that another way.
To put it more concisely, …

Going into detail
More specifically, …
Let's focus on one aspect of this …

Generalizing
Generally speaking, …
On the whole, …

Linking two points
Having dealt with A, I now want to move on to B.
So much for A, let's look at B.

Examples
A good example of this is …
We can illustrate this by …
Take X, for example.

Adding a point
In this context, it is worth mentioning …
Before we leave this subject, it's worth pointing out that …

Introducing visuals
This overhead shows …
We can see on the screen that …
This can be seen in the following transparency.

Summarizing
To summarize: …
So, to sum up: …

Finishing off
In conclusion, I'd like to …
I'd like to finish by …

INFORMATION

Things to remember:

when preparing your presentation

- the description of your product
- the image of your product
- the competition faced by your product
- the amount and type of advertising

when giving your presentation

- the way you dress
- the way you speak and move
- what you say
- what visual aids to use

6 **Give an in-house presentation on how best to promote one of the following products or services. Work in groups.**

- revolutionary new tea bag design

- new recipe for instant (i.e. powdered) whisky

- internet frozen and fast food service

- golf club with explosive device for greater distance

TEXT B 23

MAJOR BRANDS REDEFINE THEMSELVES AS A WAY OF LIFE

NIKE IS MOVING INTO CONSUMER electronics. Virgin is selling cars. Coca-Cola has launched a range of urban clothing. What next? A McDonald's bank? In simpler times, you knew where you were with brands. Nike was a pair of trainers, Virgin was a record store and Coca-Cola was the world's best-selling soft drink. Today, however, brands are taking on an additional role as big companies try to redefine them as not so much a product, more a way of life, and stretch them into new areas.

In the early years of the consumer society, a brand name on a box did little more than identify what was inside. People were looking for products that would improve their quality of life, and chose brands most likely to achieve that purpose. But as people became better off and fulfilled their basic needs, brands acquired other attributes. The functionality of the product was still important, but people also started using these brands to say something about themselves – by, for example, drinking Martini to convey the idea that they were sophisticated jet-setters.

Now, developed countries have entered a third age of branding in which many companies are making roughly the same products at roughly the same price. This means that the way a product 'works' rarely succeeds as a point of differentiation. Instead, companies are trying to make their brands stand out by emphasizing their emotional aspects, hoping consumers will identify with the set of values the brand represents. Modern brands have been more successful at doing this →

than old-established ones because they have a shorter legacy of being associated with a specific product.

The advantage of emotional brands is that companies can transfer their brand strength into other areas, increasing revenues and reducing their exposure to the lifespan of a single product.

Enterprise IG, a global branding consultancy, says the elasticity of brands is related to their position on a spectrum ranging from those rooted in solid, tangible assets to those with highly intangible, emotional qualities.

"At the one end, you have rail companies that tend to associate themselves with infrastructure and their ability to get you from A to B, and at the other end a brand like Disney that positions itself on dreams and making people have fun," says Terry Tyrrell, chairman of Enterprise IG.

Could Coca-Cola stand for something other than a fizzy drink? The company itself denies Coca-Cola Ware is an attempt to extend its brand. It says it is just part of its long-established licensing programme, under which about 320 licensees around the world produce more than 10,000 products carrying the Coca-Cola trademark.

Perhaps it is missing an opportunity. Alan Strang, managing director of Action Apparel, the UK licensee for Coca-Cola Ware, says his company has been "absolutely overwhelmed" by the response to the line, and is now negotiating with Coca-Cola to expand into new territories.

Mr Strang says the emotional attributes that youngsters seem to find appealing in Coca-Cola are its heritage, its authenticity and its global appeal. "Anything that's got a retro flavour and a flavour of being associated with global markets is fashionable at the moment," he says.

Coca-Cola is also young and cool, Mr Strang says. "Coca-Cola has always been targeted at young, fun people."

(adapted from the *Financial Times*)

7 Find words in text B to match the following.

1 put on the market (paragraph 1)
2 state of being practical and useful (paragraph 2)
3 keeping things distinct (paragraph 3)
4 enterprise giving expert advice on naming products (paragraph 5)
5 items like machines and buildings (paragraph 5)
6 highest-ranking individual in a company (paragraph 6)
7 person permitted to produce and sell something (paragraph 7)
8 aimed at (paragraph 10)

8 Refer to text B and choose the correct option.

1 What have brands come to be seen as?
   a People still think they refer primarily to particular products.
   b They are much more than only product names.
   c There is no longer any link to the products they stand for.
2 What were customers' attitudes towards products in the past?
   a As long as a product works well it's fine.
   b All that counts is an interesting product name.
   c Anything that makes life easier is good.

3 What do people associate with brand names today?
   a They indicate what a product is good for.
   b Brand names help them choose from a number of almost identical products.
   c Brands show what social group you belong to.
4 What type of product fulfils the modern function of branding best?
   a Recent ones.
   b Ones that are widely known.
   c Those with a good reputation over the years.
5 Do brands reflect both material and immaterial values today?
   a No, basically material values only.
   b Yes, definitely.
   c No, mainly immaterial values.
6 Is Coca-Cola's latest move something entirely new?
   a The company says it is merely doing what it has always been doing.
   b It is entirely new and primarily an attempt to regain lost markets.
   c It is a radical departure from its traditional business policy.
7 Will Coca-Cola's move into clothing herald a new era in its marketing strategy?
   a No, it won't last.
   b No, their clothes are only successful because of their ultra-modern design, and the company will not change its policy.
   c Well, their success may induce them to make further experiments along similar lines.

9 Discuss the following questions. Work in groups.

1 Which of the following industries do you associate with the brands in the table?

automobiles • computer technology • engineering • food retail • leisure • soft drinks • telecommunications • tobacco

The world's most valuable brands

Ranking	Global Brand	Country
1	Coca-Cola	USA
2	Microsoft	USA
3	IBM	USA
4	Intel	USA
5	Nokia	Finland
6	General Electric	USA
7	Ford	USA
8	Disney	USA
9	McDonald's	USA
10	AT&T	USA
11	Marlboro	USA
12	Mercedes	Germany

(source: *Interbrand's World's Most Valuable Brands 2000 Survey*)

2 What else do you associate with these brands?

10 What do you think a 'brandaholic' is? Are you one?

GRAMMAR

Participial and infinitive constructions

- Participial constructions (*-ing, -ed*) can be used to replace relative clauses.
  - The number of companies which specialize in marketing has been increasing steadily.
  - The number of companies **specializing** …
  - The official definition of marketing, which is taken from …
  - The official definition of marketing, **taken** from …
- Infinitive constructions are only used in relative clauses which refer to superlatives and phrases with *only*. Sometimes, the subject of the infinitive construction is introduced by *for*.
  - The best way in which you can find out about the market is by market research.
  - The best way **(for you) to find out** about the market …
  - The only thing which the company can do is to withdraw the advertisement.
  - The only thing **for the company to do** is …

11 Rewrite the following sentences using relative clauses, participial or infinitive constructions.

1. A market is a set of arrangements allowing companies to sell their goods and consumers to buy them.
2. The price which is asked for a product should not be too high.
3. Advertising is one of several instruments which are used in marketing.
4. Stores displaying their goods unattractively should not complain about poor sales figures.
5. Sponsorships are one of the most popular methods which are employed by businesses to boost sales.
6. Pens and key rings are just two of the cheap products which are often given away free.
7. The best way in which companies can improve their sales is by carrying out extensive market research.
8. A target group can be defined as a group expected to buy products and services.
9. Nike, traditionally associated with sports equipment, is now moving into consumer electronics.
10. The only thing which our advertising department can do is to hire a professional agency.

12 Translate the following sentences.

1 Marketing ist ein Begriff, der sich sehr schwer definieren lässt, weil er so umfassend ist.
2 Früher waren Markennamen wesentlich weniger bedeutend als heute, wo sie schon fast zu einem Symbol für Lebensqualität geworden sind.
3 Bei der Festsetzung von Preisen für Produkte und Dienstleistungen müssen wir auch Faktoren berücksichtigen, die auf dem Kaufverhalten der Verbraucher basieren.
4 Werbung ist nicht das einzige Marketinginstrument, das hohe Umsätze garantiert.
5 Bei bestimmten, bekannten Marken ist die Qualität des Produkts weniger entscheidend für den Verkaufserfolg als der Markenname selbst.
6 Selbst mit der genauesten bislang durchgeführten Marktuntersuchung kann man nicht alle Änderungen im Konsumentengeschmack vorhersagen.
7 Auch das Internet wird zunehmend häufig genutzt, um für Produkte zu werben, die mit der betreffenden Website eigentlich nichts zu tun haben.
8 Unternehmen, die im Fernsehen werben, vermarkten in der Regel Massenprodukte.
9 Unter den zwölf weltweit bekanntesten Markennamen sind zehn, die zu amerikanischen Unternehmen gehören.
10 Das Beste, was sie jetzt tun können, ist sich auf ihre traditionellen Markenartikel zu konzentrieren.

9 International trade

What do these headlines tell us about international trade?

US pushes for new trade talks

Forget flying the flag – we're all global now

India to expand trade ties with EU

Europe Versus United States In Steel War

China joins WTO – *at last*

TEXT A 24

Britain's overseas trade

There have been a great many changes in the pattern of Britain's overseas trade over the years. For instance, the percentage of imported food and beverages has been dropping for some time and now stands at 9 per cent. The reason is that demand has been met by domestic agriculture, and there has also been a decline in the proportion of total expenditure on food. Meanwhile, imported finished manufactures account for almost 60 per cent of the import total. Commodity imports like coal and oil as well as services make up the remaining 31 per cent.

The United States remains Britain's largest external market, accounting for 13 per cent of Britain's exports, followed by Germany, France and the Netherlands. The countries of the European Union between them take 56 per cent of all British exports. Germany tops the import table ahead of France and the Netherlands. Globally, the USA is in second place.

Britain has always been an exporter of manufactured goods. However, the composition of its exports has changed significantly. Machinery and transport equipment account for nearly half of all visible exports. Aerospace, chemicals and electronics have become major export sectors, while textiles have declined in relative importance. Britain is also Europe's biggest exporter of computers, television sets and microchips.

Service exports include a wide variety of industries: there are the traditional ones like banking, insurance, stockbroking, shipping, aviation and tourism. Recently, specialist services such as engineering consultancy, computer programming and specialist training have been added to this list. These invisible exports make a major contribution to Britain's balance of payments.

Britain's overseas sales of goods and services are equivalent to about a quarter of GDP. While its balance on invisible trade shows a healthy surplus, it traditionally imports more goods than it exports, e.g. food, electrical machinery, road vehicles and clothing. This has often led to overall deficits in its balance of payments.

Open, transparent and effective markets will help to improve Britain's competitiveness in international markets and ultimately secure economic prosperity, non-inflationary growth and full employment.

(adapted from *Britain 2001 – The Official Yearbook of the United Kingdom*)

1 Find the terms in text A to match the following.

1 international commercial transactions (paragraph 1)
2 amount of money paid (paragraph 1)
3 secondary sector products ready for use (paragraph 1)
4 goods sold abroad (paragraph 2)
5 technological advice (paragraph 4)
6 amount by which spending exceeds revenues (paragraph 5)
7 ability to succeed in the market (paragraph 6)
8 characterized by stability of money (paragraph 6)

2 Choose the correct option.

1 Almost two thirds of British imports are
   a primary sector products.
   b secondary sector products.
   c tertiary sector products.
2 Britain's overseas trade has seen
   a significant changes in food demand.
   b a decrease in the import share of food and drink.
   c an increase in the home market share for finished products.
3 Germany
   a is the leading importer of British goods.
   b exports more goods to Britain than any other country.
   c helps Britain export goods to other countries.
4 Together, the EU and the USA account for
   a 69 per cent of Britain's exports.
   b 56 per cent of Britain's exports.
   c 56 per cent of Britain's imports.
5 Britain's visible exports
   a no longer include textiles.
   b chiefly consist of vehicles.
   c include engineering products.
6 Britain's service exports
   a used to be restricted to transport services.
   b are confined to financial transactions.
   c also include advisory services.
7 The tertiary sector
   a does not significantly affect Britain's balance of payments.
   b helps Britain to achieve a more favourable balance of payments.
   c usually contributes to Britain's adverse balance of payments.
8 Britain's balance of payments
   a amounts to approximately 25 per cent of GDP.
   b shows a healthy surplus.
   c has frequently been in the red.

3 Translate the following text into German.

Britain has an open economy in which international trade plays a vital part. Its government cooperates fully with the WTO*. The share of Britain's GDP accounted for by exports and services has risen considerably over the past fifteen years. This coincides with the development in most other developed countries and shows the growing importance of international trade in an increasingly interdependent world economy.

Membership of the European Union (EU) has had a major impact on Britain's trade pattern. Since Britain joined the EEC in 1973, the percentage of Britain's exports to other EU members has risen from a third to well over half.

* WTO = World Trade Organization: global organization whose aim is to develop cross-border trade by abolishing trade barriers.

4 Complete the text with some of the terms from the following list.

agreements • coffee • cross-border • declare • embargo • formalities • grant • import • impose • obstacles • protectionism • quota • tariffs

In the past, …[1] trade was more complicated than domestic trade. Importers had to …[2] all the goods they obtained from abroad. Customs clearance required a great many …[3]. If commodities like …[4] were imported, they were usually placed in a bonded warehouse for further processing before customs duty became payable. …[5] duties were charged partly for reasons of …[6]. Preferential …[7] only applied to selected countries and certain goods. Under WTO …[8], countries were encouraged to …[9] each other most-favoured nation terms. Even if customs duties were to be abolished, there would still be major …[10] to trade, for instance different technical standards.

5 Study the Airbus illustration and answer the following questions.

1 What does this picture illustrate?
2 Why are the components produced in several countries?

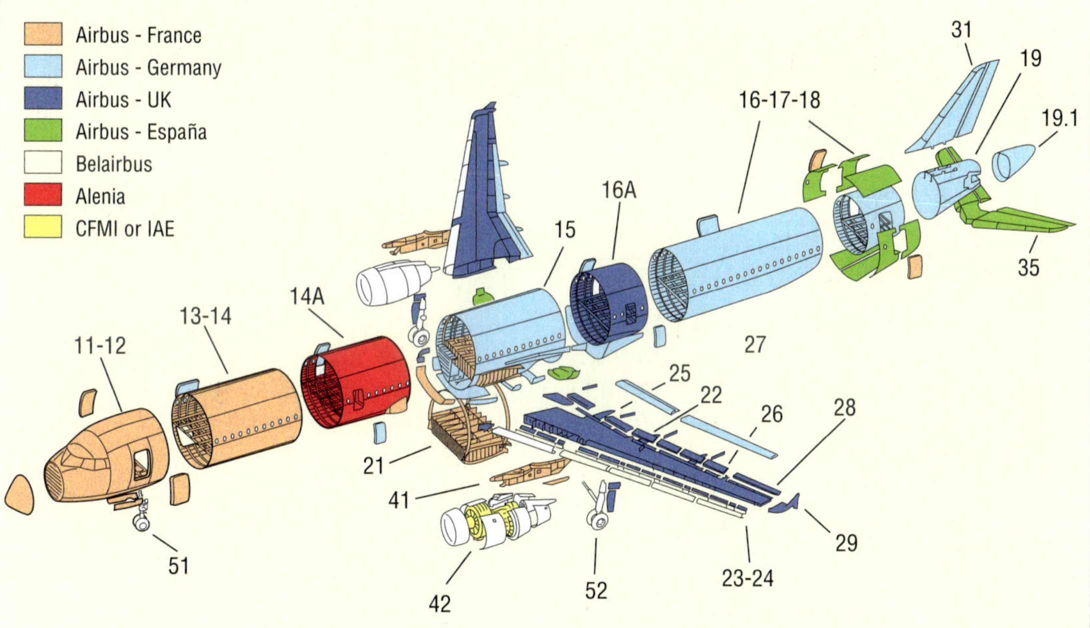

Section	Designations				
00	Aircraft G.A.	20	Wing G.A.	30	Tailplane
10	Fuselage G.A.	21	Center Section	31	Vertical Tailplane
11-12	Nose Forward Fuselage	22	Wing Box	35	Horizontal Tailplane
13-14	Forward Fuselage	23-24	Fixed + Moving Leading Edge Surface	40	Passenger Doors and Cargo Doors
14A	Forward Fuselage	25	Rear Part Fixed	41	Pylons
15	Center Fuselage	26	Spoilers	42	Pods
16A	Rear Fuselage	27	Flaps	51	Nose Landing Gear
16-17-18	Rear Fuselage	28	Ailerons	52	Main Landing Gear
19	Cone Rear Fuselage	29	Wing Tip		
19.1	Tailcone				

TEXT B 25

Globalization in the auto industry

Trading across national borders is of vital importance to all modern economies. In fact, most economies would collapse if governments adopted a policy of self-sufficiency by keeping out imports and dispensing with exports. In the second half of the 20th century, governments pursued free-trade policies by reducing and abolishing tariff and non-tariff barriers and by forming or joining trading groups like the European Common Market. The European Union is now the world's largest trading bloc, accounting for 40 per cent of world exports. Global free trade has also led to more inward and outward investment as many companies exploit the opportunities offered by universal free trade and open manufacturing facilities and/or trading subsidiaries abroad.

A good example of this trend towards globalization is the merger between Daimler Benz of Germany and Chrysler Corporation of the USA in 1998, which at the time was the biggest industrial merger in history. It created one of the world's largest automobile groups, with sales of about $130 billion and more than 400,000 employees worldwide. One of the major reasons for this merger was the saturation of the European and US automobile markets. DaimlerChrysler therefore sought to secure competitiveness and profitability by economies of scale and by gaining access to expanding markets like India and eastern Europe.

From the start of their negotiations, Daimler and Chrysler were aware that the world automobile industry was at a critical stage. Overcapacity, the financial crises in Asia and many emerging-market countries, as well as environmental concerns were all sources of uncertainty. It was thought that the resulting costs could best be met by putting the groups on a broader international footing, not least through outsourcing some production-related activities.

Until late in the twentieth century, outsourcing basically meant relying on domestic component suppliers. The ongoing abolition of trade barriers worldwide – not only within Europe and the North American Free Trade Agreement (NAFTA) area – has however led to major shifts in the production and purchase of components and automobiles away from high-cost locations like North America, western Europe and Japan. Volkswagen for instance has built production facilities in countries such as Mexico and the Czech Republic, and in 1995 General Motors formed a joint venture with a Chinese company worth $1.1 billion.

The development of the automobile industry in the past twenty years suggests that increasing globalization could soon affect many other industries and that there may be a time when the classic distinction between home and foreign trade will no longer be relevant.

6 Match the terms on the left with the definitions on the right.

1 globalization (title)	a administrative and/or technical hurdle
2 abolish (line 5)	b company belonging to another company
3 non-tariff barrier (line 5)	c do away with
4 outward investment (line 9)	d purchase goods and services from outside suppliers
5 subsidiary (line 11)	e corporate capital expenditure abroad
6 saturation (line 17)	f process by which companies expand to operate worldwide
7 outsource (line 26)	g temporary partnership to complete a project
8 joint venture (line 35)	h level beyond which demand is unlikely to increase

7 Complete the following sentences on text B.

1 … if there were no imports and exports. (paragraph 1)
2 The aim of the Common Market was … (paragraph 1)
3 Inward investment means investment by foreign companies, while … (paragraph 1)
4 … that it was difficult to sell more cars in the USA and Europe. (paragraph 2)
5 … to pool their resources. (paragraph 2)
6 Environmental concerns … (paragraph 3)
7 … to cut costs. (paragraph 3)
8 … restricted to domestic suppliers. (paragraph 4)
9 Major producers … (paragraph 4)
10 One result of increasing globalization may well be that … (paragraph 5)

8 Write short texts on these four subjects. Give examples where possible.

INFORMATION

US balance of payments (BOP) 2000

The balance of payments consists of

- the balance on current account, which is made up of the balance of visible trade and the balance of invisible trade. This lists the import and export figures for goods and services and covers items such as raw materials, manufactures, tourism and travel. The balance on current account includes interest on capital invested and dividend payments.
- the balance on financial and capital account, listing capital movements which are due over a period of years. It covers items like long-term loans as well as inward and outward investment. Inward and outward movements do not usually match. As a result, there is either a deficit or a surplus in the balance of payments.

Current account *(examples in brackets)*	**total in $**
1 Exports of visibles *(airplanes)*	**773,304m**
2 Imports of visibles *(crude oil)*	**–1,222,772m**
3 Exports of invisibles *(license fees to US corporations)*	**296,227m**
4 Imports of invisibles *(insurance premiums paid to British insurance company)*	**–215,239m**
Trade balance	**–368,480m**
5 Income receipts *(dividends earned in Japan)*	**345,394m**
6 Income payments *(rent payments to owner of office block abroad)*	**–359,050m**
7 Unilateral transfers *(government grants and private remittances to accounts held abroad)*	**–53,241m**
Current account balance	**–435,377m**
Financial and capital account	
8 Increase in foreign holdings of assets in the US *(purchase of US property by Swiss individual)*	**952,430m**
9 Increase in US-owned assets held abroad *(acquisition of Spanish company)*	**–553,349m**
Balance on financial and capital account	**399,081m**
Balance of payments	**–36,296m**

(source: *Bureau of Economic Analysis*)

9 Classify the following items under sections 1 to 9 in the box above.

1 aero engines imported from Britain *2*
2 purchase of company in Germany by US company *9*
3 money sent home by Mexican farm labourers working in the US
4 arms exported from the United States to Saudi Arabia
5 dividends earned in Switzerland
6 auto parts imported from Japan
7 insurance of US aircraft in Britain
8 sports equipment imported from China
9 money spent by UK tourists in the US
10 interest payments to French investor
11 income received in Italy by US airlines
12 takeover of US company by Spanish investor
13 transfer of US payment to UNESCO in Switzerland
14 purchase of office block in the US by Swedish investor

10 Discuss arguments for or against these slogans. Work in groups.

GRAMMAR

Adverbs

Adverbs modify

- verbs: Imports have risen **slowly**.
- adjectives: Services are **particularly** important today.
- adverbs: The manufacturing industry has been declining **extremely** rapidly.
- sentences: **Unfortunately**, embargoes are still not a thing of the past.
- prepositional phrases: As a US export destination, Mexico ranks **immediately** behind Canada.

NOTE Adjectives, not adverbs, are used after verbs like *appear, be, consider, feel, look, remain, seem, sound.*

– Export prospects remain **favourable**.

11 Complete the sentences with the appropriate adjectival or adverbial form of the words in the list.

exceeding • gradual • great • immediate • increasing • more important • ~~not surprising~~ • recent • vast

EXAMPLE *Not surprisingly*, customs duties are a major cost factor in foreign trade.

1 Embargoes are being used … often.
2 Service exports are considered … nowadays than exports of raw materials.
3 Outsourcing is developing at a(n) … fast rate.
4 Trade barriers are … being abolished.
5 Foreign trade has … increased the availability of consumer goods.
6 There have been … improvements in the performance of our subsidiaries.
7 There has been a lot of inward investment … .
8 Payment is to be effected … on receipt of the goods.

12 Translate the following sentences.

1 In der letzten Zeit spielen Rohstoffexporte wegen des Nordseeöls wieder eine größere Rolle in der britischen Handelsbilanz.
2 Gegenwärtig stellen Großbritanniens Dienstleistungsexporte einen äußerst wichtigen Wirtschaftsfaktor dar.
3 Der Handel innerhalb der Europäischen Gemeinschaft nimmt immer noch stark zu.
4 Die Investitionstätigkeit ausländischer Unternehmen in Irland wird von der Regierung für wichtig erachtet und deshalb großzügig gefördert.
5 Wegen der fast völligen Sättigung der heimischen Märkte investieren viele große Automobilhersteller zunehmend im Ausland.
6 Wahrscheinlich wird die Unterscheidung zwischen Binnen- und Außenhandel in Europa bald keine Rolle mehr spielen.
7 Größenvorteile sind bei der Standortwahl nicht immer der entscheidende Faktor.
8 Trotz der positiven wirtschaftlichen Entwicklung war die Zahlungsbilanz im vergangenen Jahr nicht nur in Großbritannien, sondern auch in den USA negativ.
9 Die USA hatten im Jahr 2000 noch eine negative Zahlungsbilanz, weil die positive Kapitalbilanz das Defizit in der Leistungsbilanz nicht ganz ausgleichen konnte.
10 Die deutsche Wirtschaft hat in den vergangenen Jahrzehnten immer einen hohen Handelsbilanzüberschuss erzielt.
11 Prozentual gesehen ist in den USA der Dienstleistungssektor wesentlich weniger wichtig für die Zahlungsbilanz als der primäre und der sekundäre Sektor.
12 Textilien werden heutzutage weitgehend aus Niedriglohnländern eingeführt.

10 Logistics

You are being sent to the USA on a two-year contract. Discuss the various options for transporting bulky items, like your bike, skis, etc.

TEXT A 26

Supply chain management

Logistics is concerned with the inbound and outbound transport of raw materials and supplies between production locations as well as movements within a plant. More simply, it is the science (and art) of ensuring that the right products reach the right place in the right quantity at the right time. It therefore also involves warehousing, stock management and information systems. Nowadays, with the continuing development of worldwide supply chains, manufacturers, retailers and other companies are demanding more from global logistics. There are two reasons for this:

- International trade has grown twice as fast as global economic output over the past decade, with many US multinationals earning more than half their revenues from overseas sales.
- Globalization means that more parts and products are being supplied by manufacturers in many different countries, complicating the coordination and on-time delivery of inbound freight.

Multinational shippers have recognized the growing importance of global logistics and also the need to look for cost savings. These include:

- choosing cheaper transport modes to meet customer requirements;
- selecting competitive carriers;
- reducing the number of third-party suppliers and choosing the best for each shipment;
- maximizing direct routing opportunities (e.g. cutting out stops at intermediate distribution centres).

Buyers demand fast and reliable delivery services, especially for high-value products such as computers, electronic equipment and automotive parts. At the same time, they want these services made available at the lowest possible cost.

Companies are finding that the best solution to their logistics problems often lies in better planning and coordination by all the parties concerned. A consignment whose departure from the factory is delayed is likely to involve extra freight costs and might still be delivered late. Improvements in supply chain management can be achieved by developing closer links between purchasing and logistics and also by determining electronically the optimum balance between production scheduling, load planning and inventory holding.

One of the main obstacles to controlling the global supply chain is the lack of door-to-door visibility of shipments. Many senders of freight claim their consignments disappear into black holes on international transit routes, and they find it difficult to locate the freight or find the causes of delays. This leads to firms carrying expensive safety stocks to meet customer and factory needs.

Reliable supply systems are being demanded for countries where there are problems with customs clearance and local delivery systems. Traditionally, forwarders, carriers and customs brokers have handled different parts of each international shipment. Attention nowadays increasingly focuses on door-to-door visibility and absolute reliability. As a result, pressure has grown for someone to manage the entire process. Satellite-based software solutions for tracking and tracing now allow the importer, exporter and forwarder to monitor this process.

Freight forwarders are also broadening their activities, with some groups, for example, adding ocean freight and customs brokerage to their air freight operations. Ocean carriers are also extending their range of services by offering forwarding services to complement existing ocean shipping and freight consolidation operations. Nowadays, freight forwarders are large, integrated logistics companies providing comprehensive one-stop freight services for their customers worldwide.

1 Give a brief explanation of the following terms from text A.

1 output (line 9)
2 inbound freight (line 14)
3 consignment (line 27)
4 inventory holding (line 32)
5 customs clearance (line 39)
6 tracking and tracing (line 43)
7 freight consolidation (line 48)
8 comprehensive one-stop freight services (lines 49–50)

2 Refer to text A and correct the following statements.

1 Economic output has grown twice as fast as international trade. (paragraph 1)
2 Globalization has made it easier to purchase parts. (paragraph 1)
3 In order to cut costs, shippers rely on their own transport facilities. (paragraph 2)
4 Substantial cost savings can only be achieved by direct routing. (paragraph 2)
5 Transport delays can be overcome simply by paying premium freight rates. (paragraph 4)
6 Production scheduling, load planning and inventory holding need to be optimized. (paragraph 4)
7 With door-to-door shipments being available every day, safety stocks are not really necessary. (paragraph 5)
8 It is only the forwarder who knows the whereabouts of consignments. (paragraph 6)
9 Major transport specialists are cutting back their operations. (paragraph 7)
10 Ocean carriers have always provided an all-inclusive service. (paragraph 7)

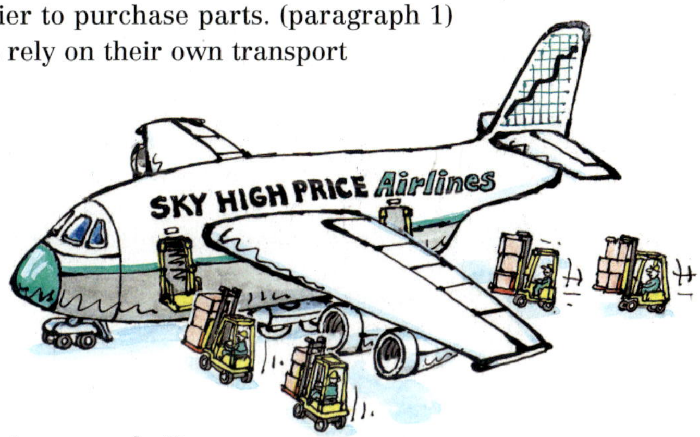

3 Complete the lists using the terms below.

cargo airline • consignee • consignor • forwarding agent • freight agent • haulage company • haulier • railway company • sender • shipping agent • shipping company

Parties involved in the transport chain

party sending the goods	party arranging transport	party moving the goods	party receiving the goods
shipper	forwarder	carrier	recipient
	shipper		

4 Find the missing words.

verb	noun	active party	recipient
consign	consignment	consigner/-or	consignee
address		xxxxxxxxxxxx	
	advice		xxxxxxxxxxxx
carry			xxxxxxxxxxxx
		consolidator	xxxxxxxxxxxx
draw	draft		
			employee
	forwarding		xxxxxxxxxxxx
		franchiser/-or	
license			
		operator	xxxxxxxxxxxx
pay			
	shipping / shipment		xxxxxxxxxxxx
		supplier	xxxxxxxxxxxx

5 Complete these sentences with words from exercise 4.

1 If the … cannot be reached, the letter will be returned to the sender.
2 Arrangements have been made for the … to pick up the … at your factory at 10 a.m. on 28 June.
3 Urgently needed goods are best … by air.
4 Your March … of computer chips arrived five days late.
5 To reduce costs, shippers often … general cargo into a full container load.
6 If FOB Felixstowe has been agreed, … to the seaport will be paid by the supplier.
7 As our stocks are running low, we need to get in a fresh … of mineral water.
8 … goods by road, although very sensible in commercial terms, is often environmentally unacceptable.
9 These two haulage companies … a fleet of 85 trucks.
10 Upon arrival of the goods, the … has to sign a freight note as proof of delivery.

6 Replace the explanations in brackets with the terms below.

buffer stocks • containerization • groupage consignments • high-bay warehouses • just-in-time (JIT) deliveries • palletizing • pick • storage and retrieval • transshipment • warehousing

Logistics today is much more than just transporting goods and raw materials from one location to another. It also involves the (putting of goods into 20/40ft steel boxes) …[1] of general cargo as well as making up (shipments of several items to different addresses in one load) …[2], breaking bulk and (storing goods) …[3]. In addition, it is concerned with collecting and distributing goods from and to manufacturers and consumers. Containerization has vastly improved the efficiency of these operations, as has (using a standard wooden or metal base) …[4] smaller items, because forklift trucks and container cranes can now be used for loading, unloading or (transfer of goods from one mode of transport onto another) …[5].

In the same way, goods storage has changed beyond recognition. Modern warehouses are located close to motorways and they are usually designed as (tall buildings to keep goods) …[6] with narrow aisles. The (putting onto and taking off shelves in a warehouse) …[7] of goods on pallets is fully mechanized. Thus, it is possible to (select) …[8] orders and to dispatch the goods within a matter of hours. As a result, manufacturers can now rely on (supply of goods at exactly the time needed) …[9] of the components they need for production, with delivery often being made direct to the assembly line. They only keep (goods which are kept in reserve) …[10] for an emergency.

7 Study the flow chart and then describe the stages one of the following raw materials goes through before it reaches the German end-user.

~~American wheat~~ • Canadian timber • Costa Rican bananas • Kenyan coffee • Nigerian crude oil

EXAMPLE *combine harvester – truck to station for rail transport to port (Chicago) – bulk carrier to Bremen – truck or train to mill – truck to bakery – van to baker's shop*

INFORMATION

The supply chain: from raw material to end-user

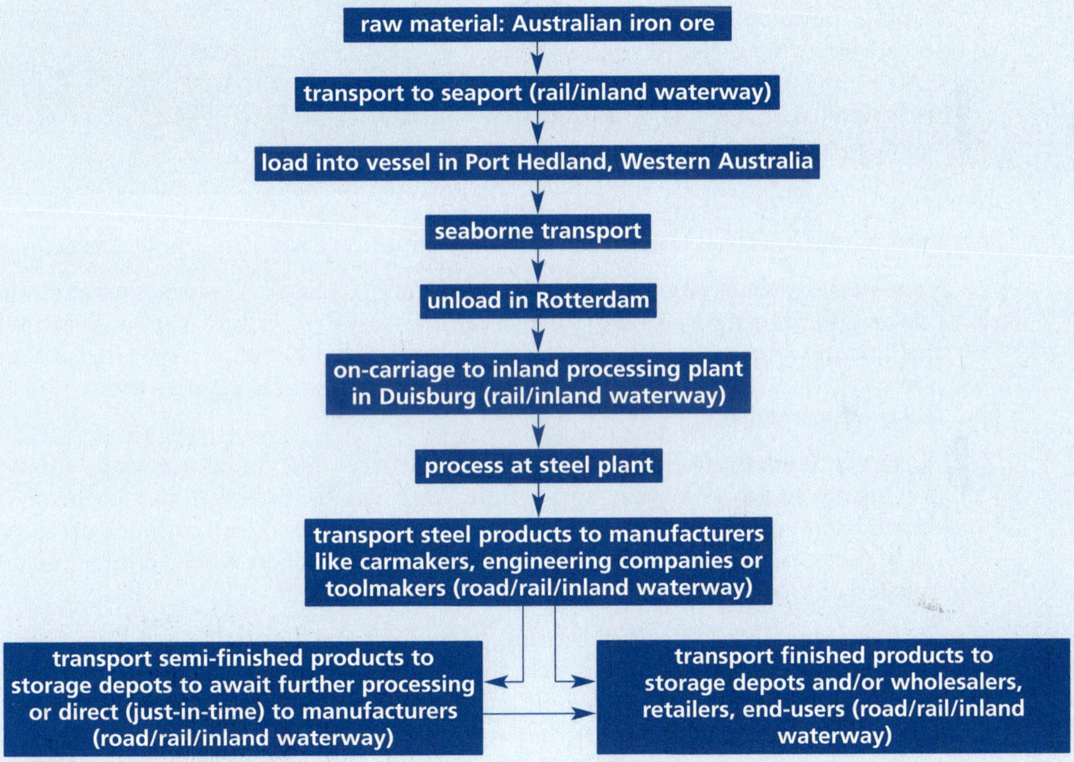

8 Write approximately 100 words on modern logistics, covering the following points.

- the importance of globalization
- cost savings
- controlling the supply chain
- a comprehensive service package

Start as follows: *Economic activities are now truly international. As a result, many logistics companies have become multinational groups with worldwide operations. …*

TEXT B 27

Europe's ports getting shipshape

Europe's ports are facing great challenges. The most immediate is to retain the business they have while meeting the demands of their shipowner users in the era of the jumbo container vessel. The two objectives overlap. The ports know that shipowners and shippers both expect high standards of service.

This has resulted in ports like Antwerp and Rotterdam making huge investments in new quays, marshalling yards and support services, while Le Havre has expanded its container facilities. Another task for Europe's leading port authorities and private stevedoring firms is to drive down costs by improving operational performance. The aim is to shorten vessel turnaround times and upgrade customer service through improved IT and security systems. In a buyer's market, the ports acknowledge that competition will continue to be fierce.

Increased productivity and lower hinterland transport costs provide the impetus for the development of intermodal services. Where this involves rail and inland water transport, there are environmental benefits. To enhance their potential, however, intermodal operations need identical regulatory as well as technical standards.

Ports are ideal locations for value-added services like bulk breaking, further processing and pre-delivery inspection. One result has been the creation of distribution parks. This focus on value-added services means that a port is no longer seen merely as the interface in the transport chain where containers are transferred from one mode of transport to another.

Environmental sensitivity concerning ports has been translated into legislation. Oil, coal, grain, animal feedstock, timber and other bulk commodities are controlled by the most stringent environmental laws. Inland navigation, an eco-friendly mode of transport, has seen increased transport volumes in recent years. The container-carrying barge is now an integral part of inland distribution at Hamburg and the Benelux ports. Iron ore can reach the blast furnaces of the Ruhr within 24 hours of being transshipped at Rotterdam in push vessels able to transport 15,000 tonnes. Car-carrying barges are also becoming a familiar sight on the Rhine.

Other developments at Europe's ports include building new terminals as well as deeper approach channels to make the ports accessible to ships drawing 15.5 metres. The predicted growth in seaborne trade is good news for Europe's ports. For some, it can't happen too soon.

9 Answer the following questions on text B.

1 What objectives do Europe's ports have to meet?
2 How have Europe's ports responded to these challenges?
3 How can operational performance be improved?
4 Why is intermodal transport becoming attractive?
5 How can intermodal services be improved?
6 What does the term 'interface' (line 32) mean in this context?
7 In what ways have environmental considerations affected the transport chain?
8 What measures have European ports taken to attract new traffic?

10 Read the statements and answer the questions. Work in groups.

1 A stevedore is defined as a person whose job is to move goods on and off ships. How do stevedoring firms (line 17) load and unload ships today?
2 Turnaround times (line 20) used to be days or even weeks. Why?
3 Hinterland transport costs (line 24) are of great importance when it comes to choosing the mode of transport. In what ways has this cost factor led to new developments?
4 Identical regulatory or technical standards (lines 27–28) have been adopted or should be adopted in rail and inland water transport. Can you think of any?
5 Processing goods in the port itself, e.g. refining oil, is a value-added service (line 29). Can you give more examples?
6 Environmentalists are very sensitive when it comes to transport, preferring some transportation modes to others. What is your opinion?

28

11 Delayed delivery: listen to the phone call and list the main points.

12 Translate this passage into German.

According to some estimates, the value of the UK's express parcels delivery market has crept past the £2 billion mark during the past year – a notable milestone in a story of continued expansion. Revenues were already on the increase last year, but if anything the statistics this year reflect an even faster growth this time round.

The higher figures do not, of course, necessarily indicate greater profitability for the parcel carriers themselves. Some parcel carriers report that volumes are increasing faster than prices, which in this sector are particularly vulnerable to competitive pressures.

Nevertheless, many of the carriers felt optimistic enough to continue opening new depots, expanding their hub depots and enlarging their truck fleets. In the case of Parcelforce, a massive £100 million has been allocated for investment in a new 'superhub' complex at Coventry, incorporating both domestic and international sorting capabilities. Securicor Omega Express is also involved in a major round of spending, which includes £30 million on a giant international hub at Hatfield, north of London.

INFORMATION

Modes of transport

Seaborne freight

- ferries over short and medium distances, fixed timetables, roll-on/roll-off (RoRo) facilities; cargo liners, usually container vessels on fixed routes, fast scheduled services; tramps chartered for specific voyages; bulk carriers and tankers for commodities like iron ore and crude oil

Inland waterways

- barges for bulk cargoes and bulky items like transformers

Road haulage

- trucks and trailers, especially articulated vehicles

Multimodal transport

- road vehicles frequently equipped with swapbodies, easy to load onto railway flatbed wagons; trailers or entire trucks carried by train (piggyback service)

Railways

- for bulk cargoes either in full trainloads or in individual box or tank wagons; also for the transport of containers and palletized loads

Airborne freight

- used for parcels, special pallets and air containers

Pipelines

- liquids and gases

13 Study the box above and say how the following commodities can best be transported. Give reasons.

1 200 newspapers from Frankfurt to Glasgow
2 2,000kgs of oranges from Jaffa (Israel) to Eindhoven (NL)
3 regular consignments of pharmaceuticals (50kgs) from Ingelheim (near Mainz) to Telford (near Birmingham)
4 a transformer measuring 25ft by 22ft by 15ft from Stafford (near Birmingham) to Esch (Luxembourg)
5 10 luxury cars from Stuttgart to Kyoto (Japan)
6 urgently needed medical supplies from Marburg to various destinations in the Congo
7 25 tonnes of toxic chemicals from Basel to Grangemouth (Scotland)
8 950,000 barrels of crude oil from Kuwait to Ingolstadt

GRAMMAR

The passive voice

- The passive voice is formed by using *be* and the past participle of the verb. The direct object of the active sentence normally becomes the subject of the passive sentence.
  - Messrs Stewart & Sons **will forward** the goods.
  - The goods **will be forwarded** by Messrs Stewart & Sons.
- The agent (identified by the preposition *by*) is often left out in passive sentences.
  - We **have chartered** a tramp to transport the equipment to Shanghai.
  - A tramp **has been chartered** (by us) to transport the equipment to Shanghai.
- If there is a personal indirect object in the active sentence, this usually becomes the subject of the passive sentence.
  - My secretary **will send** you the relevant documents as soon as possible.
  - You **will be sent** the relevant documents (by my secretary) as soon as possible.

14 Rewrite the following sentences in the passive.

1 McAlpine Construction are upgrading Dover's port facilities.
2 Barges are carrying more and more non-bulk goods.
3 You can see push vessels on all the world's major inland waterways.
4 We earn more than half our revenues from international logistics operations.
5 TransOcean Ltd have offered us an attractive freight package.
6 Most firms carry expensive buffer stocks to meet unexpected customer requirements.
7 We will send you the transport documents by airmail.
8 We are building new storage facilities in the dock area.
9 They have given us five days to get the turbines from Newcastle to Marseille.
10 Our forwarders will pick up the consignment on Wednesday.

15 Translate the following sentences.

1 Die verspätete Sendung ist gestern beim Empfänger eingegangen.
2 Normcontainer werden in der Regel mit Linienfrachtschiffen befördert.
3 Die drei neuen Fähren sind vor einem Jahr bestellt worden und inzwischen im Bau.
4 Dem Spediteur wurde ein sehr attraktives Angebot unterbreitet.
5 Früher wurden die meisten Überseesendungen in großen und kleinen Holzkisten verpackt, eine Verpackungsart, die kaum noch genutzt wird.
6 Die meisten Häfen dienten in der Vergangenheit lediglich als Schnittstelle zwischen Übersee- und Binnenverkehr.
7 Wegen der Verzögerung in der Produktion werden die Maschinen vermutlich verspätet ausgeliefert werden.
8 Alle Transportrisiken werden vom Frachtführer bzw. von dessen Versicherung getragen.
9 Von einem modernen Logistikunternehmen werden viele unterschiedliche Dienstleistungen erbracht.
10 In der Zukunft werden wahrscheinlich mehr Güter als heute im kombinierten Ladungsverkehr befördert.

11 Insurance

What types of insurance do these pictures illustrate?
Which of these do you consider necessary for yourself and why?

TEXT A 29

Modern forms of insurance

Modern forms of insurance, both personal and non-personal, only evolved in the 18th and 19th centuries. Before that, suppliers – being creditors – usually put a premium on the price of the merchandise they sold, thus covering various risks like theft, damage or loss. This system of individual underwriting was also practised by moneylenders until risk-sharing schemes were devised. One such scheme has survived to this day at Lloyd's, London's insurance market, where underwriters, the so-called Names, cover a percentage of a risk in return for a premium.

Insurance can be defined as an arrangement under which one party – the insurer – provides cover for a risk which the other party – the insured – considers too great to leave uninsured. This arrangement is laid down in a contract called the policy.

Insurance requires that a large group of identical or similar risks be covered at the same time. However, there should also be very little likelihood of large numbers of policyholders making claims at the same time. Insurance companies therefore employ mathematicians, known as actuaries, to work out the probabilities of possible losses and to calculate the appropriate premiums.

Insurance risks can be classified as follows:

- Personal risks: death, accident, sickness, disability, unemployment
- Property risks: fire, riot and civil commotion, vandalism, theft, flooding
- Transport risks: air crash, loss at sea, rail disaster, road traffic accident

While every economic unit is subject to risk, it is the smaller economic units like family businesses or small companies which need insurance most.

Financial risks like loans to customers can be covered by means of a credit insurance, while damage to and loss of property through fire, flooding, theft or vandalism are usually covered by an all-inclusive business policy.

The most important form of personal insurance apart from health insurance, which is statutory in most EU countries, is life insurance. The major types of life insurance are term insurance, which only pays out if the policyholder dies within a specific period, and endowment insurance, which combines a savings component with a risk component. In the event of the policyholder's death within a certain period, the dependants will be paid the sum stipulated in the policy in the same way as they would under a term policy. If the policyholder survives the fixed number of years, he or she will be paid out the accumulated capital including investment returns. This type of policy is often taken out by both employees and self-employed people in order to supplement their pensions.

Automobile insurance is designed to cover bodily injury and property damage liability. While third-party policies are required by law before the vehicle can be registered, comprehensive policies provide coverage even if the insured is at fault. However, the insurance company is likely to stipulate an excess, i.e. a certain amount or percentage which the insured has to pay if he or she causes an accident. US motor insurers also offer uninsured motorist coverage to protect the insured in cases where the party responsible for the damage is not insured. Under safe driver plans, the premiums may be increased or decreased in accordance with the insured's driving record. The British equivalent for safe drivers is a no-claims bonus or no-claims discount.

1 Find the missing words in text A.

1 The premium charged by suppliers was intended to … a variety of risks.
2 Insurers provide cover for risks which the … considers worth insuring.
3 Insurance is not risky as … work out the statistical likelihood of claims.
4 Damage to property caused by hooligans is usually classified as … .
5 Companies are normally covered against a variety of risks by means of … policies.
6 Employees in Germany are insured against the consequences of sickness under a … scheme.
7 Self-employed people usually take out an … insurance to provide for their old age.
8 In Britain and elsewhere, safe drivers are rewarded by being granted a … .

2 Why, in your opinion, …?

1 … is insurance indispensable?
2 … are insurance companies unlikely to operate at a loss?
3 … are loans sometimes covered by special policies?
4 … are endowment policies so popular?
5 … do comprehensive vehicle policies stipulate an excess?
6 … is uninsured motorist coverage to be recommended in the USA?
7 … are automobile premiums raised or lowered for individual policyholders?

Imperial Motor Insurance

What you need to know before you fill in a proposal form.

The best deal for you

As intermediaries, we don't work for any single insurance company – we work for you. Our goal is to find the best quality cover at the best price. Your age, the car you drive, where you live, your occupation, your no-claims discount are all important factors that influence the premium you pay.

YOUR COVER AT A GLANCE

	Type of insurance		
	third party	**third party and theft**	**comprehensive**
1 Accidental damage cover. Damage to your car and accessories as well as the cost of towing your car to the nearest recommended garage.			✓
2 Loss of or damage to your car by fire, theft or attempted theft.		✓	✓
3 Windscreen cover. When damage only relates to the windscreen or other windows, your no-claims discount will not normally be affected.			✓
4 Loss of or damage to rugs, clothing and personal belongings while they are in your car.			✓
5 Personal injury to other people. Your liability for death or injury to other people.	✓	✓	✓
6 Damage to other people's property.	✓	✓	✓
7 Passenger negligence. The liability of passengers in your car for accidents caused by them.	✓	✓	✓
8 Driving other cars. Your liability to others while driving a car not owned by you or hired to you under a hire purchase agreement.	✓	✓	✓
9 Legal defence. Unlimited legal defence costs.	✓	✓	✓
10 Personal accident cover. Specific financial payments (irrespective of liability) to you or your spouse for death or loss of limb or eye.			✓
11 Medical expenses up to £1000 incurred by you or your passengers.			✓

3 Translate sections 1 to 11 in the brochure on page 88.

4 Assuming you have a car, which motor insurance cover would suit your personal needs best and why?

30

5 Phoning an insurance hotline: listen to the dialogue and complete the form below.

NIAGARA INSURANCE

1 Policyholder's name: ....

2 Policy number: ....

3 Scene of accident: ....

4 Who caused accident? ....

5 Other driver's insurance and policy number: ....

6 Was anyone injured? ....

7 Damage to insured vehicle? ....

8 Were the police called? ....

TEXT B

31

Swiss Re plans life insurance sales online

Swiss Re is making plans to sell life insurance over the internet in the US and is likely to announce an ambitious joint venture with a high-technology company in the next few months.

The move by one of the world's largest insurance groups will challenge the traditional idea that life insurance cannot be sold over the internet, resulting in the sector being slow to offer products online.

Traditionally, insurance has been seen as a product that needs agents to convince customers that they require it. In addition, insurers have not been able to achieve the speed and efficiency gains seen in other industries due to the need in almost all life policies to ask prospective policyholders to undergo blood and other medical tests.

As a result, approval of life policy proposals can often take a month. However, Swiss Re is planning to offer some policies of up to $250,000 that do not require blood tests.

Its US life insurance executives said they hoped to approve 60–70 per cent of applications almost immediately once applicants had answered nine medical questions online.

It hoped also to increase the percentage of immediate approvals by completing a deal with a partner that had access to patients' medical records. The executives said they were confident they could overcome privacy concerns.

The insurance group's US executives said sales of its simple "term life" products would still be viewed as wholesale – customers would be buying them through established insurance brokers, e.g. Fidelity or Charles Schwab.

At present, Swiss Re has no forecasts of how much life insurance it will sell over the internet. Swiss Re believes the simplicity of its products and background checks will open the market faster. It said it had already gained regulatory approval from a number of states – it needs permission from all 50 – to start the internet project.

(adapted from the *Financial Times*)

6 Explain the following terms and phrases from text B.

1 joint venture (lines 3–4)
2 offer products online (line 10)
3 efficiency gain (line 15)
4 prospective policyholder (line 17)
5 policy proposal (lines 19–20)
6 approve an application (lines 25–26)
7 complete a deal (lines 30–31)
8 privacy concern (line 34)
9 insurance broker (line 39)
10 background check (line 44)

7 Use text B and your own knowledge to answer the questions.

1 What plans does Swiss Re have to expand its insurance business?
2 Why may selling life insurance over the internet be difficult?
3 What, in your opinion, is the advantage of selling an insurance product online?
4 Explain the function of an insurance agent.
5 In what respect are life insurance products different from other products?
6 How can the approval of applications for life insurance be speeded up?
7 Explain why privacy could be an issue in connection with life policies.
8 Why do you think Swiss Re requires regulatory approval to sell life insurance online?

8 Use the role card below to phone an insurance agent about insurance for your new house. The agent's card is on page 134.

Client

- *just moved into new house – kinds of insurance required?*
- *request for explanation of types of cover*
- *burglary?*
- *anything not covered?*
- *premiums and discounts?*
- *cover for how long?*
- *thank agent – how to proceed further?*

32

Now listen to the model answer.

9 Choose the correct terms to complete this insurance letter.

Christopher Jennings Ltd
INSURANCE BROKERS
17 Broad Street, Cheam Village, Surrey SM3 7VL
Tel: 020 8436 5757 Fax: 020 8421 1525 Email: cjennings@bt-internet.com

Broker Ref / FENX01HQ01

Ms Jane Fenwick
15 Coldstream Rise
Inverness IV4 2XA

15 May 2002

Dear Ms Fenwick

Home Contents Policy No. all/06/213783

We write in conjunction with the above policy which ...[1] on 1 June 2002.

Your existing insurance company is ...[2] renewal at an annual ...[3] of £160.53 and in order to maintain your ...[4] we would ask that this be paid on or before the above date. Please make cheques payable to Christopher Jennings Ltd.

It is the policy of our company to examine renewal premiums to ensure that they remain competitive. All classes of insurance have ...[5] a number of rate increases over the past 12 months. However, having carried out our survey, we can confirm that your existing company continues to be ...[6] and would recommend renewal with them.

We enclose our renewal papers, which provide details of your ...[7] sums insured, and would suggest that this may be an ...[8] time to consider whether any adjustments need to be made. In the ...[9] of a claim, difficulties could arise if the items ...[10] are not adequately covered.

THE PREMIUM INCLUDES A £3.00 SERVICE CHARGE.

We look forward to hearing from you shortly.

Yours sincerely

G.Pell

Gillian Pelham

1	a becomes payable	b falls due for renewal	c is overdue
2	a insuring	b offering	c selling
3	a bonus	b discount	c premium
4	a cover	b safety	c security
5	a experienced	b undergone	c witnessed
6	a cheap	b competitive	c inexpensive
7	a actual	b current	c latest
8	a acceptable	b adequate	c ideal
9	a event	b likelihood	c situation
10	a assured	b insured	c taken out

10 Write a reply to the letter based on the following outline.

- acknowledge receipt
- agree to renewal proposal
- ask for amount insured to be raised by 10 per cent to cover additional items purchased for your flat
- end with polite phrase

GRAMMAR

Converting adjectives into nouns

Adjectives can be converted into nouns by adding the definite article.

- group/collective nouns in the plural: the rich, the poor, the unemployed
- singular nouns denoting abstract concepts: the inevitable, the unthinkable
- a small number of singular or plural nouns denoting persons, often in a legal context: the insured, the deceased, the undersigned

NOTE the easiest thing, the only thing

11 Use these adjectives to complete the following sentences.

best • deceased • ideal • impossible • insured • poor • reasonably well-off • unemployed • unexpected

1 I'm certain ... would be to take out an endowment policy.
2 ... can claim unemployment benefit if they have contributed to the statutory social security scheme.
3 The dependants of ... will be entitled to the sum assured under this policy.
4 While private insurance plans are something that ... might opt for, ... will ultimately depend on the state for relief.
5 As a driver, you must always be prepared for ... .
6 I'm afraid this is asking for ... .
7 Before receiving the policy itself, ... will receive a cover note, which will enable him or her to have the vehicle registered.
8 ... would be to take out a comprehensive motor policy to cover for all eventualities.

12 Translate the following sentences.

1 Eine Police ist ein Versicherungsvertrag zwischen Versicherungsgeber und -nehmer.
2 Versicherungsmathematiker kalkulieren die Prämien auf der Grundlage der eingetretenen und zu erwartenden Schadensfälle.
3 Eine Hausratversicherung bietet Versicherungsschutz gegen Risiken wie Einbruch, Diebstahl, Feuer auch dann, wenn der Schaden außerhalb der Wohnung eingetreten ist.
4 Das Einzige, das Sie unter diesen Umständen tun können, ist es, eine Kapitallebensversicherung abzuschließen.
5 Unsere Superplus-Police deckt nicht nur Risiken wie den Verlust von Wertsachen ab, sondern auch Schäden, die durch mutwillige Zerstörung verursacht worden sind.
6 Auch bei einer Kfz-Vollkaskoversicherung muss der Versicherungsnehmer in der Regel einen Teil des Schadens tragen, den er an seinem eigenen Fahrzeug verursacht hat.
7 Der Swiss Re-Konzern hofft, demnächst mehr Lebensversicherungspolicen an Interessenten über das Internet zu verkaufen.
8 Sollte das Unerwartete eintreten, dann ist eine Versicherungssumme von 1 Mio € immerhin etwas für die Hinterbliebenen.

12 Forms of business organization

What do the abbreviations after the names stand for?

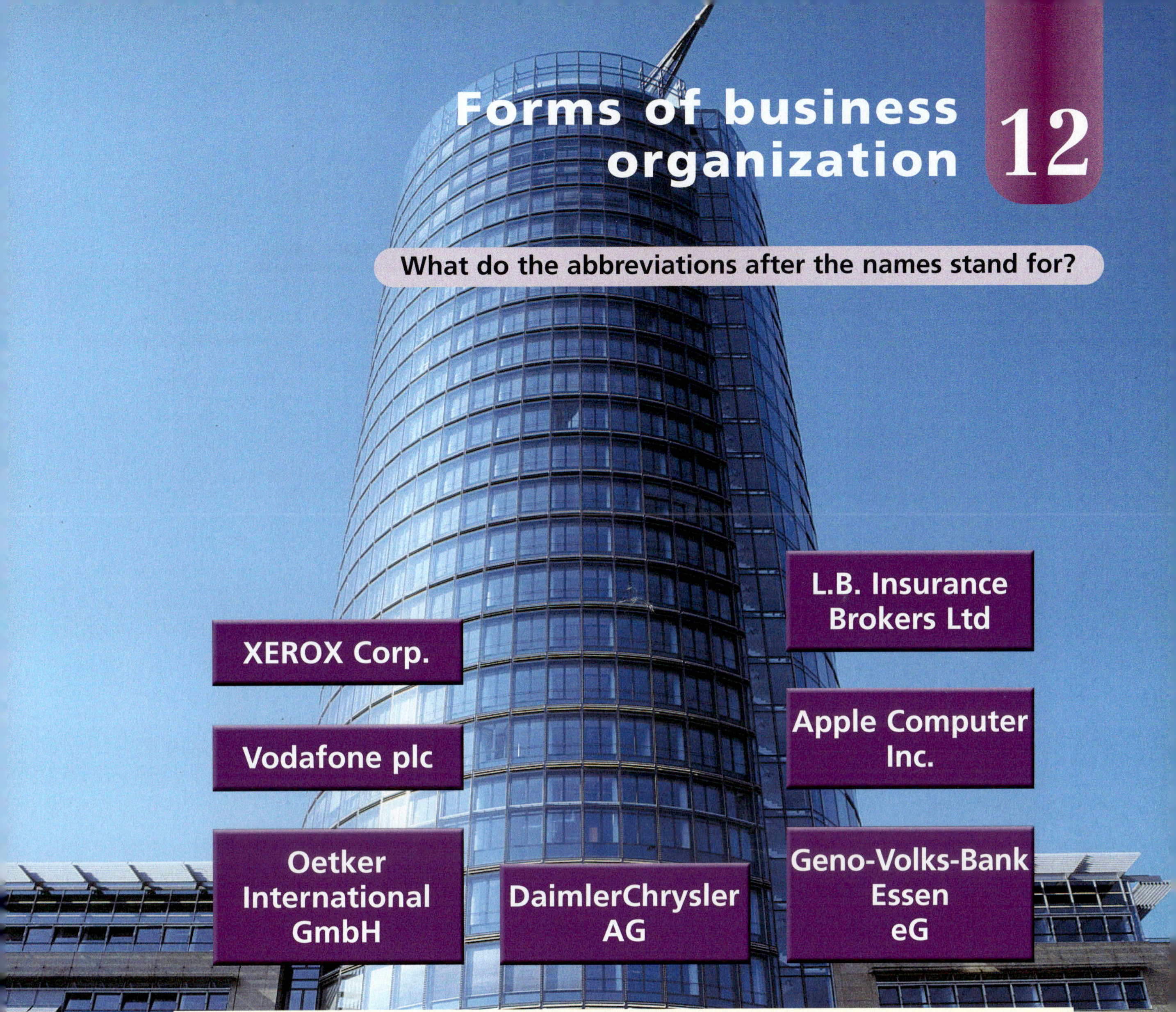

TEXT A 33

Survey of business organizations in the UK

Sole traders or sole proprietors run their businesses alone and may employ any number of people to help. Farmers, builders, hairdressers, insurance brokers and restaurant owners for instance usually operate as sole traders. However, despite their very large number, their contribution to GNP is relatively small.

Partnerships are owned by more than one person. **General partnerships** are typically set up in the professions – by lawyers, accountants, doctors and estate agents. The formalities required for setting up a partnership are minimal, although often a deed of partnership is drawn up, which states partners' rights – such as the allocation of profits, the responsibilities of the various partners and the procedure for ending the partnership or taking on new partners. All the partners are usually involved in running the firm and the liability of each partner is unlimited.

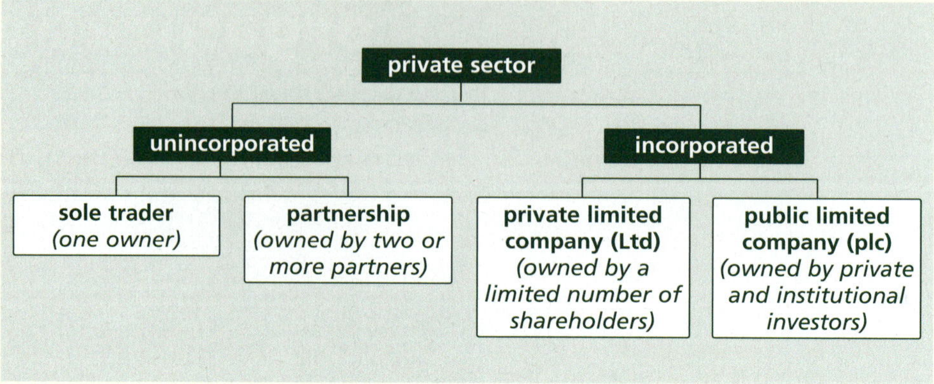

Limited partnerships are businesses in which the liability of at least one partner – the general partner – is unlimited. The liability of the other partners – the limited partners – is restricted to the amounts they have invested. The general partner is responsible for managing the firm.

Private limited companies are owned by a limited number of shareholders, often the members of a family. The shares cannot be sold without the consent of the other shareholders. Profits are divided among the shareholders according to their respective stakes in the company. Each shareholder's liability is limited to the amount of capital invested. A private limited company is set up by registration with the Registrar of Companies, a government department which issues a certificate of incorporation. In contrast to partnerships and sole traders, a private limited company is a distinct legal entity, which means that it can sue and be sued. It is supervised and managed by a board of directors, usually with a chairperson in a non-executive function and a chief executive.

Public limited companies are the most complex form of business organization. Of the some 500,000 limited companies in the UK, only 3 per cent are public limited companies. If a plc is to be formed, a number of documents must be filed with the Registrar of Companies, who then issues a certificate of incorporation. For the company to be listed on the stock exchange, a prospectus must be drawn up advertising the company to potential investors and inviting them to subscribe for shares. Once the stock exchange has granted a company's application to be admitted to the official list, it becomes a plc. The minimum share capital of a plc is £50,000.

A plc is owned by all those who have shares in the company. These can be bought and sold on the stock exchange, which also means that entire companies can be bought, i.e. taken over by other companies; the bidder just needs to buy a majority of the company's shares.

Other forms of business organization include

- **co-operative societies:** owned and run by their members, who receive a dividend for their investment. Co-operatives are chiefly confined to agriculture, food retailing and banking.
- **friendly societies:** non-profit-making organizations founded and operated for the benefit of their members. These mutual organizations are typically building societies or insurance companies. In recent times, many friendly societies have been converted into public limited companies.
- **public-sector organizations:** state-owned as well as government-controlled organizations like the Royal Mail, the NHS and the BBC. While in the past a large variety of enterprises like British Rail, British Coal and British Steel belonged to this category, these industries are now part of the private sector.

1 Complete the following puzzle with terms from text A.

Across

1 incorporated business
2 government department issuing a certificate of incorporation
3 dividing up the surplus at the end of a business year
4 register of companies whose shares are bought and sold on the stock exchange
5 form of business involving two or more owners, usually with unlimited liability
6 fully liable part-owner of a business
7 business which can sue and be sued
8 body responsible for supervising and running a company
9 person in a company with overall responsibility for the day-to-day running of a company
10 person owning and running a business

Down

11 Provide a definition for the solution.

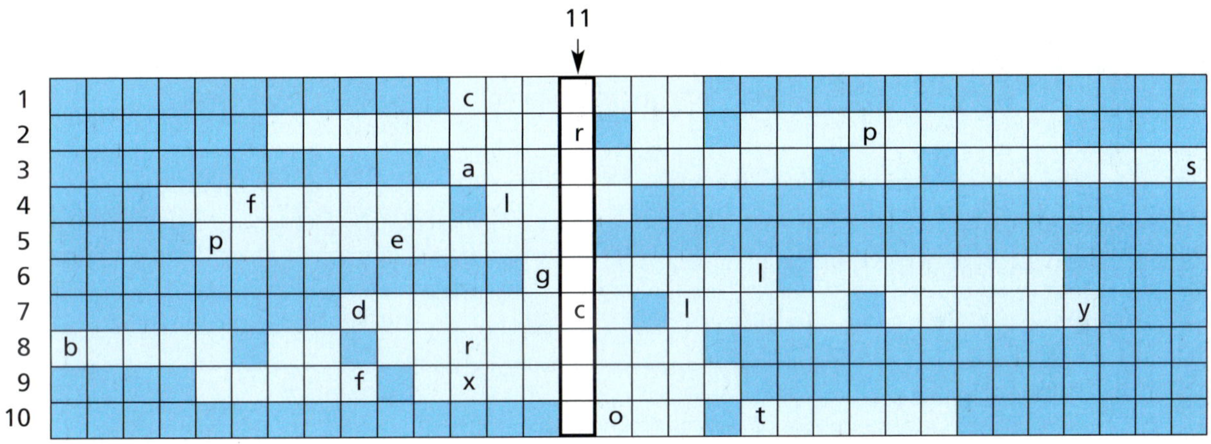

2 Study text A and advise the parties below on the form of business most suited to their situation. Work in groups.

EXAMPLE Bridget, Chris, John, Matthew and Paul have inherited a small construction business from their uncle. They are all interested in owning and expanding this business. The expansion would cost some £30,000.

We suggest that you set up a private limited company and raise the necessary capital by either putting up the money between you or inviting others to become shareholders. The main advantage is that your liability will be restricted to the capital you have invested.

1 Mary Mitchell worked as a hairdresser for several years but was made redundant. She spent six months looking for a new job but then decided to set up her own business after inheriting £10,000.
2 After three years as employees of a wholesale chain, Michael Bratchell and Jennifer McGregor decide to set up a jointly owned wholesale business.
3 After ten successful years in business, Media Systems Ltd decide to expand their business considerably. They need to raise £1,000,000 for their project.

INFORMATION

German, British and US company terminology

German	British	US
AG	**public limited company (plc)**	**corporation**
Aktionär/in	shareholder, stockholder	shareholder, stockholder
Aufsichtsrat	*supervisory board**	*supervisory board*
Aufsichtsratsmitglied	*member of the supervisory board* non-executive director	*member of the supervisory board* non-executive director
Aufsichtsratsvorsitzende/r	*chairman/chairwoman of the supervisory board*	president
Finanzvorstand	director of finance, chief financial officer, CFO	vice-president finance chief financial officer, CFO
Vorstand	executive board	executive board
Vorstandsmitglied	member of the executive board, executive director	vice-president
Vorstandsvorsitzende/r	chief executive (officer), CEO	chief executive officer, CEO
GmbH	**private limited company (Ltd)**	**close(d) corporation, private/ privately held corporation**
Geschäftsführer/in	managing director, general manager	managing director, general manager
Gesellschafter/in	shareholder	shareholder
OHG	**general/ordinary partnership**	**general partnership**
Teilhaber/in	partner	partner
KG	**limited/special partnership**	**limited partnership**
Kommanditist/in	limited partner	limited partner
Komplementär/in	general partner	general partner
Einzelkaufmann/frau	**sole trader/proprietorship**	**proprietorship**
Versicherungsverein auf Gegenseitigkeit (VVaG)	**mutual insurance company**	**mutual insurance company**
Genossenschaft (eG)	**cooperative**	**cooperative**

* The terms in *italics* are translations of German institutions.

3 Complete the text with some of the terms from the list below. In some cases, the plural form is necessary.

annual general meeting (AGM) • board • chairman/chairwoman • chief executive (CEO) • close corporation • company • corporation • director • executive • non-executive director • president • private limited company • ~~public limited company~~ • share • shareholder • stake • stock • stockholder • supervisory

As a rule, *public limited companies* [1] in the UK have only one board of directors with a …[2] in a purely supervisory function. In the USA, businesses whose …[3] are quoted on the stock exchange are called …[4]. German AGs have both a …[5] board and an …[6] board. In the USA and the UK, the person responsible for running the company is usually referred to as the …[7]. At least once a year, public limited companies in the UK and open corporations in the USA must invite their …[8] to an …[9] where the annual report is presented, the board is discharged, the company's …[10] are elected and profits are allocated. In a …[11], the various shareholders – often the members of one family – cannot sell their …[12] in the company without the consent of the other shareholders.

4 Translate the above text into German.

Notice of Annual General Meeting

The Annual General Meeting of McTel plc will be held at the Balmoral Hotel, Princes Street, Edinburgh EH12 5AC on Friday, 10 May 2002 at 2.00 p.m. to consider the following:

Resolution 1
THAT the accounts and reports of the directors and the auditors for the year ending 31 December 2001 be received and approved.

Resolution 2
THAT the final dividend of 11.25 pence per share recommended by the directors be declared payable to holders of ordinary shares.

Resolution 3
THAT Sir Anthony Campbell, Mrs Mary Cameron and Lady Susan Blair be re-elected as directors.

Resolution 4
THAT Reid & Kennedy be re-appointed as auditors of the Company from the conclusion of this meeting until the conclusion of the next general meeting, at which accounts are laid before the shareholders in accordance with the provisions of the Companies Act 1985, and their remuneration be fixed by the Board.

Any other business

By order of the Board

C.R. LEAR
Company Secretary

81 Caledonian Road, London EC1A 7AG

22 MARCH 2002

A member entitled to attend and vote is entitled to appoint a proxy or proxies to attend and to vote instead of him or her. A proxy need not be a member of the Company.

5 Read the notice of the AGM above and correct these statements.

1 The extraordinary general meeting of McTel plc will be held on 10 May 2002.
2 Shareholders will only have to vote on the directors' report.
3 The board decides the dividend to be paid.
4 Four directors are standing for re-election.
5 Auditors are appointed by the AGM for two years.
6 Shareholders can only vote if they attend the AGM.
7 The notice is signed by the chief executive.
8 The company's head office is in Edinburgh.

TEXT B 34

Xerox optimistic as losses below estimates

Xerox, the troubled US copier and printer manufacturer, on Thursday inspired a 37 per cent leap in its share price by reporting better than expected results for the first quarter. By midday in New York on Thursday, the stock rose $2.43 to $8.83, its highest level since last November.

The results for the three months to March 31 showed the benefits of the company's recovery plan, consisting of cost reductions, asset sales and improved operating performance. "About $2bn of assets have been sold. We're ahead of schedule and gaining ground in the marketplace," Paul Allaire, chairman and chief executive, told analysts.

The group reported a loss of 12 cents a share, less than half the 28 cent loss expected. Operating income was 30 cents per share in the same period last year.

Including restructuring charges and a gain on the sale of half Xerox's stake in Fuji Xerox, its Japanese joint venture, the company recorded first-quarter earnings of 19 cents a share, compared with a loss in the equivalent period of 38 cents.

Xerox faced an unexpected crisis last year because the poor execution of a restructuring plan, slackening demand and an accounting scandal at its Mexican unit used up cash and undermined investor confidence.

Xerox revenues in the first quarter were down 8 per cent at $4.16bn, compared with $4.5bn. The good news is that the company managed to reduce inventory by $150m in the three months to end-March, normally a period when stocks increase. The group also laid off 4,300 workers in the first quarter, 300 more than expected, and Anne Mulcahy, chief operating officer, said further staff reductions were expected.

Mr Allaire said the Xerox group would report "similar" operating income in the second quarter. He stuck by his forecast that the group would be profitable for the full year. The group's gross operating margin had declined in the past year from 41.3 per cent a year ago to 33.5 per cent, partly due to weak results from the high-end copier systems Xerox produces and a weak performance in developing markets.

Ms Mulcahy conceded that operating conditions were still challenging in many markets but she said the group would be able to improve margins in the second half. She added that, having prevented the cash crisis with asset sales, future disposals were less urgent. "We will only proceed with additional asset sales if they make overall sense," she said.

(adapted from the *Financial Times*)

6 Match the definitions with the following terms from text B.

asset (line 11) • operating performance (line 12) • restructuring charge (line 21) • revenue (line 33) • inventory (line 36) • chief operating officer (lines 41–42) • margin (line 49) • disposal (line 60)

1 any item that has money value
2 amount of money to be spent on reorganizing a business
3 executive in charge of production
4 difference between cost price and selling price
5 results from ordinary business activities
6 stock in hand
7 amount of money received
8 sale of assets

7 Study text B and ask questions to match the following answers.

1 … because its results in the first three months of this year were very good.
2 They are doing better than expected.
3 The company turned a severe loss into a healthy profit.
4 … because, among other things, there was a major scandal involving bookkeeping in one of its foreign subsidiaries.
5 There is now cautious optimism concerning the company's future.
6 There are going to be further job cuts.
7 … poor margins and weak foreign markets.
8 Yes, but only if it makes overall sense.

8 Write a report of about 200 words on the figures below.

Tesco's five-year record

	1997	1998	1999	2000	2001
Turnover	£13,118m	£14,971m	£15,835m	£16,958m	£22,773m
Operating profit	£760m	£875m	£919m	£993m	£1,100m
Operating margin	5.8%	5.8%	5.8%	5.9%	6.0%
Profit after taxation	£520m	£532m	£606m	£674m	£767m
Profit per employee	£8,487	£8,755	£8,771	£9,160	£9,649
Number of stores	568	586	639	659	692
Share price year end	116p	172p	177p	169p	271p

Begin your report as follows:
Turnover for the period under review …

VOCABULARY

Time period
late nineties • past year(s) • period/year under review • first half/quarter • same period last year

Movement
be higher/lower • be up/down • decrease • edge up/down • exceed • fall • increase • post/report a profit/loss • rise • weaken

Amount/Percentage
by … per cent • from … to …

Degree
considerable • constant • dramatic • gradual • marked • moderate • sharp • stable • steady • substantial • unchanged

Comparison
in comparison to/with • in contrast to • similar

9 Translate the following text into German.

Tesco's sales for the seven weeks ending 5th January 2002 increased by 11%. This growth was driven by all four parts of the company's strategy: a continued strong core UK performance, increasing non-food sales, strong performance across our international business and the success of retailing services. We remain on track to achieve our year-end targets. International sales were up 31.2% over the Christmas and New Year period, in line with our plans. We now have 102 international hypermarkets, giving us over 10 million sq. ft. of sales space. We are on target to have more space overseas than in the UK by the end of 2003.

(www.tesco.com)

GRAMMAR

Conditional clauses

There are basically two types of conditional clauses:

- Factual conditional clauses are used if the fulfilment of the condition is possible.
  - If you **form** a public limited company, you **(will) have to publish** annual reports.
- Hypothetical conditional clauses are used if the fulfilment of the condition is unlikely or impossible.
  - If I **were/was** you, I **would set up** a partnership. (reference to present or future)
  - If I **had bought** telecom shares, I **would have lost** quite a bit of money. (reference to past)
  - **Had** we **invested** in this business, we **would be** millionaires now. (reference to past and present)

NOTE Varying degrees of improbability can be expressed by *were to* and *should*.

- If the AGM **were to reject** the proposed dividend, we **would sell** our shares.
- If anything **should happen** to the chief executive, he **would have to be replaced** as soon as possible.

NOTE *will* and *would* are used after *if* to express a polite request.

- If you **will/would sign** on the dotted line, …
- We should be greatly obliged if you **would forward** the goods by air.

10 Complete the sentences using the correct tense of the verbs in brackets.

1 If a sole trader needs more capital, he or she (set up) … a partnership.
2 If the auditors discover irregularities in the company's financial conduct, they (have to) … inform the AGM.
3 If the general partner was not fully liable, creditors (lose) … a lot of money in the event of bankruptcy.
4 If the corporation had invested sufficiently in the past, it (not have to) … file for bankruptcy last month.
5 Should the AGM not discharge the directors, they (have to) … step down.
6 Had last year's results not been so disappointing, the chief executive (not be dismissed) … last month.
7 If the board of directors (not be re-elected) …, investors might lose all confidence in the company.
8 If you (want) … to sell your shares in a private limited company, you will have to get the other shareholders' permission.
9 If we had not taken over our main competitor, we (be) … in serious difficulties now.
10 If you operate as a sole trader, you (be fully liable) … for any losses.
11 We would be very pleased if you (grant) … our application for a short-term loan.
12 If you (just take) … a seat, I will be with you in a minute.

"Apparently, it was one hell of a board meeting."

11 Translate the following sentences.

1 Einzelunternehmen haben in der Regel größere Schwierigkeiten bei der Kreditbeschaffung als offene Handelsgesellschaften und Kommanditgesellschaften.
2 Bei der Kommanditgesellschaft haftet ein Teilhaber – der Komplementär – unbeschränkt für alle Verbindlichkeiten der Firma, während die Haftung der Kommanditisten auf die Höhe ihrer Einlage beschränkt ist.
3 Die Industrie- und Handelskammer wies darauf hin, dass es vorteilhafter sein könnte, eine offene Handelsgesellschaft zu gründen, obwohl dann alle Teilhaber voll hafteten.
4 Bei einer amerikanischen Aktiengesellschaft entscheidet nicht die Hauptversammlung, sondern der Vorstand über die Höhe der auszuschüttenden Dividende.
5 Hätte die Regierung die Eisenbahn nicht privatisiert, wäre vermutlich mehr in die Infrastruktur investiert worden.
6 Wäre das Weihnachtsgeschäft nicht so gut gewesen, müssten wir unsere Gewinnerwartungen sicher deutlich nach unten korrigieren.
7 Wenn wir nicht planten, Unternehmensbeteiligungen zu veräußern, würde uns die Sanierung des Unternehmens wohl nicht gelingen.
8 Wenn das Geschäftsergebnis nicht so unbefriedigend ausgefallen wäre, wäre die Dividende für das abgelaufene Geschäftsjahr nicht so niedrig gewesen.
9 Genossenschaften sind häufiger in der Landwirtschaft als im Bauwesen anzutreffen.
10 Welche Vorteile hätte ich als Versicherungsnehmer, wenn ich alle meine Versicherungen bei einer VVaG abschlösse?
11 Gesellschaften mit beschränkter Haftung sind in Großbritannien häufig im Besitz von Familien. Sie sind daher eher klein.
12 Wenn zwei Großunternehmen fusionieren, kann leicht ein Monopol entstehen. Daher schreitet in solchen Fällen oft die Kartellbehörde ein.

13 Money and markets

Explain the following:
FTSE 100 DAX 30 NIKKEI EUROSTOXX 50 DOW JONES

TEXT A 35

Stock markets: past, present and future

Many people do not understand how the stock market works. But there is no mystique to this institution. In fact, it is little more than a high-powered fruit and vegetable market, with the same basic parts: suppliers (companies), wholesalers (marketmakers), stallholders (stockbrokers) and customers (investors) – an organized market for the sale and purchase of securities such as equities and bonds.

The first exchanges appeared in Europe in the 15th century. The stock market in Britain began in the coffee houses of London. In 1760, a group of 150 share dealers formed a club at Jonathan's Coffee House in the City, where they met to buy and sell shares.

People who buy shares on the stock market invest money in companies. The financial risk is limited to the value of their investment and they cannot be held liable for any of the debts of that company beyond the value of their shareholding. Having shares in a company makes a shareholder a part-owner of that company, with a right to say how it is run. This right is exercised at shareholders' general meetings. Shareholders also share in any profits that are made, which are paid in the form of a dividend.

The traders operating on the stock market are popularly divided into so-called bulls and bears. Bulls buy shares as they speculate on rising prices – a bull market – while the bears anticipate a downward change in the market – a bear market – by selling shares in good time, hoping eventually to buy them back at a lower price.

Today, most of the major stock markets are fully electronic. In fact, floor trading may become a thing of the past as electronic communications networks create new forms of trading. These virtual markets offer a way to trade for a fraction of what it costs, for example, on the New York Stock Exchange (NYSE) or the technology stock market, Nasdaq*. There is no need for specialist marketmakers to serve as middlemen as they do in floor trading or in computer trading rooms and the savings in transaction costs can be immense.

So, what does the future hold for stock markets? There is a drive to create strategic alliances between national stock exchanges. And it is almost inconceivable that national exchanges as we know them today will still be around after 2010. Every step towards virtual trading has led to greater volatility with faster global dealing on ever lower margins. Communities of financial expertise will survive in places like London, New York and Frankfurt. But ultimately, global online trading around the clock is likely to replace these geographical centres.

* Nasdaq = National Association of Securities Dealers Automated Quotations

1 Explain the following terms from text A.

1 marketmaker (line 4)
2 securities (line 5)
3 equities (line 6)
4 exchange (line 7)
5 shareholding (line 14)
6 floor trading (line 23)
7 virtual market (line 25)
8 trading room (line 29)
9 volatility (line 33)
10 global dealing (line 34)

2 Ask one question on each of the six paragraphs in text A.

EXAMPLE *Why can you compare the stock market to a fruit and vegetable market?*

3 Ask and answer your questions from exercise 2. Work in pairs.

EXAMPLE ... *because the people involved in a fruit and vegetable market – suppliers, wholesalers, stallholders and customers – have the same sort of role to play as on the stock market.*

4 Match the terms in the list with the 'clues' below.

blue chip • bonds • commodities • futures market • gilts • hedging • initial public offering (IPO) • price-earnings ratio (p/e) • unit trust • yield

1 not the little thing in your computer: security of a first-class company, holders receive dividends
2 all that glitters is not gold: securities issued by the UK government, considered very safe, holders receive interest
3 going public: first ever sale of a company's shares on the stock exchange
4 find out how profitable it is: money earned from your investment in relation to the amount originally put in

5 for once you can rely on the promises made by governments or companies: the money borrowed will be paid back, with interest
6 a small slice of the big cake is yours: fund managers put your money into stocks and shares
7 works like a row of bushes to protect you from the wind: investors seek protection against future losses
8 buy now – pay later: place where you can buy or sell contracts for the delivery of commodities in three or six months' time
9 dig them up or cut them down: raw materials like oil, grain, timber, coffee, iron ore
10 you must be good at maths to work it out: relationship between a company's reported profits per share and the current price of this security

5 Find the German equivalents for the terms above.

6 Translate the following sentences into German.

1 Although stock markets were generally weak, there was little change in the prices of blue chips.
2 As all the indications point towards an uptrend in the European markets, we can expect the number of IPOs to rise as well.
3 Traditionally, the yield of corporate bonds is slightly higher than that of government bonds.
4 Ahead of the Bank of England meeting in London, there was little activity in the gilts market.
5 With a price-earnings ratio of more than 70, this bio-technology share seems to be a speculative investment.
6 Investing in unit trusts can help spread the risk, but unit prices cannot altogether escape market trends.
7 Oil futures fell sharply yesterday on news that there had been a big increase in US stockpiles.
8 Hedging operations provided some activity in the market for coal, with buyers trying to secure contracts at current price levels.

VOCABULARY

Verbs signifying rising movements

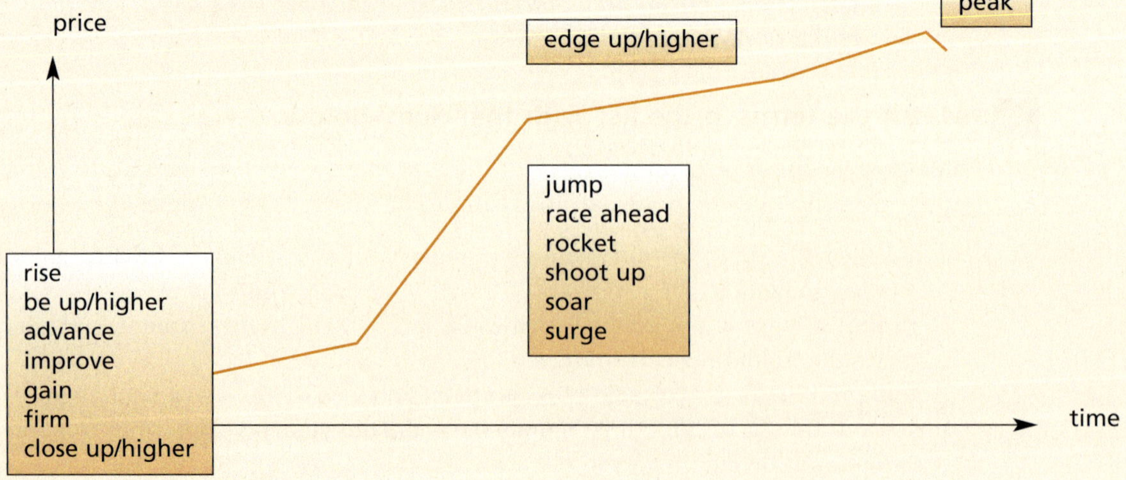

Verbs signifying falling movements

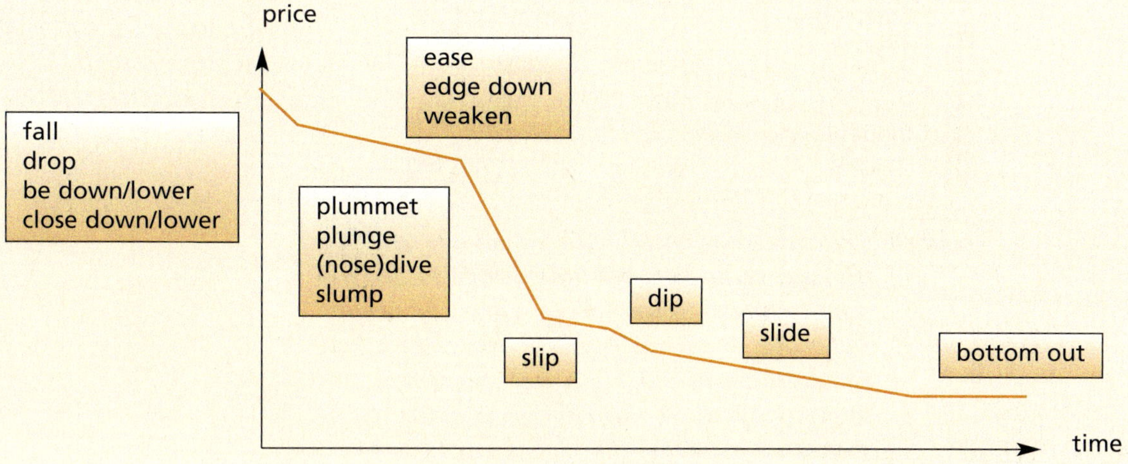

7 Complete the following sentences with the correct prepositions.

1 Share prices ... Singapore gained 21.86 points ... Thursday.
2 The euro rose ... 0.9127 US cents, its highest ... 22 May.
3 Shares ... Nokia jumped 4.2 per cent ... €21.96 yesterday.
4 Crude oil fell 16 cents ... $24.80 a barrel ... London yesterday.
5 ... July, the Dow Jones edged up 0.2 per cent ... 10,522.81.
6 Infineon was down ... most of the day but ended 0.5 per cent higher ... €40.42.
7 ... midsession, the Dow Jones Industrial Average was up 67.54 points ... 9,629.06.
8 Tech shares surged ... new heights ... Wall Street on Friday.

8 Form sentences describing 'yesterday's' changes in the share prices below. Use a different verb for each sentence.

stock	change (%)	price (pence)	change (pence)
British Airways	1.9	321	6

EXAMPLE *Shares in British Airways ended 1.9 per cent or six pence higher at 321p yesterday.*

stock	change (%)	price (pence)	change (pence)
1 Abbey National	1.9	1145	21
2 BT	3.4	527.3	17.5
3 Cadbury	4.2	495	20
4 EMI	– 2.1	445	– 9.5
5 Man Group	5.89	881.5	49
6 Pearson	– 2.0	1205	– 25
7 Safeway	– 6.78	306	– 22.25
8 Scottish & Newcastle	3.8	538.5	19.7
9 Shell Transport	– 0.4	542	– 2.1
10 Vodafone	5.3	203.2	10.5

9 Explain the chart movements below.

VOCABULARY

unchanged	short-lived
volatile	stage a rally
come under pressure	slightly
erratic movement	steadily
modest/good gains	steeply
sharply	underlying trend

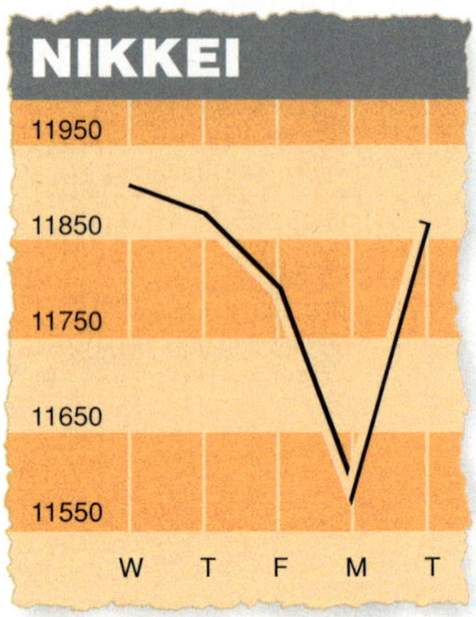

EXAMPLE *On Wednesday, the Nikkei opened at 11,890. For the next three days, the index came under considerable pressure, falling sharply by around 100 points. By the beginning of the week, it had nosedived to around 11,570 but staged an impressive rally on Monday. On Tuesday, it opened at just above the 11,850 mark.*

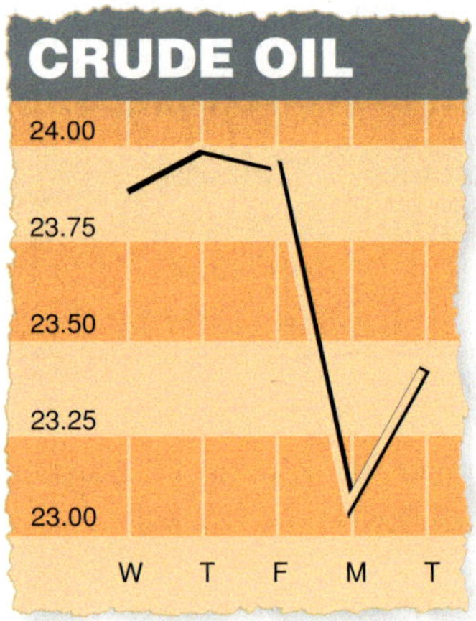

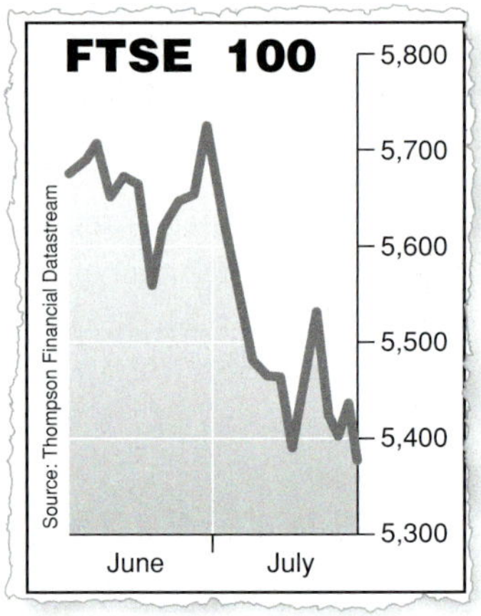

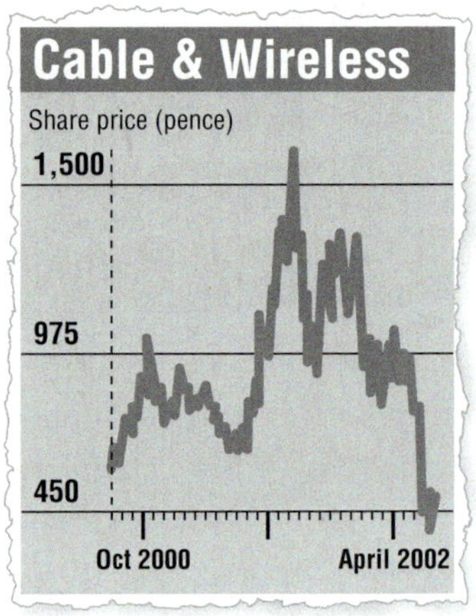

TEXT B 36

The functions of central banks

These days central bankers seem all powerful. In most rich countries they go about their business without interference from politicians. And their success in bringing down inflation has earned them great respect. Time and again, decisions taken by central banks, especially the Federal Reserve Board (the Fed) in the USA, the European Central Bank (ECB) and the Bank of England, have had a considerable influence on the financial markets.

The main functions of central banks are to control the money supply (the total amount of money available to the national economy) and to ensure steady and stable economic growth without risking periods of recession or inflation. Most central banks set monetary policy targets aimed at keeping inflation low. The European Central Bank has the statutory goal of 'price stability'. The Fed also has a duty to support employment and economic growth. Governments have usually adopted a policy of not interfering with central bank policy.

In pursuing their policies central banks can make use of the following instruments:

- fixing short-term interest rates for their customers, the banks. The discount rate is charged for loans to the banks which are secured by commercial paper (e.g. bills of exchange) or government securities. When the central bank raises these rates, the banks must charge their customers higher interest rates and vice versa. And this means that borrowing money becomes dearer or cheaper.

- influencing the amount of money available to the economy by increasing or decreasing the percentage of customer deposits that commercial banks must make available to the central bank.
- engaging in open market operations. Central banks control interest rates and – as a result – the money supply. By buying or selling government bonds on the open market, they influence the volume and the price of credit available in the economy. Buyers in such open market transactions – banks, insurance companies or large corporations – purchase these bonds and therefore have less money available for loans or investment projects.

European Central Bank

10 Read these statements on text B and decide if a or b is more accurate.

1 a Governments exercise strict control over the activities of central banks.
  b Governments do not usually interfere in the activities of central banks.
2 a Keeping inflation down has earned central bankers much praise.
  b Central bankers have won great respect for reducing inflation.
3 a The money supply is an important tool of economic policy.
  b All economic activity in a national economy depends on the money supply.
4 a Low inflation is the top priority with most central banks.
  b Keeping inflation low is one of the two top priorities, the other being securing employment and economic growth.
5 a The interest rates charged by commercial banks chiefly depend on the central bank's discount rate.
  b Commercial banks fix interest rates depending on the demand for credit.
6 a For reasons of monetary policy, central banks must have access to a percentage of customer deposits at commercial banks.
  b Central banks use customer deposits to finance their activities.
7 a Central banks use open market operations primarily to increase their earnings.
  b Open market operations serve monetary policy goals, i.e. to increase or decrease the money supply.
8 a If banks, insurance companies and big corporations buy government bonds, there will be less money available for loans and investments.
  b Corporate investments depend on how much money is available on the open market.

GRAMMAR

Word order: the position of adverbs and adverbial phrases

- Adverbs of place and definite time come at the beginning or end of a sentence. If an adverb of place and one of definite time are next to each other, the sequence is normally 'place before time'.
  - **Yesterday**, equities soared **on the London Stock Exchange**.
  - Investors have not engaged in heavy selling in **Frankfurt today**.
- Adverbs of manner come before the (full) verb if they are not stressed.
  - I **wisely** decided to sell my shares.

  They are placed after the verb if they are stressed.
  - Are you sure you acted **wisely** when selling your stocks?
- Adverbs of indefinite time come before the full verb.
  - We've **always** opted for blue chips rather than high-risk securities.

  If an adverb of indefinite time is stressed, it is usually placed at the beginning of the sentence.
  - **Lately**, the stock market has not seemed all that attractive.
- After 'negative' adverbs (e.g. hardly, never, rarely, seldom) the usual word order is inverted.
  - **Only rarely** will private investors go for that type of stock.

  This type of construction can be avoided by using *It is* … .
  - **It is only** after presenting their results that companies can be judged properly.
- Long adverbs and many adverbial phrases usually come at the beginning or end of a sentence.
  - **As a rule**, trading starts on Monday morning.

  Adverbial phrases may be placed in the middle of a sentence, in which case commas or dashes are used.
  - It is safe to assume that, **in the prevailing investment climate**, securities will eventually regain last year's levels.

11 Form sentences by putting the parts below into the correct order. The first word is capitalized.

1 about corporate earnings / the high-tech sector / have weighed down / Worries / this week
2 in future / of a higher quality / coming to the stock market / companies in the dotcom sector / will be / It is hoped that
3 at the end of September / fresh money / have found it hard / many companies / Since the IPO market collapse / to come up with
4 yesterday / were up / at the close of trading / Stock market prices / sharply / in Tokyo
5 entirely / For some central bankers / is not / the current situation / negative
6 central bank sources / in the immediate future / is unlikely / According to / a cut in interest rates
7 are likely to show / figures from Italy and Germany / In Europe / in the months ahead / will probably recede / that inflationary pressures
8 close to / Brazil / 1m tonnes / global cotton supplier / Nearly two decades ago / with an annual production of / was an established

12 Complete the following text with some of the terms from the list below.

brought down • central bank • core rate • federal bank • inflation • interest rate • peak • percentage • rate cuts • reduce • slipped • swing • taken down

UK inflation has fallen sharply, raising borrowers' hopes for further cuts in interest rates. Expectations of further monetary easing were driven even higher by news that the ...[1] of inflation, which excludes goods whose prices tend to ...[2] wildly, also fell for the first time this year.

The underlying rate of retail price inflation, which excludes mortgage interest payments, fell by 0.3 ...[3] points to 2.3 per cent in September, the Office for National Statistics said yesterday. Inflation was ...[4] even more sharply, following August's quarter-point ...[5] cut by the Bank of England, the UK ...[6], which prompted mortgage lenders to ...[7] their rates. The inflation rate fell by 0.4 percentage points to 1.7 per cent, and is set to be pushed down still more by further ...[8].

Core inflation, excluding petrol and food prices, ...[9] by one fifth of a percentage point from an August ...[10] of 2.9 per cent.

Bank of England

13 Translate the following sentences.

1 Nur der New Yorker Technologiemarkt Nasdaq hatte gestern einen leichten Kursanstieg zu verzeichnen. Der Index stieg um 18 Punkte auf 2487.
2 Die Senkung der wichtigsten Zinsen um einen halben Prozentpunkt durch die EZB führte zu einem kurzfristigen Anstieg der Aktienkurse an den wichtigsten europäischen Börsen.
3 Analysten gehen davon aus, dass das milliardenschwere Investitionsprogramm der japanischen Regierung nicht ohne Auswirkungen auf den Aktienmarkt in Tokio bleiben wird.
4 Das Börsengeschehen wird zurzeit einzig und allein von den großen Kapitalanlegern bestimmt. Die Kleinanleger halten sich schon seit Monaten auffallend zurück.
5 Die Rohstoffpreise an der Terminbörse sind in den letzten Monaten stetig gestiegen, so dass die Experten schon vor einem Anstieg der Investitionsgüterpreise warnen.
6 Die rasante Entwicklung der Börsenkurse um die Jahrtausendwende hat viele neue Anleger dazu veranlasst, ihre Ersparnisse in Aktien anzulegen.
7 Kaum hatte das Unternehmen seine Gewinnwarnung veröffentlicht, gingen an den meisten großen Börsen die Kurse für Telekommunikationswerte dramatisch zurück. Lediglich die Kurse der großen Unternehmen konnten sich bis zum Ende der Börsensitzung leicht erholen.
8 Die Ölpreise sind am Rotterdamer Markt in den letzten Wochen kontinuierlich gestiegen, weil sich amerikanische Unternehmen hier eindecken.

14 Taxation

Robin Hood robbed the rich to help the poor. Does this apply to modern forms of taxation?

TEXT A 37

Tax systems

Governments levy taxes in order to fund tasks that individuals and corporations are unable or unwilling to pay for, e.g. security, education, welfare and infrastructure. Moreover, taxes serve to bring about a more equal distribution of income and wealth as well as to achieve economic policy goals.

Taxes can be classified in various ways, the most common distinction being that between direct and indirect taxes. Income tax and corporation tax are the most important examples of direct tax, while sales taxes, especially value-added tax (VAT), are usually cited as typical indirect taxes. Those individuals and companies who are required to pay a specific tax do not always bear the burden in the long run. After a tax is imposed, this burden may well be shifted onto others, for instance, in the form of higher prices. Sometimes the price of a commodity contains several taxes. Thus, the pump price of petrol includes both fuel tax and VAT.

Income tax is the most important element in most countries' tax systems, accounting for approximately half their revenues. While, as a rule, all income, from whatever source, is subject to income tax, there are a number of exemptions and deductions which effectively reduce individual taxable incomes. Rate structures and tax bands vary from country to country and are also frequently changed for political reasons. However, most countries have adopted systems according to which taxpayers in higher income brackets pay a greater share of their incomes by way of tax. Moreover, single persons have a higher tax liability than married couples filing joint returns. Retirement incomes are usually taxed at a lower level, or even tax-exempted below a certain threshold.

Corporation tax is also a major source of income for governments. Again, while the effective rates are subject to change, they likewise depend on the taxable income of the corporations concerned. The tax base is arrived at by deducting from gross income all expenses incurred in securing this income, e.g. wages and salaries, repairs, rents, costs of materials, interest payments and, of course, taxes. It is only the net income on profit which is liable for corporation tax. In addition, all corporation tax regimes allow deductions for depreciation. In general, assets are not fully deductible in the year they were acquired, but must be written off over several years.

Sales taxes and **excise duties** are the most important types of indirect tax in terms of revenue. Excises are levied on certain commodities for both revenue-raising and political purposes. Thus, taxes on alcoholic beverages and tobacco products can be quite high in certain countries.

Value-added tax in the EU has been adopted as the uniform sales tax in order to harmonize taxation and to facilitate intra-European trade. While the rates of VAT vary from country to country, the way this 'cascading tax' operates is the same. (See page 112.)

There are still a great many other taxes which companies or individuals have to pay, e.g. taxes on property, commercial rates, inheritance tax, capital transfer tax as well as taxes on gambling and entertainment.

As they say, the taxman is always with us.

1 Replace the items in colour with words and phrases from text A.

1 National and local governments raise taxes to pay for goods and services individuals cannot finance themselves.
2 The aim is to achieve a more balanced spread of earnings and wealth.
3 The extra cost caused by a tax is usually transferred to the consumer.
4 In some cases, the price of a product includes more than one tax.
5 Income tax often accounts for more than 50 per cent of a nation's tax take.
6 Income tax must be paid on all types of income.
7 Often old-age pensions are not liable for tax.
8 Capital goods purchased within a given year are usually set off over a period of several years.
9 Excise duties are imposed on quite a few goods and services.
10 Taxes on real estate are levied by local authorities.

2 Use information from text A and your own experience to answer the following questions.

1 Which of the following are paid for out of tax revenues: telephone networks, canals, pop concerts, art museums, nursery schools, fire services?
2 Which of these are direct and which are indirect taxes: church tax, fuel tax, cigarette tax, inheritance tax?
3 Which of these people normally pay tax at a higher or lower rate: secretary, company director, police officer, government minister, student working part-time, old-age pensioner, successful young business person?

3 Go to www.inlandrevenue.gov.uk/rates/it.htm to find the UK income tax rates, bands and allowances. Then work out the tax liability for the following people and explain the procedure.

EXAMPLE *(based on taxyear 2001–2002)*
Single person, 25, annual income £19,000
Annual income: £19,000 – £4,535 (personal allowance) = £14,465 (taxable income)

Liability: first £1,250 at 10 per cent:	*£125*
Remaining £13,215 at 22 per cent:	*£2,907*
TOTAL	*£3,032*

1 Married couple (50 and 51), no children, annual joint income: £38,500
2 Married couple (35 and 30), 2 children, annual joint income: £39,000

'Before you say no, let me outline some of the tax benefits...'

INFORMATION

VAT – a cascading tax

The following example is simplified in two respects:

- there is no reference to a specific country
- the tax rate is 10%

1 Farmer Charles A. charges the Aqua mineral water company €1 for every hectolitre of mineral water taken from a spring on his land. In the year under review, his receipts amount to €15,000. As this amount is way below the VAT threshold, he is not liable for VAT.

2 The Aqua mineral water company has paid 10% VAT on a variety of items in the year under review (transport, empty bottles, energy, advertising, bottling machines, etc.) – the total cost being €110,000, which includes 10% VAT, i.e. €10,000 (input tax). The company sells bottled mineral water worth €220,000 to its sole customer, the Cent supermarket chain. This amount includes 10% VAT, i.e. €20,000 (output tax). Aqua's accounting department deducts the input tax included in the cost of purchases from the output tax on the sales price. This leaves a balance of €10,000, which is remitted to the tax authorities.

3 The Cent chain of supermarkets sells goods worth €11m in the year under review. This figure includes 10% VAT (output tax), i.e. €1m. Having bought goods (not only mineral water) to the value of €5.5m, which includes €0.5m VAT, they are liable for VAT in the same way as their suppliers:

  €1.0m output tax on sales
– €0.5m input tax paid on purchases
= €0.5m VAT to be remitted to the tax authorities

4 Joe B. buys a bottle of Aqua mineral water. The price – €1.10 – includes 10% VAT. Unfortunately, Joe B. can't claim any tax back.

4 Go to www.europa.eu.int/comm/dg10/publications/brochures/voy2000txt_en.html to find the standard VAT rates in the European Union. Write a short text summarizing the information.

TEXT B 38

Tax advice for Britons abroad

WHO, IN THE EYES of the Inland Revenue, lives in Britain? The answer is not as simple as it seems. Those who sell up and move away do not automatically become non-residents. And the rules differ according to which type of tax is discussed. A Briton who works overseas for a full tax year would normally be considered non-resident and therefore exempt from income tax.

However, to qualify you must not spend more than 180 days in Britain during that tax year or, if you are abroad for four years or more, an average of 90 days annually. And any income received from work undertaken in Britain during this period would still be subject to British tax, as would income generated from, say, renting out your British home. However, expatriates still qualify for personal allowances and can offset maintenance expenses against their tax obligations.

For those retiring overseas, to qualify as a non-resident you must remain away from Britain for three consecutive tax years, with the same rules about visiting. However, to escape capital gains tax (CGT) on, for example, the sale of a British property, the qualifying period rises to five tax years. And inheritance tax (IHT) is decided on where the Revenue considers you are 'domiciled', not where you are resident. So a person who was born in Britain but who has lived abroad for 20 years, yet still maintains a property in the UK and visits family here regularly, is likely to be classed as 'British-domiciled' and his or her worldwide assets are liable to face IHT.

At present, over 80 countries have double taxation agreements with Britain, so that income is not subject to two sets of tax. This is good news for those receiving an income from a pension or savings and investments, but non-residents forfeit British tax relief on pension contributions and this affects their eligibility to save through a tax-saving scheme.

(adapted from *BBC on Air*)

5 Which of the options are closest in meaning to these terms from text B?

1 considered	a taken into account	b regarded as	c respected as
2 be exempt from	a does not need to pay	b should not pay	c must not pay
3 qualify	a reach	b apply	c be entitled to
4 subject to	a responsible for	b liable for	c dependent on
5 offset … against	a claim … against	b deduct … from	c allow … against
6 obligations	a liabilities	b rates	c forms
7 property	a ownership	b possession	c real estate
8 assets	a advantages	b gains	c items owned
9 forfeit	a do without	b lose	c miss
10 eligibility	a entitlement	b choice	c loss

6 True or false? Correct these statements on text B where necessary.

1 In order to become a non-resident for tax purposes, you should get rid of all your property in the UK.
2 Working abroad for at least twelve months enables you to escape the Inland Revenue, at least as far as income tax is concerned.
3 If you manage to stay abroad for 90 to 180 days, you will be exempt from income tax for up to four years.
4 Earned as well as rental income received in the UK is regarded as liable for tax by the Inland Revenue.
5 The cost of repairing your home in Wales can be deducted from any rental income generated by letting it.
6 Old-age pensioners living in Spain must not spend more than 90 days in the UK if they are to avoid income tax.
7 If you sell your British home in order to retire abroad, make sure you stay away from Britain for three years in succession to avoid paying CGT.
8 It is hard for native Britons to avoid inheritance tax.
9 Any overseas investments left to 'British-domiciled' heirs will attract the Inland Revenue's attention.
10 Those who are classified as living abroad for tax purposes also stand to lose some of the advantages offered by the British tax regime.

7 Describe the sources of revenue in the UK as illustrated in the pie chart.

VOCABULARY

Verbs: account for, add up to, amount to, contribute to, represent

Phrases: almost insignificant, a mere, a quarter, as little/much as, by far the largest/smallest, no less/more than, more/less than, one sixth

UK sources of revenue 2001

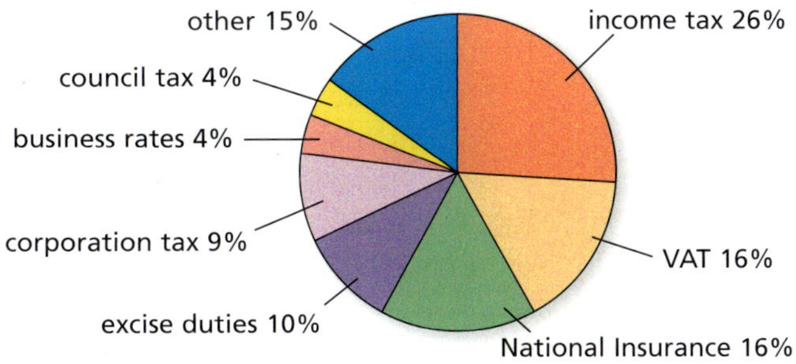

8 Do you think the respective shares of US government spending are justified?

US federal expenditures 2001

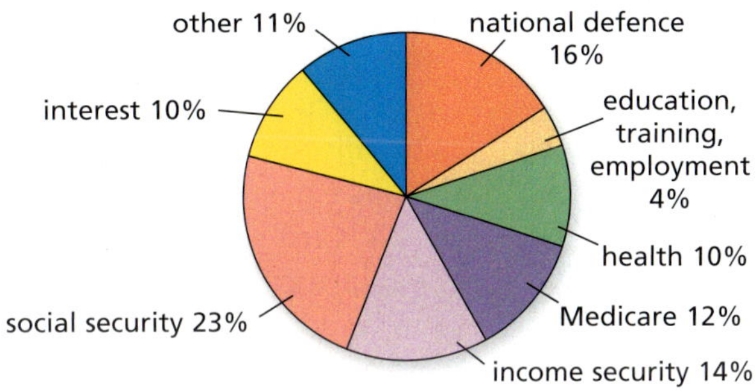

GRAMMAR

The indefinite and the definite article

- The indefinite article is used before countable nouns in order to indicate group membership.
  - John Dolittle has decided to become **a** tax adviser.
- It is also used in connection with quantity statements.
  - You only need to file your tax return once **a** year.
- The definite article is used to refer to a specific group or institution.
  - In the end, **the** taxpayer will always foot the bill.
  - **The** Inland Revenue collects all direct taxes in GB.
- If people or things are referred to in general, the nouns in question are used without articles.
  - Taxpayers sometimes move abroad in order to avoid **tax**.
  - In Germany, even if you don't go to **church**, you may still be liable for **church tax**.

9 Choose the correct option.

1 Once you start paying tax, you are hooked for
   a life.
   b the life.
   c a life.

2 If you don't know how to complete this form, just ask for
   a the advice.
   b an advice.
   c advice.

3 For serious tax evasion, you might be sent to
 a a prison.
 b prison.
 c the prison.
4 Direct federal taxes are collected by
 a Internal Revenue Service.
 b the Internal Revenue Service.
 c an Internal Revenue Service.
5 In spite of all the protests, our minister of finance is still in
 a office.
 b an office.
 c the office.
6 My knowledge of the tax system is based on what I learned at
 a university.
 b a university.
 c the university.
7 All items except food are taxed at
 a a standard rate of VAT.
 b standard rate of VAT.
 c the standard rate of VAT.
8 Many employees make a lot of phone calls at
 a the work.
 b a work.
 c work.

10 Translate the following sentences.

1 Die in westlichen Industriestaaten heute erhobenen Steuern dienen nicht nur der Finanzierung von öffentlichen Ausgaben, sondern auch einer gerechteren Verteilung von Einkommen und Wohlstand.
2 Die Einkommensteuer ist nach wie vor die ergiebigste Steuerquelle, gefolgt von der Mehrwertsteuer, wobei die letztere immer wichtiger wird.
3 Einmal im Jahr sind Steuerzahler gehalten, der Finanzbehörde gegenüber ihre Einkünfte offen zu legen, damit die Einkommensteuer berechnet werden kann.
4 Einkünfte aller Art unterliegen der Einkommensteuer. Die tatsächliche Höhe des steuerpflichtigen Einkommens kann jedoch dadurch verringert werden, dass z.B. Werbungskosten geltend gemacht werden.
5 Alleinstehende zahlen in der Regel mehr Steuern als Verheiratete, die sich gemeinsam veranlagen lassen.
6 Wirtschaftsgüter sind ebenfalls steuerlich absetzbar. Allerdings können sie in der Regel nur über einen Zeitraum von mehreren Jahren abgeschrieben werden.
7 Wenn Sie ein Haus oder eine Wohnung im Ausland besitzen, dann können Sie die Kosten für Unterhaltung und Reparatur gegen Mieteinnahmen verrechnen.
8 Die Erbschaftsteuer wurde in Großbritannien zu Beginn des zwanzigsten Jahrhunderts eingeführt und sie hat tatsächlich zu einer erheblichen Umverteilung von Eigentum geführt.

The environment 15

global warming
- temperature
- carbon dioxide
- climate change
- toxic substances
- earth's atmosphere
- ozone layer
- emissions
- fossil fuels
- greenhouse effect

Use the above diagram to explain what global warming is.

TEXT A 39

Business and the environment

ENVIRONMENTAL issues have become a permanent part of the social, political and business agenda.

- The world's population is twice what it was only 35 years ago and is likely to double again within three decades.
- The build-up of atmospheric carbon dioxide has widely reported implications for climate change.
- The diminution of the Earth's protective ozone layer will remain with us for most of this century, even though the CFC gases (chlorofluorocarbons) used in aerosols and refrigerators are being phased out.

These changes, together with the destruction of natural habitats, for example by logging and farming, are causing the extinction of many species. While the consequences for humans are unknown, scientists agree they are likely to be harmful, perhaps seriously so. And there will be increasing pressure to minimize mankind's footprint on the natural environment.

Businesses will have to focus more on environmental issues. At a minimum, managers should conduct an 'environmental audit' of the ways in which their company interacts with the environment. This begins with a review of all the wastes and emissions the company produces. Managers should then examine the life cycles of their products, researching where the components of the product end up and how the uses of the product affect the environment. Do they lead to wastes or emissions that could be reduced by different designs? Could transportation or packaging be reduced? Does waste disposal damage the environment?

Carrying out an environmental audit can allow the company to see ways of turning possible problems into profit opportunities. Reducing waste products can save costs. In many cases, savings on materials have more than offset the cost of waste reduction, and profits have increased. Recycling also has profit potential. If components are designed to be recycled and reused, the cost of materials falls substantially, while the environmental image of the company is enhanced. New energy sources, new power sources for vehicles and an increasing emphasis on minimal environmental footprints will create new products and markets.

Environmental problems influence the way we live and do business, and responses to them are already shaping strategies in several industries, such as power and transportation. In the future, more and more aspects of business life will be shaped by constraints imposed by our dependence on the environment. This can be the basis for uncovering opportunities that help both the company and the environment – waste reduction, sale rather than disposal of by-products, recycling initiatives and many others. It can help companies to do well by doing good.

(adapted from the *Financial Times Mastering Management* series)

1 Explain the following terms and phrases from text A.

1 diminution of the ozone layer (lines 11–12)
2 natural habitat (line 19)
3 extinction of species (lines 21–22)
4 minimize mankind's footprint (lines 26–27)
5 environmental audit (line 32)
6 life cycle (line 37)
7 waste disposal (line 45)
8 recycling initiative (lines 78–79)

2 Study text A and complete the following sentences.

1 The ozone layer will continue to become thinner although ...
2 Many kinds of plants and animals will die out because ...
3 Those in charge of industrial companies should try to work out how ...
4 Managers should also ask themselves whether ...
5 The result of carrying out an environmental audit might well be that ...
6 Non-labour costs could be reduced considerably if ...
7 Business life will be increasingly determined by outside factors which ...
8 By doing the environmentally right thing, companies stand to gain because ...

3 Explain the difference between the following terms and give examples to illustrate the difference.

1 by-product – waste product
2 diminution – depletion
3 environment – habitat
4 recycle – reuse
5 toxic substances – noxious substances
6 waste disposal – waste reduction

4 Complete the brochure with some of these verbs.

deal with • dispose of • eliminate • ~~give~~ • increase • involve • meet • minimize • monitor • recycle • reduce • reuse

Quality and Green Issues

Tetley & Burton Logistics are committed to minimizing damage to the environment and have developed the following standards for good environmental management:

1 *Give* careful consideration to the environment in corporate decision-making.
2 ... all relevant environmental standards.
3 ... the impact of its activities on the environment.
4 ... management and employees by making individuals aware of their own environmental responsibilities.
5 ... vehicle emissions.
6 ... energy efficiency.
7 ... the use of non-renewable resources.
8 ... the use of pollutants (including CFCs in refrigeration plants).
9 ... materials wherever possible.

T & B LOGISTICS

TEXT B 40

Inside the heap: the sociology of rubbish

The sociology of trash is simple: the rich make it, the poor deal with it. The rich who make it are generally considered 'clean'; the poor who deal with it are considered 'dirty'. It's a topsy-turvy sociology. But then the whole issue of trash is pretty much upside-down and back-to-front. For a start, there is the economics of waste. We tend to think of industrial production as being mainly about manufacturers making things we need – or just want – which we then buy. This is what keeps money circulating and the economic roundabout going round.

What if, for instance, it weren't production that led to economic growth, but waste? Now that seems crazy. Not so crazy though, if you take the example of the United States. For every 100 kilograms of products manufactured, 3,200 kilograms of waste is created. "We are far better at making waste than at making products," concludes Paul Mawken, author, business person and environmentalist.

Western lifestyles that are currently being exported all over the world are phenomenally wasteful. Citizens in the US, world leader in trashing, waste a million pounds (450,000 kilograms) in weight per person per year. If you live in the rich, industrialized part of the world, your consumption – and the pollution you leave behind – is tremendous. A person living in the industrial world will consume 19 times more aluminium, 13 times more iron and steel, 10 times more energy, 6 times more meat and 3 times more fresh water than their fellow human beings living in the developing world.

A trip to a major landfill site is not everyone's idea of an excursion. But what you see there are the most amazing mountains of waste, much of it plastic-seeming. This is where most waste goes – holes in the ground that no one wants in their backyard. With reason: landfills are full of danger. They emit methane, they overheat, they leak – which becomes increasingly ominous as the quantity of chemical products dumped into landfills in the industrial world is expected to double between 1990 and 2005.

Countries which are short of land, like Japan and Belgium, favour incinerating rubbish. This is no better; many experts say it's a lot worse. It creates air pollution, releasing toxins and dioxins into the atmosphere. A few years ago, the US raised the alert. The big country had run out of landfill sites. This was in spite of it exporting waste to Canada and Mexico and, of course, many parts of the developing world. In this the US is not alone. Most developed countries export their waste.

Many people are responding by trying to alter their personal habits. Recycling is on the increase – though it varies widely from region to region. In parts of Britain recycling has crept up to 5 per cent of household waste; in parts of Australia it's 15 per cent. But in some areas of Canada it's closer to 80 per cent.

There are practical things that we, as individuals, can do – like recycle, reuse, consume carefully and generally consume less. But there also needs to be a major mind-shift in the way our economies and our societies operate. We need, metaphorically speaking, to take the lid off the rubbish bin. Only then will we get down to tackling the beast in the bin.

(adapted from *BBC on Air*)

5 Match the definitions with these terms from text B.

consume • dump • environmentalist • incinerating • landfill site • pollution • release • rubbish bin • trashing • wasteful

1 result of adding harmful substances to soil, water or air
2 sb actively involved in green issues
3 producing waste
4 area where waste material is buried under layers of earth
5 excessive in the use of resources
6 dispose of things in an irresponsible manner
7 burning
8 allow sth to escape
9 use
10 container used for all kinds of domestic waste

6 What do the following figures from text B refer to?

1 3,200
2 450,000
3 19
4 10
5 3
6 2005
7 5
8 80

7 True or false? Correct these statements on text B where necessary.

1 The poor produce next to no rubbish.
2 The issue of waste is an appropriate subject for economic analysis.
3 The volume of waste is determined by the volume of production.
4 The consumption of valuable resources – ranging from water to aluminium – is 3 per cent to 19 per cent higher in industrialized countries than in developing countries.
5 Landfill sites are surprisingly popular places to visit.
6 Ominous chemicals usually end up in incinerators.
7 Quite a few developing countries have been importing garbage from the USA.
8 On the face of it, inhabitants in developing countries behave in an environmentally responsible way.
9 Parts of Britain and Australia still have a long way to go as far as recycling is concerned.
10 'Taking the lid off the rubbish bin' will only increase the number of environmental problems.

8 Do the crossword puzzle and then work out the environmental slogan.

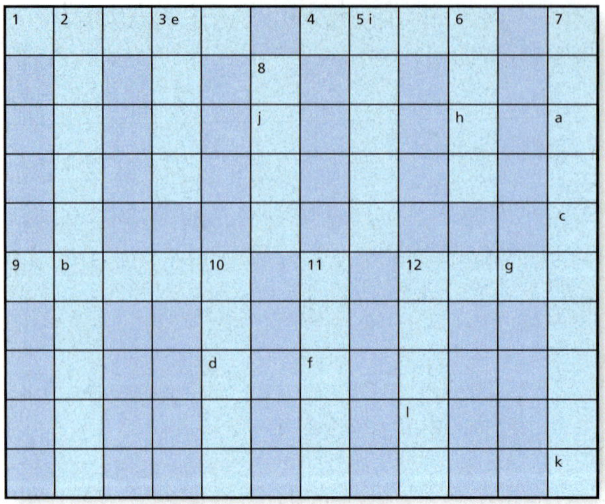

Across

1 environmentally friendly colour
4 gases found in aerosol sprays
9 powered by the sun
12 conserve

Down

2 ecologically sensitive area of trees
3 expel
5 emissions from car exhausts
6 abbreviation for small and medium-sized enterprises
7 burn
8 dispose of irresponsibly
10 dangerous
11 opposite of clean
12 leak of oil or other toxic substance

Slogan

a b c d e f g h   i j k l !

9 Use this role card to arrange the transportation of waste materials with the manager of a specialist company. The manager's card is on page 134.

Caller

- *enquire about suitability of company: what types of waste it specializes in*
- *explain what waste has to be disposed: four lorryloads of asbestos*
- *consider environmental risks of transport by truck*
- *request details of company safety standards and staff qualifications*
- *ask about disposal sites and costs involved*

41

Now listen to the model answer.

GRAMMAR

all, every, each, any

- *all* is used before plural nouns if the total number of persons or things concerned is referred to.
  - **All** the companies dealing with toxic waste …
  - **All** cases of contamination must be taken seriously.

It is also used before nouns in the singular, especially if they denote something that consists of several components.

  - We've been attending a conference on the environment **all** week.

- *every* denotes every single 'member' of a real group whose total size is not always known (but larger than two) and where the emphasis is on what these members have in common.
  - **Every** bit of glass will be recycled.
  - Our rubbish is collected **every** Wednesday.
- *each* denotes every single member of a small group where the emphasis is on what separates these members from each other.
  - **Each** member of the committee has a different set of responsibilities.
- *any* denotes a conceivable member of a group.
  - **Any** company can apply for environmental subsidies.

10 Complete the following sentences, using *all*, *every*, *each* or *any*.

1 There is an ecological as well as an economic dimension to … industrial product.
2 In analyzing the environmental impact of the items produced, … the waste generated by manufacturing processes should be taken into account.
3 … attempt to clean up the mess left by former industries is bound to be costly.
4 … landfill site in this country is a nuisance which must be dealt with.
5 Not … the companies accused of polluting the environment have promised to mend their ways.
6 … known types of incinerator emit noxious gases.
7 … citizen 'consumes' huge amounts of steel, aluminium and energy, although they might not be aware of it.
8 This steel plant pollutes the air … day and … night … day of the week.
9 … site specializes in a particular type of waste.
10 Take … case of pollution – they're … extremely difficult to deal with.

11 Translate the following text into German.

The Business in the Environment organization is today publishing its fifth Corporate Environmental Commitment list, assessing companies on their efforts to minimize their impact on the world in terms of pollution and depletion of natural resources. The aim of the index is "to encourage companies to reduce the damage they cause to the environment whilst gaining competitive advantage through effective management processes".

"The most important thing we have achieved is to get companies to think about the environment and their performance and about the wider implications of what they do," says Belinda Howell, director of BiE.

The number of companies taking part in the survey has grown each year to the point where the list represents 78 per cent of the top 350 companies listed on the stock exchange. Those that refuse to take part are named and shamed for the first time this year.

(adapted from *The Guardian*)

12 Discuss one of the following issues. Work in groups.

1 Jobs versus the environment

The last big employer in your area, a smelting plant that emits deadly toxic materials, may have to close because the authorities say that the health of the local people is more important than the jobs. Unemployment in the area already stands at 40% and the smelter provides hundreds of jobs.
If you had to choose between jobs and the environment, which would you choose? Would you support a campaign to close down the last major employer? Or would you want the factory to remain open?

2 The car versus the environment

Representatives of the groups below discuss the future of the motor car as a credible form of transport.

- federation of car dealers
- airports authority
- road haulage association
- environmentalist group
- railway transport group
- association of bus companies

13 Use the internet to find out about the green policies of a company of your choice. Summarize your findings and present them in class.

14 Translate the following sentences.

1 Bei der Produktion von Konsumgütern fallen pro Kilo zusätzlich 32 kg Müll an.
2 In der Vergangenheit ist fast der gesamte Müll der Industriestaaten auf Deponien verbracht worden.
3 Jedes Müllverbrennungssystem – und sei es auch noch so gut – setzt schädliche Substanzen frei.
4 Jedes Mitgliedsland der EU muss die vereinbarten, von Brüssel überwachten Umweltauflagen einhalten.
5 Umweltschützer kämpfen schon seit Jahren für eine Verkehrspolitik, deren Ziel es ist, mehr Güter per Bahn zu befördern.
6 Nachhaltige Herstellungsverfahren mögen höhere Kosten verursachen. Aus Umweltgründen sollten sie jedoch subventioniert werden.
7 Haushaltsmüll wird in fast jedem EU-Mitgliedsland getrennt und bis auf den Restmüll der Kreislaufwirtschaft zugeführt.
8 Die Sprecherin des Chemieunternehmens sagte, ihr Unternehmen sei in Umweltdingen engagierter als jedes andere Unternehmen dieser Branche.
9 Wir müssen alle Anstrengungen unternehmen, um in der Öffentlichkeit nicht als Umweltverschmutzer gebrandmarkt zu werden.
10 Falls nötig, können Sie unsere Umweltabteilung jederzeit anrufen.

The European Union 16

Find the member states of the EU on the map above.
Do you as an individual benefit from the EU, and if so how?

TEXT A 42

Doing business in the European Union

From its modest beginnings as not much more than a customs union, the European Union has become a single market. It has the euro as its currency in most of its member states and a number of joint institutions, free trade between member states, and a common external tariff on goods and services imported from outside.

The common external tariff is placed on all imports into the EU. If tariffs were different for different EU states, this might lead to problems. For example, if Germany had a 10 per cent tariff and France a 20 per cent tariff, then a US corporation exporting goods to France could use Germany as a transit country, paying the lower tariff, and then forward them to its French customers without paying any further duty.

For businesses, membership of the EU has many advantages.

- Businesses in EU states have free access to markets which would otherwise be protected by tariffs or quotas. In this way French businesses, for example, have access to all other EU markets. This provides them with the opportunity to operate in EU markets basically as they would at home. A Paris-based firm can operate in Berlin or Bilbao in much the same way as it would in Lyon or Lille.
- Businesses have full access to all the factors of production (land, labour and capital) in any of the member states. For instance, a Swedish business can purchase cheap land in southern Portugal for a new factory location, hire skilled designers from Italy or buy capital equipment from France.
- The EU provides businesses with a large market of around 378 million consumers and so businesses can profit from massive economies of scale.
- Businesses are protected from competitors from outside this area by the common external tariff. Such protection allows them to be sheltered from the potentially damaging effects of unfair competition. On the other hand, increased competition from businesses in other EU states may act as an incentive to increase efficiency.

There are, however, also disadvantages for businesses in the EU.

- Foreign businesses will have access to a member country's market. Such competition may reduce the market share which domestic businesses have established.
- Protection from external tariffs is not always beneficial to businesses operating from within the EU. This is because being sheltered from external competition may result in fewer incentives for a business to become more efficient.
- Businesses have to comply with harmonized standards and regulations concerning taxation, quality, hygiene, safety and the environment.

Yet overall, as the large number of applicants for entry in the past has shown, the advantages of EU membership – for countries, companies and individuals – appear to far outweigh the disadvantages.

1 Find the terms in text A which are explained below.

1. market without restrictions concerning the movement of persons, goods and capital
2. country through which goods are transported to another country
3. dispatch and transport
4. limit placed by a government on imports and/or exports of goods to or from a country
5. machinery, instruments and vehicles owned and used by a company to manufacture goods
6. savings through production in large numbers
7. something that gives an employee or a company the desire to improve performance
8. having a helpful effect

2 Answer the following questions on text A.

European Parliament

1 Why would it be incorrect to describe the EU as a customs union?
2 In what way might non-EU states benefit if there were no common external tariff?
3 Why is a single market particularly useful for businesses wishing to expand?
4 What is the advantage of the common external tariff for businesses in EU states?
5 What is the likely effect of competition within the EU?
6 In what way can a country's EU membership harm that country's businesses?
7 What are the potentially negative results of the common external tariff?
8 What norms and rules must businesses observe when operating in the EU?

3 Complete the text using the correct tense of the verbs in brackets.

The history of the European Union (start) …[1] in 1952, when the European Coal and Steel Community (be set up) …[2] by six countries. Under the Treaty of Rome, these countries – Belgium, France, Germany, Italy, the Netherlands and Luxembourg – (establish) …[3] the European Economic Community, whose aim (be) …[4] not only the creation of a Common Market and a Common Agricultural Policy, but also 'ever closer union'.

In 1973, the UK, Eire and Denmark (become) …[5] members of what (come) …[6] to be known as the EC, followed by Greece in 1979 and Spain and Portugal in 1985. If the UK (join) …[7] earlier, things (take) …[8] a different turn, especially with regard to agriculture.

In 1995, Austria, Sweden and Finland successfully (apply) …[9] for membership. Their applications for accession to the EU (not meet) …[10] with any opposition as they (fulfil) …[11] all the criteria.

New Year's Day 1993 (see) …[12] the introduction of the Single Market after national VAT tax regimes (be harmonized) …[13]. Since then, border controls (more or less disappear) …[14], especially between countries that, in 1985, (sign up) …[15] to the Schengen agreement on the movement of people and cross-border police powers. At the time it (be argued) …[16] that such freedom of movement (lead) …[17] to a steep rise in cross-border crime, but, by and large, these fears (not materialize) …[18] so far. The 1992 Treaty of Maastricht (create) …[19] the European Union, thus making progress towards 'ever closer union' as originally envisaged by the Treaty of Rome. Eastern European countries (have) …[20] to meet all the criteria if they (wish) …[21] to become full members of the EU. It remains to be seen, however, whether politicians of all countries and political persuasions (have) …[22] the courage to create a really united Europe.

4 Use these items to replace the words and phrases in brackets.

agenda • agreements • applied • body • budget • coordinates • disputes • draft • driving force • exchange • implementing • in co-decision • legislate • monetary policy • operation • revenues • suffrage • supervision

European Parliament

Elected every five years by direct universal (right to vote) …[1], the European Parliament is the expression of the democratic will of the Union's 378 million citizens. It shares with the Council the power to (pass laws) …[2] as well as budgetary control and it exercises democratic (control) …[3] over the Commission.

Council of the European Union

(also referred to as the Council of Ministers)

The Council is the EU's main decision-making (organ) …[4]. It is the Union's legislative body; for a wide range of EU issues, it exercises the legislative power (jointly) …[5] with the European Parliament. It concludes important international (treaties) …[6] on behalf of the EU, and it (harmonizes) …[7] the broad economic policies of the member states. According to the matters on the (list of business to be discussed) …[8] , the Council meets in different compositions: foreign affairs, finance, education, telecommunications, etc.

European Commission

The Commission is the (authority initiating change) …[9] in the Union's institutional system. It has the right to (draw up) …[10] legislation. It is the Union's executive body and is responsible for (putting into practice) …[11] European legislation. Finally, it represents the Union on the international stage.

Court of Justice

The Court of Justice ensures that Community law is uniformly interpreted and effectively (administered) …[12]. It has jurisdiction in (controversies) …[13] involving member states, EU institutions, businesses and individuals.

Court of Auditors

The Court of Auditors checks that all the Union's (receipts) …[14] have been received and all its expenditure incurred in a lawful and regular manner and that the financial management of the EU (estimate of revenues and expenditures) …[15] is sound.

European Central Bank

The European Bank defines and implements European (strategies concerning financial matters) …[16]; it conducts foreign (currency) …[17] operations and ensures the smooth (functioning) …[18] of payment systems.

(adapted from http://europa.eu.int/inst-en.htm)

INFORMATION

Country	Inhabitants in millions (2001)	GDP per head
European Union	378.0	100
Austria	8.2	111
Belgium	10.3	113
Denmark	5.4	114
Finland	5.2	102
France	59.0	109
Germany	82.3	104
Greece	10.6	77
Ireland	3.8	96
Italy	57.8	98
Luxembourg	0.4	162
Netherlands	16.0	109
Portugal	10.0	70
Spain	40.1	80
Sweden	8.9	99
United Kingdom	59.9	102
Czech Republic	10.3	60
Estonia	1.4	38
Hungary	10.0	52
Poland	38.6	39
Slovenia	2.0	71

(source: http://europa.eu.int/comm/eurostat)

5 Complete the following sentences with the appropriate adjectives and nouns. In some cases, the above list will be useful.

EXAMPLES 80 per cent of the 59.9 million *Britons* live in urban areas.
Many *Portuguese* live in or near the capital Lisbon.

1 Although Germany (360,000 km^2) is much smaller than Sweden (450,000 km^2) and Spain (492,000 km^2), there are more … than … and … together.
2 EU membership of the 2 million … would not be a serious financial problem for the other member countries.
3 Although English is spoken everywhere in Ireland, quite a few people in this country speak … as well.
4 Many of the 16m people in the … speak English and German in addition to … .
5 Although … and … share the same language, people in – say – Vienna and Berlin are radically different.
6 GDP per head achieved by the 1.4m … is about one third of the EU average and about half the figure for the 10.6m … .
7 The 3.8m … have benefited greatly from joining the EU. Now, their per capita GDP is almost as high as that of the 57.8m … .
8 The …, the … and the … achieve a per capita GDP which is between 9 and 12 percentage points higher than that of the 59.9m … .
9 With a per capita GDP of 109 the … and the … are well above the EU average.
10 The … and the … also have an identical GDP per head.

6 Use the table on page 129 and your own knowledge to answer the questions.

1 Which countries have a GDP per head above the EU average?
2 Why is Poland's EU membership more problematic than that of Slovenia?
3 Why is Luxembourg way ahead in terms of GDP per head?
4 Would it be correct to say that agricultural countries have a lower GDP per head than the others? Give reasons.
5 Are the large EU countries economically stronger than the small ones? Give reasons.

INFORMATION

Trade statistics

Origin of goods in per cent of total imports*

Exporting country / Importing country	B	F	D	I	NL	E	UK	Total		USA
France	7	–	15	9		10	10	51		9
Germany	5	10	–	7	9		7	38		8.5
Greece		9	15	16	6		6	52		5
Ireland		4	6		3		31	44		16
Italy	5	13	19	–	6	4	6	53		5
Spain		18	16	9		–	8	51		5
UK		9	13	5	7		–	34		13

Destination of goods in per cent of total exports*

Importing country / Exporting country	B	F	D	I	NL	E	UK	Total		USA
France	10	–	18	10		8	9	55		10
Germany	5	11	–	7.5	7.5	4.5	8.5	44		10
Greece		4	16	14	3		6	43		6
Ireland	6	8	15	3	6		20	58		14
Italy	3	13	17	–	3	6	7	49		10
Spain		20	13	9		–	8	50		4
UK	5	10	12	5	8		–	40		15

* The tables only list countries with a percentage of at least 2 per cent.

(source: *Fischer Weltalmanach*)

7 Study the tables above and write a text on one of the following topics.

1 The importance of any two of the countries above as EU trading partners.
2 The role of the USA as an EU trading partner.

TEXT B 43

Still Europeans

EUROPEANS ARE unable or unwilling to move around their continent. Only 0.4 per cent of the European Union's population move to another country to work each year. In the US, mobility from state to state is six times higher. Many economic and cultural barriers to mobility are still in place. Governments should rally behind European Commission plans to dismantle them.

The demand for labour mobility in Europe is growing for three reasons. First, in a single market with a single currency, the integration of many sectors and industries is intensifying. Businesses increasingly have operations in more than one country. They and their employees would benefit from operating under compatible rules.

Second, the rapid development of high-technology, new-economy industries has created new skills gaps. The EU believes there will be 1.7m vacancies in Europe's information technology sector alone by 2003. The International Labour Organization has calculated that the skilled labour shortage in new-economy industries has cost £73bn in lost growth since 1998.

Third, there are wide divergences in economic performance across the euro-zone. Indeed, the one-size-fits-all interest-rate policy could be exacerbating them. Thus booming Ireland hopes to employ 300,000 immigrants in the first half of the decade, filling 75 per cent of vacancies. It remains to be seen whether German builders will flock to Dublin, a reversal of historic flows. Many critics of the euro say the project will not succeed unless people are willing to travel abroad to find work.

The EU should do more to remove the obstacles to mobility. Governments should use bilateral treaties to smooth out tax barriers, particularly with regard to pension contributions. Supplementary pensions should be made truly portable. The mutual recognition of qualifications must be made to function in practice. And businesses must work more closely with the public sector to close skills gaps.

But governments can do little about the biggest deterrents: the bother of finding new schools, housing or jobs for spouses. Mobility is thus likely to benefit only the highly skilled or the highly motivated. Like immigration into Europe, it is increasingly selective.

The onus is therefore on governments to make their static workforces more adaptable through training, lifelong learning and wage flexibility and by encouraging older workers to stay in the labour market. This might also help to avoid some of the problems associated with mobility in the US, such as rootlessness, dependency and crime.

(adapted from the *Financial Times*)

8 Match the definitions and synonyms below with these terms from text B.

compatible • deterrent • dismantle • exacerbate • onus • portable • rootlessness • skills gap • smooth out • supplementary

1 abolish gradually
2 additional
3 anything that makes people decide not to do something
4 burden
5 harmonize
6 make worse
7 shortage of well-trained labour
8 state of not feeling at home anywhere
9 suited
10 transferable

9 True or false? Correct these statements on text B where necessary.

1 Europeans are much more mobile than Americans.
2 More and more businesses are operating in a number of member countries.
3 Within the EU, there is general agreement that any barriers to improving mobility ought to be removed.
4 For many of the jobs in new industries there are not enough qualified staff.
5 Increasingly, Europeans are taking up jobs in other EU member countries.
6 Governments cannot do much about improving their citizens' attitudes towards mobility.
7 Social problems are the only real drawback immigrants face in their new country.
8 If governments wish to avoid the negative consequences of mobility as found in the USA, they will have to take a number of steps.

10 List the main points of each paragraph in text B.

11 A young Spanish teacher wants to work in Germany. Give her or him advice on the aspects below. Work in groups.

health • housing • job prospects • qualifications • way of life

12 Translate the following text into German.

WHAT IS THE EUROPEAN UNION?

The European Union is a unique, treaty-based system that defines economic and political cooperation among its member states. The Union is the latest stage in a process of integration begun in the 1950s by Belgium, France, Germany, Italy, Luxembourg, and the Netherlands, whose leading representatives signed the original treaties establishing various forms of European integration.

These treaties gave life to the novel concept that, by creating communities of shared sovereignty in matters of coal and steel production, trade, and nuclear energy, another war in Europe would be unthinkable. While common EU policies have evolved in a number of other sectors since then, the fundamental goal of the Union remains the same: to create an ever closer union among the peoples of Europe.

13 Translate the following sentences.

1 Europa könnte als einheitlicher Wirtschaftsraum kaum funktionieren, wenn nicht schon vor 50 Jahren der gemeinsame Außenzoll eingeführt worden wäre.
2 Wenn sie gefragt würden, welche Vorteile Europa ihnen bietet, würden die meisten Leute antworten, dass sie es eigentlich nicht wüssten.
3 Bedauerlicherweise weiß kaum jemand in der EU, dass sich die EU vorwiegend durch Einnahmen aus dem gemeinsamen Außenzoll und einem kleinen Anteil am Mehrwertsteueraufkommen finanziert.
4 Kurz nach dem Beitritt Großbritanniens zur EU sind die Nahrungsmittelpreise dort erheblich gestiegen, weil Importe aus den Commonwealth-Ländern nun verzollt werden mussten.
5 Es wird manchmal behauptet, dass die EU nur dazu dient, Konkurrenten aus Amerika und Asien den Zugang zu einem Markt von 378 Mill. Verbrauchern zu erschweren.
6 Leider hat das Europäische Parlament nicht die Kompetenzen, die mit denen der nationalen Parlamente der Mitgliedstaaten vergleichbar wären.
7 Es wird weithin angenommen, dass freie Stellen in der Informationstechnologie nur besetzt werden können, wenn die grenzüberschreitende Arbeitsmobilität größer wird.
8 Nur durch lebenslanges Lernen – insbesondere das Lernen anderer europäischer Sprachen – können Arbeitnehmer in Zukunft in Europa Arbeitsplätze finden.
9 Inzwischen können auch Einzelpersonen und nicht nur Unternehmen den Europäischen Gerichtshof anrufen.
10 Unter den Beitrittskandidaten weisen die mitteleuropäischen Länder Polen, Slowenien, die Tschechische Republik und Ungarn den höchsten Entwicklungsstand auf. Daher wurden sehr früh Beitrittsverhandlungen mit ihnen aufgenommen.

Role cards

Unit 3, exercise 9

Reservations manager

- *offer assistance*
- *double room available*
- *rooms face garden, away from restaurant, bar & disco area*
- *conference room available 18/8; state-of-the-art equipment*
- *rates: rooms £140 per room and night; conference room including refreshments £100 per day*
- *confirmation: ask caller for email address*
- *thank caller for booking*

Unit 6, exercise 10

Personnel manager

- *vacancies for experienced call centre staff with language skills*
- *member of team handling calls from across Europe*
- *processing + coordinating bookings for international airline*
- *£16,500, overtime bonuses, shift work*
- *22 days' paid holiday for full-time staff*
- *location just outside Sheffield*
- *300 staff*
- *operates 365 days a year*
- *on average 60,000 calls a week*

Unit 11, exercise 8

Agent

- *need for buildings and home contents insurance*
- *buildings insurance: cover against fire, storm damage, burst water pipes, lightning, etc.*
- *home contents insurance: accidental damage to home and contents*
- *burglary part of home contents policy*
- *exclusions depend on scope of cover: certain valuables, expensive jewellery and large amounts of cash excluded*
- *attractive rates, depending on area and value of house and contents insured*
- *duration of cover: 12 months with automatic renewal*
- *proposal form to be filled in and forwarded – phone for further information*

Unit 15, exercise 9

Manager of transportation company

- *company specializes in: liquid bulk, petroleum, gases, hazardous & non-hazardous waste materials*
- *full service provided: consultation, transportation, warehousing, disposal*
- *state-of-the-art vehicles designed to transport hazardous waste safely*
- *fully trained and experienced staff*
- *competitive rates*
- *use regional landfill disposal sites controlled by environmental safety officials*

08 ▪ Unit 3, exercise 8

RECEPTIONIST Rutland Hotel, good afternoon. What can I do for you?

CALLER Hello, could you put me through to reservations, please?

RESERVATIONS Reservations. Linda speaking. How can I help you?

CALLER I'd like to book a number of rooms for October. Have you got any vacancies?

RESERVATIONS When exactly were you thinking of coming and how many rooms do you require?

CALLER We'll be attending a conference in Manchester from Monday, October 2nd to Thursday, October 5th. So we'll need accommodation for three nights, four singles and two doubles, if possible.

RESERVATIONS I'll just check. ... That'll be all right.

CALLER And what are your rates for the different rooms?

RESERVATIONS Singles are £145 per night, doubles are £195, including full English breakfast.

CALLER Right. I'll book those rooms.

RESERVATIONS Fine. In whose name shall I make the booking?

CALLER It's for our company. Steinbeck & Co.

RESERVATIONS Could you spell that, please?

CALLER S-T-E-I-N-B-E-C-K.

RESERVATIONS And your name and telephone number, sir?

CALLER Horst Weber. And the telephone number is 0049 234 264057.

RESERVATIONS Thank you, Mr Weber. Let me just repeat the telephone number: it's 0049 234 264057. Could I also have your email address, please, and then we can confirm your booking?

CALLER Yes, certainly. It's steinbeck@t-online.de – have you got that?

RESERVATIONS Yes, steinbeck@t-online.de – thanks. We'll be sending your confirmation later today, Mr Weber.

CALLER Thanks. Bye.

RESERVATIONS Thank you. Goodbye.

09 ▪ Unit 3, exercise 9

RESERVATIONS Reservations, good afternoon. How can I help you?

CALLER Good afternoon, this is Julia Schmidt from Kaufstadt AG. I'd like to book accommodation for our sales director, and reserve a conference room for a one-day meeting.

RESERVATIONS Yes, certainly. When would you like the accommodation and conference facilities?

CALLER When? The conference is scheduled for 18th August. The accommodation would be for two nights from 17th to 19th August. And could the room please be in a quiet part of the hotel?

RESERVATIONS Yes, of course. The rates per room and night are £140, and I'll book one of the rooms overlooking the garden; very peaceful.

CALLER £140 per room? That sounds reasonable. I presume that includes breakfast.

RESERVATIONS Yes, either full Scottish or Continental, the choice is yours. The conference room rate is £100 per day and that includes refreshments.

CALLER £100? OK. What refreshments are included in the price?

RESERVATIONS Soft drinks, tea and coffee. Snacks and meals would cost extra of course.

CALLER Fine. Could you please send me an email to confirm the booking?

RESERVATIONS Yes, no problem. What's your email address, please?

CALLER It's kaufstadt@t-online.de

RESERVATIONS kaufstadt@t-online.de – right, I'll do that immediately. Thank you for doing business with us. We look forward to welcoming you to the Mackintosh Hotel. Goodbye.

CALLER Thanks. Bye.

11 ▪ Unit 4, exercise 7

RECEPTIONIST Welcome to First Bank Direct Banking. If you require the balance of your main account, please press zero. If you wish to use the push button service, press one. Or to speak to a Direct Banking adviser, press two. Please wait for one of our Direct Banking advisers to help you.

TOM RAYNER Good evening. First Bank Direct Banking. My name is Tom Rayner. How can I help you?

SHEILA MYERS I'd like to check the balance of my account.

TOM RAYNER May I confirm your name, madam?

SHEILA MYERS Mrs Sheila Myers.

TOM RAYNER And can I have your account number?

SHEILA MYERS 2-0-5-4-2-7-9-8

TOM RAYNER Thank you. Just a moment, please. ... It is £1,069.78. Anything else I can do for you, madam?

SHEILA MYERS Yes, I would also like to make a remittance.

TOM RAYNER That's no problem. Who is the remittance to go to?

SHEILA MYERS To Johnstone & Co Ltd, 10 Market Street, Perth.

TOM RAYNER Could you just spell the name, please.

SHEILA MYERS J-O-H-N-S-T-O-N-E.

TOM RAYNER OK. I've got that. And the name of the bank?

SHEILA MYERS The Perth branch of the Clydesdale Bank.

TOM RAYNER Yes ... And the account number?

SHEILA MYERS The number is 6-0-5-5-7-8-6-4.

TOM RAYNER Let me just repeat: 6-0-5-5-7-8-6-4. And the sort code?

SHEILA MYERS The sort code is 85-46-80.

TOM RAYNER Yes, 8-5-4-6-8-0. And the amount you wish to transfer?

SHEILA MYERS £552.75.

TOM RAYNER Fine. So that's £552.75 to Johnstone & Co Ltd in Perth at the Perth branch of the Clydesdale Bank. The account number is 60557864. And the sort code is 85-46-80.

SHEILA MYERS That's correct.

TOM RAYNER Can I do anything else for you?

SHEILA MYERS No. That's all. Thank you very much.

TOM RAYNER You're welcome, Mrs Myers. Thank you for calling Direct Banking.

13 ▪ Unit 4, exercise 12

This is Simon Kendal from the Avon Bank in Bristol. Sorry to be ringing on a Friday afternoon. I'm phoning about your account with us, number 4763603. You asked us to check some items on the statement we sent you a few days ago. I've looked into the matter, and – yes – there are two payments which have been wrongly entered. The entry for 4 March, which we booked in your favour, should have read £10,475 and not £475. And I'm afraid there was a second keying-in error on 17 March. The correct entry is £1005.75.
So, your account is well in the black, and we won't, of course, make any interest charges. We have also processed your transfer to Harper's & Sons. Please accept our apologies for these unfortunate errors. Thank you and have a nice weekend.

15 ▪ Unit 5, exercise 11

BROWN Good morning, Mr Price, this is Adèle Brown at People Search. You applied to us for a job as a sales manager a couple of weeks ago. We have now made a shortlist of candidates and were wondering if you would be able to come for an interview next Thursday at 10 o'clock?

PRICE Oh, that's good news. The 17th? Let me just check. Yes, of course. Where will the interview be held?

BROWN We'll be conducting interviews at the Howard Hotel in George Street in Edinburgh. Do you know it? It's only about five minutes' walk from Waverley Station.

PRICE Yes, I think so. I'm pretty sure I'll find it. Could you tell me where you are running the interviews in the hotel?

BROWN Just ask at the reception when you get there. They'll show you to where we are.

PRICE Fine. Could you possibly tell me who'll be interviewing me and how long the interview will last?

BROWN I believe it will be either Peter Miller or John Fisher. They'll be in charge of all the interviews. The interview shouldn't take much longer than half an hour.

PRICE I'll probably still take the day off. Do you know if there will be any tests?

BROWN Oh, I'm sorry, I'm not absolutely sure

about that. But I'll find out and phone you back.

PRICE Excellent. Could you call me on my mobile? The number is 06752 734668.

BROWN I'll just repeat that: 06752 734668.

PRICE Yes, that's correct. And thank you very much for calling.

BROWN Not at all. And the best of luck on Thursday, Mr Price.

18 ▪ Unit 6, exercise 10

Personnel Manager = PM

CALLER Hello, I'm phoning about the vacancy advertised on your website.

PM Well, we have several vacancies for experienced call centre workers with foreign-language skills as we handle calls from all over Europe.

CALLER As for foreign languages, I'm fluent in French and my German isn't too bad, either.

PM What about call centre experience? Have you ever worked in a call centre?

CALLER Yes, I have, on a part-time basis that is, while I was studying. Now that I've graduated I could work full-time, starting next week.

PM You would be required to handle and process bookings for an international airline.

CALLER That would be no problem because I've done that sort of thing before. ... Um ... Could you tell me something about the salary, hours, overtime, flexitime, that sort of thing?

PM We can offer a salary of £16,500 per annum plus overtime bonuses. Mind you, you'll be required to work shifts ... and ... yes ... we have a flexitime system.

CALLER That sounds OK. What about holidays?

PM Our full-time staff are entitled to 22 days' paid holiday. ... Is there anything else you'd like to know?

CALLER Hm, yes ... is the call centre in Sheffield itself? ... And ... do you work around the clock?

PM As I said, we work shifts – 365 days, incidentally – and we handle something like 60,000 calls a week with a staff of 300. Our premises are not in Sheffield itself, but on the outskirts. Perhaps you could pop in next week to discuss things.

CALLER Yes, I'll do that. What's the address?

PM 25 Hallam Road. It's easy to reach by public transport or by car. If you take the ...

21 ▪ Unit 7, exercise 12

Hello, ... I ... um ... assume you speak English. I'm ... um ... I'm phoning on behalf of Cardiff Computers Limited. I found your website and would like to place an order for a hamper with you. The hamper is to be presented to the manager of our Munich branch, Herr Schmitt, next Wednesday. We've opted for the Alpine hamper – order No. 2/779/50X – I repeat 2/779/50X – at a price of €100, plus €25 for delivery within the Munich area. Do you think you could swap the bottle of gin for a bottle of whisky, say White & Mackay? Oh, by the way, could you deliver the hamper to our subsidiary in Schillergasse 15? Perhaps you could confirm our order by phone – the number is 01222 336 1389 – I repeat – 01222 336 1389 or to our email address: cardcomp@freeserve.co.uk
I look forward to hearing from you on Monday because it's perhaps too late now. After all, it's Friday 5 p.m. our time. Bye for now. Oh, I forgot: my name is David Thomas. Bye.

28 ▪ Unit 10, exercise 11

SIMMONDS Laura Simmonds. Purchasing department. Hello. What can I do for you?

BAUER Hansemann & Meier, Bauer speaking.

SIMMONDS Yes. What can I do for you?

BAUER I'm phoning about a consignment which we had shipped to you for onward delivery to our customer in Stafford.

SIMMONDS Yes?

BAUER Well, you see the problem is that the consignment hasn't been delivered yet. And our customer is getting rather worried because they need the goods urgently.

SIMMONDS OK. Let me just take down the details. You are Herr Bau...??

BAUER Bauer, B-A-U-E-R, of Hansemann & Meier in Neuss in Germany. As far as we know, the goods were part of a container load to your Stafford depot.

And the shipment was arranged by our forwarding agent Eurologis here in Neuss.

SIMMONDS Right. Now, could I just take down the names and any other details that you may have?

BAUER Yes, of course.

SIMMONDS Right. Perhaps you could let me have the consignee's name first.

BAUER It's Banerjee Ltd in Stafford.

SIMMONDS And how do you spell the name, please?

BAUER B-A-N-E-R-J-E-E, in Stafford, 57 Stoke Road.

SIMMONDS Right I've got that. Then I need the name of your forwarding agent.

BAUER It's Eurologis from Neuss.

SIMMONDS And could you spell that too, please?

BAUER No problem. The first part is EURO like the euro, and the second is logis as in logistics. And their office is in Neuss N-E-U-S-S, Am Hafen 19. That is A-M, new word H-A-F-E-N; number 19.

SIMMONDS OK, I think I've got that. And when was the consignment shipped?

BAUER That was three days ago by air from Düsseldorf to Birmingham. You see, as I said, the matter is rather urgent.

SIMMONDS I understand that. So, three days ago you say, that would have been on the 27th.

BAUER Yes, that's correct.

SIMMONDS OK. I'll see what I can do. I'll first check on our computer and then we'll contact our depot at Birmingham airport. I'm sure we'll be able to trace your consignment very quickly. And could you just let me have your phone number? I'll call you back as soon as possible.

BAUER Yes, of course. The area code is 2131, and the number is 5 84 38. And don't forget the country code for Germany.

SIMMONDS So that's 0049 for Germany and then 2131 – 5 84 38 ...

30 ▪ Unit 11, exercise 5

Insurance Clerk = IC

RECEPTIONIST Niagara Insurance. How can I help you?

TOURIST Hello, I'm phoning because we've had an accident with our rented car. I couldn't get through to the rental company.

RECEPTIONIST I'll put you through to our claims department. Please hold.

TOURIST Thank you.

IC Claims department, Sally speaking. What can I do for you?

TOURIST Well, we've had an accident with our rented car and we don't know what to do next.

IC All right, I need your policy number, please.

TOURIST Sure, just a minute ... It's CL 0-1-5-5-4-5-2-7-8-6 XL.

IC I'll just read that back to you. Your policy number is CL 0-1-5-5-4-5-2-7-8-6 XL ... and may I have your name the way it's printed on the policy?

TOURIST The name is Frank Obermüller.

IC Could you spell that, please?

TOURIST F-R-A-N-K O-B-E-R-M-U umlaut-L-L-E-R.

IC U – what?

TOURIST That's okay, just write U-E.

IC Thank you, Mr Obermüller. Now I need your present location and a brief description of the accident.

TOURIST I'm phoning from Oakland near San Francisco. We must have taken the wrong turn on the freeway and were suddenly in the center of Oakland, when this huge old car drove right onto the street from somebody's front yard. I mean, there was no driveway or anything, he just drove right over the sidewalk and the curb and hit us. The door was badly damaged and won't open any more.

IC Did you call the police, and was anybody injured?

TOURIST We're all right, and the driver of the other car just ran off, but he seemed all right. And yes, we called the police, who told us to contact the rental company or you.

IC It's a good thing you took out our uninsured driver's policy, because it sounds like you might have been hit by an unregistered, uninsured vehicle. But there's no need to worry. Everything is covered, including a taxi to the airport for you to pick up a replacement vehicle from your rental company. We'll get in touch with them right away.

TOURIST Thank you.

IC If the police are still on the scene, it would be good if I could talk to them.

32 ▪ Unit 11, exercise 8

AGENT Bristol Union Insurance, Marion Mitchell speaking. How can I help?

CLIENT Good morning. This is Dave Saunders. I've just bought a new house near the coast and was wondering what kind of insurance I would need.

AGENT Well, most importantly, you will need buildings and home contents insurance cover.

CLIENT OK, fine. Could you explain them in a little more detail?

AGENT Sure. The buildings insurance covers damage to your property caused by fire, storm, burst water pipes and lightning. The home contents insurance, as the name implies, covers accidental damage to home and contents.

CLIENT Does the insurance cover burglary?

AGENT Yes, it does. It's part of the home contents policy.

CLIENT Is there anything that is not covered by the policies?

AGENT Exclusions? They really depend on the level of cover. Valuables will be insured up to a certain amount. Expensive jewellery and large amounts of cash would not be covered however.

CLIENT How much would my premium payments come to? And would there be any discounts?

AGENT Our rates are particularly attractive, and depending of course on where you live and the value of the property as well as the level of cover for the contents, I am sure we could offer you a competitive premium. If you have a burglar alarm installed, that will reduce the monthly premium payment.

CLIENT How long would the cover last?

AGENT The insurance cover usually lasts for twelve months and then you will be asked to renew your policy. You may of course have your policy renewed automatically, if you wish.

CLIENT Well, thank you very much for all your help, Ms Mitchell. How do we go on from here?

AGENT Just fill in the proposal form and return it to us.

CLIENT Fine. I'll do that right away.

AGENT And feel free to give me a call if you have any more questions.

CLIENT Thanks for all your help.

41 ▪ Unit 15, exercise 9

RECEPTION Hello, Burton and Taylor Ltd. Can I help you?

CLIENT Hello. This is John Trevors from Carlton Builders. Could I speak to the manager, please? I would like to find out about the possibility of having some waste material removed from a building site.

RECEPTION Yes, certainly. I'll put you through to Mr Taylor. He will help you.

* * *

MANAGER Jim Taylor speaking.

CLIENT This is John Trevors from Carlton Builders. We've got some waste to dispose of and I was wondering whether you could handle that sort of thing. But first I would like to know what types of waste you specialize in.

MANAGER We deal with all kinds of waste really, liquids, gases, hazardous and non-hazardous materials. And we also provide a full range of services, consultation, transportation, storage, and disposal. Our staff are fully trained and very experienced.

CLIENT That's good to know, because the kind of waste we need to dispose of is rather difficult to handle. You see, we have about four lorryloads of asbestos to be removed from a site where we are doing some refurbishment work at the moment. And I don't need to tell you about the kind of risk that is involved with asbestos. And especially when it has to be moved by road.

MANAGER Well, I know what you mean. But you can rest assured. We've got all the necessary equipment, and with our state-of-the art vehicles I don't foresee any problems at all. And, as I said, our staff are well trained and experienced in dealing with that sort of thing.

CLIENT And what about the costs?

MANAGER We have very competitive rates. But, in the end, the exact figure depends on the volume to be moved and the equipment we'll need. I would suggest that I come out and inspect the stuff to get an idea of the work involved and then prepare an estimate.

CLIENT That sounds like a good idea. By the way, could you tell me where you put the waste?

MANAGER Certainly, we'll use the nearest disposal site in the area that will accept asbestos building waste. All the disposal sites we use are regularly inspected by local safety officials. So everything is quite safe and above board, if that's what you are worried about.

CLIENT Well, I was actually. But now about the estimate …

Translation texts

Introduction

Why translate?

Translating is a key activity at all levels of the business world today and this fact is reflected in the prominence given to translation assignments in this textbook.

Reasons for selection

The sixteen English and German texts that follow (eight English, eight German) have been chosen with two aims in mind: to complement many of the topics covered in this textbook, and to serve as practice examination texts.

Criteria for selection

In terms of length, subject matter, source and degree of difficulty, all the texts correspond to the German Chamber of Commerce (IHK) translation examination task at foreign language correspondent level.

Dictionaries

It is also important to note that students should be allowed to consult any general or specialist German/English English/German dictionary or dictionaries they consider will help them produce a good translation.

Time permitted

In line with IHK examination requirements, students should be allowed 60 minutes to do each of the translation assignments.

English/German translation texts

Subject: Personal banking / Unit 4

Source: *The Guardian*

Barclays held out the possibility of levying some charges on new cash machines last night as it, along with two of its rivals, caved in to public pressure by ditching planned charges on its existing network.

The bank's decision not to introduce a £1 surcharge on rivals' customers using its machines from next year followed exactly one year of negative publicity about the controversial plan, which had threatened to destabilize the entire Link cash machine network.

However, while most of the 28,000 cash machines in the Link network will be free from next year, after Lloyds TSB last night also bowed to peer pressure, Barclays was careful not to rule out charges in the future.

Yesterday's statements by Barclays and Lloyds TSB followed confirmation by HSBC last week that it would not introduce disloyalty charges.

Barclays had already stopped levying a disloyalty fee on its own customers when they use rivals' machines, a move which industry experts have estimated will lose it £50m a year in income. The Bank planned to recoup the loss by introducing a surcharge on rivals' customers using its own machines, but was forced to delay the charge until January 2001 after furious rows with other Link members.

Subject: Retailing / Unit 7

Source: *Sunday Times*

Supermarket loyalty cards fail to encourage shoppers to stick with one particular chain, research shows. The results of a survey carried out by Mori for the Black Sun consultancy group showed that, while more than half of British shoppers held loyalty cards, 69 per cent of the cardholders said they were not influenced by them when it came to deciding where to shop. Almost nine out of ten cardholders said they were more concerned with getting a better price for goods than with collecting loyalty points. Those who did use their loyalty cards were also forgetful about cashing in on the points they collected, the researchers found. More than 25 per cent of those questioned said they rarely or never redeemed their points. The results of the survey will confirm analysts' fears that loyalty schemes are an ineffective way of keeping customers. But despite the negative sentiment, Marks & Spencer will soon launch a loyalty card that will combine a rewards points programme with a credit card. And Tesco last month claimed a coup when it won the right to offer Air Miles to cardholders. But other supermarket groups have gone the other way. Safeway dropped its loyalty card scheme in 2000, while Waitrose has always resisted the idea of loyalty schemes, insisting they are a waste of time.

Subject: International trade / Unit 9

Source: *The Guardian*

America's big three carmakers yesterday went head to head in the battle to acquire South Korea's Daewoo Motor and with it a leading position in one of Asia's most important vehicle markets.

Ford entered the bidding on its own, General Motors teamed up with its new strategic partner, Fiat, while DaimlerChrysler joined forces with Hyundai as part of a broader alliance between the two companies.

The automotive business is up for sale in the wake of financial problems which hit the Daewoo group, one of South Korea's biggest industrial conglomerates.

The team auctioning the motor business has said it will cut the list of bidders to one or two at the end of this week and a final decision is expected to be announced in September.

Although Daewoo Motors is heavily in debt, it has attracted the interest of the big three, mainly because of its strength in Asia. It also has production capacity in eastern Europe.

With the markets in the US and Europe seen as close to saturation, the big car companies are keen to build up their operations in regions which appear to offer higher growth opportunities.

"There are four centres of top quality auto production in the world and South Korea happens to be one of the four, along with North America, Europe and Japan," according to Meera Kumar, spokeswoman for the Ford bid team.

Subject: Insurance / Unit 11

Source: *Sunday Times*

The latest heavy storms are almost certain to mean higher household insurance premiums, while those living in areas prone to flooding may be refused cover altogether. More than 3,000 homes have already been flooded in the worst downpours for 50 years and thousands more are at imminent risk if the rain continues.

Most damage will be covered by your buildings and contents insurance. Buildings cover will pay for damage to the building and garages, while contents cover will pay for removable items such as furniture and electrical equipment.

But be wary when making emergency repairs. Insurers should fund reasonable emergency costs immediately, such as getting a builder to throw a tarpaulin over a leaking roof. But do not make any repairs without first getting approval from the insurer as this may jeopardize your claim. Many insurers provide 24-hour emergency helplines to put customers in touch with tradespeople who can carry out emergency repairs. The average claim for flood damage is about £6,000 and carpets account for most of this.

Between 950,000 and 1.2 million British homes are in danger of inland flooding, at a potential cost of £35 billion, according to a report by the Association of British Insurers.

Subject: Company report / Unit 12

Source: *P&O Princess Cruises plc,* Annual Review and Summary Financial Statements

Princess Cruises was among the first companies to recognize the increasing demand for personal choice in cruising and to create a product that caters for this trend. In 1995, we introduced Sun Princess, a class of vessel characterized by a high proportion of balcony cabins and a wide choice of dining, entertainment and other activities. This was followed by the Grand Princess design, which further developed the concept of providing choice and a personalized experience for cruise passengers.

We have continued to invest in a fleet designed to satisfy the demand for flexibility and personal choice. Over the next four years, six new ships will join the fleet with the introduction of the first, Golden Princess, in May 2001. We expect that the introduction of these new ships will result in greater economies of scale and, together with other initiatives, will improve our overall cost structure.

Princess's strong level of brand awareness will be reinforced by a major new marketing campaign starting in January 2001. The new campaign aims to position Princess as the cruise company that focuses on individual choice and to create a sense of community, particularly among Princess's principal target market of experienced travellers.

Subject: Interest rates and inflation / Unit 13

Source: *International Herald Tribune*

Inflation in the euro zone increased in April to its highest level since November, intensifying pressure on the European Central Bank to cut interest rates. Euro-zone consumer prices rose 2.9 percent last month, up from 2.6 percent in March and 1.9 percent a year ago, according to Eurostat, the European Union's statistical agency in Brussels.

The April figure matched November's record inflation rate for the 12 nations that share the euro, the highest level since the single currency was introduced in January 1999. The inflation report is likely to delay further interest rate cuts by the ECB and is something of an embarrassment to the central bank. Last Thursday, it announced a surprise reduction in its main interest rate, saying inflationary pressures would diminish and citing a need to stimulate growth in the euro zone. The rate cut followed months of international criticism that the ECB had contributed to Europe's economic slowdown by adhering so long to its tight-money policies.

The inflation figures create a strong incentive to keep interest rates unchanged for weeks if not months, even if the European economies go further into recession.

Subject: The environment / Unit 15

Source: *The Scotsman*

Scotland is bottom of the world recycling league and must introduce tough new targets to cut the landfill dumping of rubbish, environmental campaigners urged today. The country recycled or composted just 6.1 per cent of its household waste last year, with a third of the local councils recycling less than in the previous 12 months. Although the total was one per cent higher than the previous year, Friends of the Earth Scotland said it compared to eight per cent in England and Wales, 31.5 per cent in the United States and 52 per cent in Switzerland. Other countries are also far ahead of Scotland, partly because of the more limited availability and higher cost of landfill, with the Netherlands and Austria recycling 45 per cent of their domestic waste.

Rates varied widely within Scotland, with Perth and Kinross managing almost 18 per cent in 2000, up from 15.6 per cent the previous year, and Aberdeenshire increasing from 5.6 per cent to 16.4 per cent. However, the worst performers slipped back further last year, with the Highlands' total dropping from 2.2 per cent to two per cent.

Much of Scotland's waste is tipped into landfill sites, which have been a cheap and plentiful disposal option but were linked last month with increased rates of birth defects in children.

Subject: The European Union / Unit 16

Source: *The Guardian*

Competition commissioner Mario Monti yesterday put the European automotive industry on notice to expect radical reform in the way cars are sold when regulations expire next year. Though Mr Monti was careful to stress he was "open-minded" about the need for any changes to the "block-exemption" mechanism which governs car distribution within the European Union, his criticism leaves little doubt that changes are on the way.

The competition commission's investigations showed that the assumptions underlying the present regime – which Mr Monti described as the highway code for car distribution – were open to question and its objectives were not being achieved.

The block-exemption scheme which was renewed for a seven-year period in 1995 gives the automotive industry exemption from the competition provisions of the Treaty of Rome and allows car manufacturers to sell vehicles only through their own dealer networks. But the system is not delivering the expected improvements in competition, Mr Monti said.

The three assumptions on which the regime rests are that it provides effective competition, that dealers must provide after-sales service, and that brand specialists are needed to repair cars.

German/English translation texts

Subject: The tourist industry / Unit 3

Source: www.schweizertouristik.ch

Der Flugverkehr wird im nächsten Jahr um gut zehn Prozent zurückgehen, das globale Wachstum um 1,7 Prozent schrumpfen, mindestens 8,8 Millionen Arbeitsplätze werden verloren gehen. Die Prognosen, die den Delegierten der World Tourism Convention auf der australischen Insel Tasmanien kürzlich präsentiert wurden, hätten pessimistischer nicht sein können. Kein Ereignis der jüngeren Geschichte hat derart dramatische Konsequenzen für die Tourismusindustrie wie die Terroranschläge vom 11. September 2001. Laut Rick Miller, dem Präsidenten des World Travel and Tourism Council, befindet sich die Reise- und Tourismusindustrie in der größten Krise ihrer Geschichte.

Der Tourismus hat sich in den letzten 40 Jahren zu einem der weltweit wichtigsten Wirtschaftszweige entwickelt. Flogen 1960 noch 69 Millionen Passagiere, waren es im letzten Jahr bereits über 669 Millionen. Die Tourismusindustrie ist für elf Prozent des globalen Bruttoinlandproduktes verantwortlich. 260 Millionen Menschen sind in diesem Wirtschaftszweig beschäftigt. Doch wenn die Experten richtig liegen, werden diese Zahlen innerhalb der kommenden Monate und Jahre weltweit massiv reduziert. Die Angst der Bevölkerung, wieder in ein Flugzeug zu steigen, habe schwerste Konsequenzen für die gesamte Tourismusindustrie, meinten mehrere Fachleute.

Subject: Recruitment / Unit 5

Source: *Süddeutsche Zeitung*

„Bei uns gehen mittlerweile 60 Prozent der Bewerbungen online ein", sagt Dagmar Zey, bei Philips für das Internet-Recruiting zuständig. Kein Einzelfall. Der Wandel vom Recruiting zum E-Cruiting ist voll im Gange: Nach einer Studie des US-Marktforschungsunternehmen iLogos nutzen 73 Prozent der europäischen Großunternehmen bereits das Internet zur Bewerbersuche, in den USA sind es sogar 90 Prozent. Die klassische Papierbewerbung ist zwar noch nicht verschwunden, doch die Zahl der E-Mail-Bewerbungen hat selbst bei Old-Economy-Konzernen gleichgezogen. Tendenz steigend.

Dabei ist die frei formulierte E-Mail-Bewerbung mit Dateianhang, vom Bewerber zusammengestellt und per Mausklick an eine beliebige Anzahl von Firmen geschickt, schon wieder auf dem Rückzug. Zu viele unvollständige Bewerbungen trafen in den Personalabteilungen an. Viele Firmen haben daraus ihre Konsequenzen gezogen: Das Pharmaunternehmen Merck beispielsweise schickt E-Mail-Bewerbungen inzwischen mit dem Bescheid zurück, man solle doch bitte den Weg über das E-Formular gehen. Dieses Formular filtert interessante Bewerber schnell heraus. Bis zu einer Stunde dauert es, das persönliche Profil einzugeben. Zeugnisse usw. bringt man zum Bewerbungsgespräch mit.

Subject: Modern forms of work / Unit 6

Source: "Das körperlose Jahrhundert", Conference and Incentive Management

Das Phänomen der Telearbeit wird Europa in den kommenden zehn Jahren vor neue – auch kommunikative – Herausforderungen stellen. Unternehmen erzielen deutliche Kostensenkungen, wenn sie möglichst viele ihrer Mitarbeiter zu Hause arbeiten lassen. Die Technik erlaubt eine perfekte Online-Anbindung, das Unternehmen spart Organisations- und Bürokosten in beträchtlichem Umfang. Zugleich werden damit aber auch bestehende Kommunikationsstrukturen auf den Kopf gestellt. Der Ideen- und Gedankenaustausch mit Kollegen wird weitgehend durch die sterile Online-Sprache des heimischen Computers ersetzt. Millionen Menschen in online-vernetzten Wohnungen führen zu isolierten Familienvätern und -müttern. Die Dauerpräsenz zu Hause könnte sich als Bumerang erweisen.

Einschneidende Veränderungen in unserer Arbeitswelt haben den heutigen Fortschritt möglich gemacht. Jetzt fordern uns diese Entwicklungen ernsthaft heraus. Wir müssen uns fragen, ob dieser neue Fortschritt wünschenswert ist. Der Mensch ist im Grunde ein kommunikatives Wesen. Deshalb bleiben die Begegnungen von Angesicht zu Angesicht in den Unternehmen und auf Kongressen ein wichtiger Bestandteil unseres Berufsalltags.

Subject: Retailing / Unit 7

Source: *Frankfurter Allgemeine Zeitung*

Lego, Europas größter Spielwarenhersteller glaubt wieder an den Fachhandel. Der Verkaufsleiter für Zentraleuropa, Dirk Engehausen, meinte kürzlich, er sei überzeugt, dass der Fachhandel in Zentraleuropa auch weiterhin eine wichtige Rolle spielen werde. In den vergangenen Jahren hatte man bei Lego Pläne diskutiert, sich aus dem Fachhandel, über den Lego in den Ländern Deutschland, Österreich und Schweiz etwa ein Drittel seines Umsatzes erzielt, zurückzuziehen. So kündigte Engehausen jetzt an, man werde das Lego-Ersatzeilprogramm, das bisher nur im Internet erhältlich ist, auch über den Fachhandel verkaufen. Einzelhändler, die den Verkauf von Legoprodukten besonders förderten, sollten künftig durch besondere Konditionen belohnt werden. Mehrfach hatte es in der Vergangenheit heftige Kritik am Lego-Internetangebot gegeben. Man darf wohl davon ausgehen, dass sich die Erwartungen an den elektronischen Handel nicht erfüllt haben.

Das Unternehmen hat soeben ein sehr erfolgreiches Jahr hinter sich. Der Umsatzzuwachs beruht aber nicht nur auf dem Erfolg von Lizenzproduktionen wie Harry Potter oder Star Wars, sondern besonders auf dem Erfolg der Marke Lego. Das vergangene Jahr war das Umsatzstärkste in der Geschichte des Unternehmens, der Zuwachs betrug rund 10 Prozent.

Subject: International trade / Unit 9

Source: *Frankfurter Allgemeine Zeitung*

Im vergangenen Jahr erzielte der deutsche Außenhandel einen Rekordüberschuss. Nach Informationen des statistischen Bundesamtes erreichte der Überschuss die Höhe von 93,9 Milliarden Euro nach 59,3 Milliarden im Jahr zuvor. Insgesamt wurden Güter im Wert von 637 Milliarden Euro ausgeführt, das sind 6,6 Prozent mehr als im Jahr zuvor. Der Wert der Einfuhren stieg dagegen nur um 0,9 Prozent auf 543 Milliarden Euro. Somit ist der hohe deutsche Außenhandelsüberschuss vor allem auf den schwachen Import zurückzuführen. Ursache hierfür ist die schwache konjunkturelle Entwicklung in Deutschland ebenso wie der deutliche Rückgang der Rohölpreise. Doch auch die Exporte sind wegen der schwächeren Weltwirtschaft langsamer gestiegen als noch ein Jahr zuvor. Für das kommende Jahr hofft die Exportwirtschaft auf eine Belebung der Konjunktur und damit der Exportnachfrage vor allem in den Vereinigten Staaten und in den Ländern Südostasiens.

Erstmals seit 1990 erzielte Deutschland im vergangenen Jahr wieder einen Leistungsbilanzüberschuss. Dem hohen Handelsbilanzüberschuss stand ein im Vergleich zum Vorjahr leicht höheres Dienstleistungsbilanzdefizit gegenüber. Insgesamt zeigte die Leistungsbilanz einen Überschuss von 11 Milliarden Euro. Im Jahr zuvor hatte das Defizit noch bei 20 Milliarden Euro gelegen.

Subject: Logistics / Unit 10

Source: Nachrichten-Börse. Informationen zum Konzern Deutsche Post World Net

Unternehmen produzieren in vielen Ländern und haben ihre Kunden in aller Welt. Ein Beispiel ist die Autoindustrie. Täglich laufen Tausende Wagen von den Bändern – in Deutschland und in Übersee. Die großen Autohersteller betreiben unter anderem in Südamerika ihre Produktionsstätten. Ein entscheidender Faktor dafür, dass die Bänder nicht stillstehen, ist die rechtzeitige Lieferung der Fahrzeugteile. Dafür sorgt Danzas AEI Intercontinental als Dienstleister der Automobil-Zulieferindustrie.

Danzas holt die Autoteile regelmäßig bei den Herstellern in ganz Deutschland ab und fährt sie zu einem zentralen Knotenpunkt. Dort wird die Ware für die Verladung in 40-Fuß-Container zusammengestellt. Lange Lagerzeiten darf es nicht geben, so dass zwischen der Anlieferung der Ware und der Abfahrt des Lkw mit einer Sammelladung höchstens 24 Stunden vergehen.

Der Lkw fährt nach Rotterdam, von wo es per Schiff weitergeht. In Brasilien oder Mexiko angekommen, hat Danzas alles für die Zollabwicklung vorbereitet. Die „letzte Meile“ zum Standort der Fahrzeugproduktion erfolgt wieder per Lkw. Da es für den Zulieferer manchmal um Stunden geht, bietet Danzas als weltweit größtes Luftfrachtunternehmen auch die Lieferung per Flugzeug an.

Subject: Forms of business organization / Unit 12

Source: *Westdeutsche Allgemeine Zeitung*

In Deutschland sind Frauen in den Führungsetagen großer Unternehmen nach wie vor die Ausnahme. Das gilt nicht nur in Branchen, die als typisch männlich gelten wie Kohle, Stahl, Maschinenbau, Automobilbau, Bauwirtschaft, sondern auch in Branchen, die als „frauenfreundlicher“ gelten wie z.B. Tourismus, Verlagswesen, Lebensmittelindustrie. Ganz anders ist das in angelsächsischen Ländern. Hier gibt es schon seit Jahren Frauen in den Spitzenpositionen börsennotierter Unternehmen. In Deutschland wird man Mühe haben, Frauen auf der Vorstandsebene der 30 im Dax vertretenen Firmen zu finden. Dabei sind Frauen so qualifiziert wie selten. Der Frauenanteil bei Hochschulabsolventen ist in den letzten zehn Jahren beständig gestiegen. In einigen Studiengängen liegt er deutlich über 50 Prozent. Dennoch wird dieses Potenzial von der Wirtschaft kaum genutzt, denn nur 11 Prozent der Führungspositionen in Deutschland werden von Frauen besetzt. Damit liegt Deutschland im europäischen Vergleich im unteren Drittel. Wenn Frauen Spitzenpositionen erreichen, verdanken sie das – neben unternehmerischen und analytischen Fähigkeiten – vor allem ihrem Durchsetzungsvermögen. Die als typisch weiblich geltenden Stärken wie Teamfähigkeit und Einfühlungsvermögen sind weniger wichtig.

Subject: The environment / Unit 15

Source: *Frankfurter Allgemeine Zeitung*

Der Anteil des „Ökostroms“ an der gesamten Stromerzeugung in Deutschland ist im vergangenen Jahr auf 7,25 Prozent gestiegen. Im Jahr 2000 waren 7,1 Prozent des gesamten Stromverbrauchs in Deutschland aus den erneuerbaren Energieträgern Wasser, Wind, Biomasse, Müll und Photovoltaik erzeugt worden. Das meldete der Verband der Elektrizitätswirtschaft am Montag nach ersten Schätzungen. Trotz ungünstiger Witterungsbedingungen sei 2001 mit mehr als 36 Milliarden Kilowattstunden 2 Prozent mehr „Ökostrom“ produziert worden als im Jahr zuvor.

Rückläufig war nach Angaben des Verbandes die Stromerzeugung aus Wasserkraft. Im Vergleich zum regenreichen Jahr 2000 sei im vergangenen Jahr 9 Prozent weniger Strom erzeugt worden. Die Ausbeute aus Wind sei im windarmen Jahr 2001 sogar um ein Fünftel geringer gewesen als üblich. Die Produktionssteigerung der Windenergie um 21 Prozent von 9,5 auf 11,5 Milliarden Kilowattstunden beruhe allein auf neuen Windkraftanlagen, teilte der VDEW mit. Im vergangenen Jahr waren nach Angaben des Bundesverbands Windenergie 2079 neue Windräder mit einer Gesamtleistung von 2,7 Megawatt errichtet worden. Wie das Deutsche Atomforum am Montag mitteilte, haben die 19 deutschen Atomkraftwerke im vergangenen Jahr mit 171,3 Milliarden Kilowattstunden so viel Strom erzeugt wie nie zuvor.

Chronological word list

Alles in dieser Liste wird so übersetzt, wie es im Text- und Übungszusammenhang erscheint.

Abkürzungen:
1A = Unit 1, Text A; 1B = Unit 1, Text B; 1.3 = Unit 1, Exercise 3; Info = Information;
Gr = Grammar; V = Vocabulary; UPh = Useful Phrases

Unit 1 Trade and industry: past and present

7

evolution	Entwicklung	*1A*
tribe	Stamm	*1A*
basic need	Grundbedürfnis	*1A*
self-sufficient	autark, selbstversorgend	*1A*
to emerge	entstehen	*1A*
division of labour	Arbeitsteilung	*1A*
barter	Tauschhandel	*1A*
medium of exchange	Tauschmittel	*1A*
to conduct	durchführen	*1A*
business transaction	Geschäft(svorgang)	*1A*
efficiently	effizient	*1A*
primary production	Grundstoffindustrie	*1A*
extraction	Gewinnung	*1A*
secondary production	Sekundärgüterproduktion, gewerbliche Erzeugung	*1A*
conversion	Umwandlung	*1A*
finished product	Fertigerzeugnis	*1A*
tertiary production	Erbringung von Dienstleistungen	*1A*
distribution	Verteilung, Vertrieb	*1A*
manufacturing sector	gewerblicher Sektor	*1A*

8

predominant	vorherrschend	*1A*
location	Standort, Lage	*1A*
available	verfügbar	*1A*
expansion	Ausbau, Ausweitung	*1A*
shift	Verschiebung	*1A*
to overtake	überholen	*1A*
national income	Volkseinkommen	*1A*
health care	Gesundheitsfürsorge	*1A*
entertainment	Unterhaltungsindustrie	*1A*
growth industry	Wachstumsindustrie, Wachstumsbranche	*1A*
teleworking	Telearbeit	*1A*
to replace	ersetzen	*1A*
emphasis	Schwerpunkt, Betonung	*1A*
unprecedented	beispiellos, ohnegleichen	*1A*
agrarian society	Agrargesellschaft	*1A*
to progress	fortschreiten	*1A*
to predict	vorhersagen, voraussagen	*1A*
drawback	Nachteil	*1.1*
to affect	beeinflussen	*1.1*
extent	Ausmaß	*1.1*
dependent on	abhängig von	*1.2*
agriculture	Landwirtschaft	*1.2*
to achieve	erreichen	*1.2*
satisfactory	zufriedenstellend	*1.2*

9

assembly-line worker	Fließbandarbeiter(in)	*1.3*
bricklayer	Maurer	*1.3*
insurance agent	Versicherungsvertreter(in)	*1.3*
nurse	Krankenschwester, Krankenpfleger	*1.3*
TV presenter	Fernsehredakteur(in), Fernsehmoderator(in)	*1.3*
chemicals	Chemieerzeugnisse	*1.3*
domestic trade	Binnenhandel	*1.3*
education	Erziehungswesen	*1.3*
foreign trade	Außenhandel	*1.3*
forestry	Forstwirtschaft	*1.3*
insurance	Versicherung	*1.3*
nursing	(Kranken)Pflege	*1.3*
pharmaceuticals	Arzneimittel, Pharmaprodukte	*1.3*
retailing	Einzelhandel	*1.3*
roadbuilding	Straßenbau	*1.3*
wholesaling	Großhandel	*1.3*
exhaustive	Abbau-	*1.3*
non-exhaustive	erneuerbar	*1.3*
manufacturing	Fertigung, Produktion; gewerbliche Industrie	*1.3*
construction	Bauwirtschaft	*1.3*
utilities	Versorgungsunternehmen	*1.3*
aid to trade	kommerzielle Dienstleistung	*1.3*
oil drilling	Ölproduktion	*1.3*
quarrying	Gewinnung von Steinen und Erden	*1.3*
automaking	Automobilherstellung	*1.3*
complementary	sich ergänzend	*1 Info*
planned economy	Planwirtschaft	*1 Info*
production target	Produktionsziel	*1 Info*
competition	Wettbewerb, Konkurrenz	*1 Info*
means of production	Produktionsmittel	*1 Info*
staple foods	Grundnahrungsmittel	*1 Info*
free-market economy	freie Marktwirtschaft	*1 Info*
to accumulate	ansammeln	*1 Info*
availability	Verfügbarkeit	*1 Info*
supply and demand	Angebot und Nachfrage	*1 Info*
interference	Einmischung	*1 Info*
driving force	treibende Kraft	*1 Info*

10

start-up	neugegründetes Unternehmen	*1B*

swapping	Tauschen	*1B*
currency	Währung	*1B*
revival	Wiederbelebung	*1B*
printing shop	Druckerei	*1B*
purchase	Erwerb, Kauf	*1B*
brochure	Prospekt, Broschüre	*1B*
in return	im Gegenzug	*1B*
exchange	Börse	*1B*
to scale to new levels	zu neuen Höhen bringen	*1B*
eventually	schließlich	*1B*
bidding	Angebot(sabgabe)	*1B*
to sign up	beitreten	*1B*
credit	Kreditwürdigkeit	*1B*
transaction fee	Bearbeitungsgebühr	*1B*
accessible	zugänglich	*1B*
challenge	Herausforderung	*1B*
critical mass	Mindestanzahl	*1B*
customer	Kunde, Kundin	*1B*
player	Anbieter	*1B*
small-business	Kleinunternehmens-, mittelständisch	*1B*
to acquire	erwerben	*1B*
client	Kunde, Kundin, Klient(in)	*1B*
varied	verschiedenartig	*1B*
tax advice	Steuerberatung	*1B*
advertising space	Werbefläche	*1B*
to be unlikely to do sth	etwas wohl nicht tun	*1B*
tricky	schwierig	*1B*
hard sell	schwer zu verkaufen	*1B*
reluctant	widerwillig	*1B*
to lock up	(Kapital) binden	*1B*
online-only	nur on-line verfügbar	*1B*
site	Webseite	*1B*
reservation	Vorbehalt	*1B*
to overcome	überwinden, ausräumen	*1B*
regulator	Aufsichtsbehörde	*1B*
exchange control	Devisenkontrolle	*1B*
black market	Schwarzmarkt	*1B*

11

old-fashioned	altmodisch	*1.5*
wholehearted	uneingeschränkt	*1.6*
to associate	verbinden, assoziieren	*1.7*
approach	Methode	*1.7*
impact	Auswirkung	*1.9*
primarily	vorwiegend	*1.9*
economics	Wirtschaftswissenschaften	*1 Gr*
mathematics	Mathematik	*1 Gr*
politics	Politik	*1 Gr*
statistics	Statistik	*1.Gr*
merchandise	(Handels)Ware	*1 Gr*
to precede	vorausgehen	*1 Gr*
item	Posten, Stück, Artikel	*1 Gr*
labour costs	Arbeitskosten	*1 Gr*
to retain	beibehalten	*1 Gr*
criterion	Kriterium	*1 Gr*
premises	Betriebsgelände	*1 Gr*
savings	Ersparnisse; Einsparungen	*1 Gr*
surroundings	Umgebung	*1 Gr*
to denote	bezeichnen	*1 Gr*
board	Behörde, Ausschuss	*1 Gr*
Metropolitan Police	Londoner Polizei	*1 Gr*
to found	gründen	*1 Gr*
to sweep to victory	einen leichten hohen Sieg erringen	*1 Gr*
to make up	ausmachen, bilden	*1 Gr*
majority	Mehrheit	*1 Gr*
applicant	Bewerber(in)	*1 Gr*
to reduce	reduzieren, vermindern	*1 Gr*
to insure	versichern	*1.10*

Unit 2 The UK and the USA: facts and figures

14

population	Bevölkerung	*2A*
approximately	ungefähr, annähernd	*2A*
surface area	(Land)Fläche	*2A*
urbanized	verstädtert	*2A*
gross national product (GNP)	Bruttosozialprodukt (BSP)	*2A*
gross national income (GNI)	Bruttosozialprodukt (BSP)	*2A*
to lag behind	hinterher hinken	*2A*
per capita	pro Kopf	*2A*
to account for	ausmachen, auf ... entfallen	*2A*
workforce	Beschäftigte, Erwerbstätige; Belegschaft	*2A*
production level	Produktionsniveau	*2A*
grain farming	Getreideanbau	*2A*
livestock farming	Viehzucht, Viehwirtschaft	*2A*
cattle	Rinder	*2A*
poultry	Geflügel	*2A*
on a large scale	in großem Umfang	*2A*
food requirements	Nahrungsmittelbedarf	*2A*
to contribute	beisteuern, beitragen	*2A*
exploitation	Ausbeutung, Abbau	*2A*
to enable	befähigen, erlauben, ermöglichen	*2A*
fuel	Brennstoff	*2A*
to predominate	vorherrschen, stark geprägt sein durch	*2A*
manufacture	Produkt, Erzeugnis	*2A*
aerospace equipment	Erzeugnisse der Luft- und Raumfahrtindustrie	*2A*
information technology (IT)	Informationstechnologie	*2A*
telecommunications equipment	Fernmeldeausrüstung	*2A*
precision instrument	feinmechanisches Produkt	*2A*
cutback	Kürzung	*2A*
smokestack industry	alte Industrie, Schwerindustrie	*2A*
high-tech industry	Hochtechnologieindustrie	*2A*
to offset	ausgleichen	*2A*
job loss	Arbeitsplatzverlust	*2A*
to prefer	vorziehen	*2A*
corridor	Korridor, Gürtel	*2A*
notable	bemerkenswert, auffallend	*2A*
exception	Ausnahme	*2A*
to locate	(sich) ansiedeln; errichten	*2A*

factory	Fabrik	*2A*
sector	(Industrie)Branche, Industriezweig	*2A*
transport	Transportgewerbe, Transportwirtschaft	*2A*
to benefit from	Nutzen ziehen aus, profitieren von	*2A*

15

to transfer	übertragen	*2.1*
to balance out	ausgleichen	*2.1*
set of figures	Statistik	*2 Info*
striking	auffällig	*2 Info*
employment figures	Beschäftigtenzahlen	*2.3*
table	Statistik, Tabelle	*2.3*

16

countless	unzählig	*2B*
survey	Umfrage	*2B*
hub	Zentrum, Knotenpunkt	*2B*
economically strong	wirtschaftsstark, wirtschaftlich bedeutend	*2B*
decade	Jahrzehnt	*2B*
analyst	Analyst(in)	*2B*
to surpass	übertreffen	*2B*
ambitious	ehrgeizig; gewagt	*2B*
prediction	Vorhersage, Prognose	*2B*
to top	übertreffen	*2B*
to indicate	darauf hindeuten, erkennen lassen, anzeigen	*2B*
on track	auf Kurs	*2B*
home sales	Verkauf von Wohnungen/Eigenheimen	*2B*
cost of living	Lebenshaltungskosten	*2B*
substantial	beträchtlich, erheblich	*2B*
urban	städtisch	*2B*
aside from	neben, außer	*2B*
pro-business	unternehmensfreundlich	*2B*
attitude	Haltung	*2B*
tax structure	Steuersystem	*2B*
labour force	Arbeitskräfte	*2B*
reasonably priced	zu vernünftigen Preisen	*2B*
commercial land	Gewerbefläche, Industriegrundstück	*2B*
consolidated	gemeinsam, konzertiert	*2B*
effort	Anstrengung	*2B*
destination	Ziel; Standort	*2B*
to relocate	Standort verändern, umsiedeln	*2B*
developer	Erschließungsgesellschaft	*2B*
mixed-use	für gemischte Nutzung	*2B*
business park	Gewerbepark	*2B*
Development Authority	Entwicklungsbehörde	*2B*
to assist	unterstützen, helfen	*2B*
non-gaming	nicht mit Glücksspiel verbunden	*2B*
to create jobs	Arbeitsplätze schaffen	*2B*
vast	überwiegend	*2B*
to represent	stellen, ausmachen	*2B*
to prosper	Erfolg haben, florieren	*2B*
indicator	Anzeichen	*2B*
retail	Einzelhandel	*2B*
retail store	Einzelhandelsgeschäft	*2B*
to outpace	übertreffen, übersteigen	*2B*
expectation	Erwartung	*2B*
mega resort	Riesen-Freizeitanlage	*2B*
gross revenue	Bruttoeinnahmen	*2B*
to generate	entstehen	*2B*
lifeblood	Lebensnerv; Haupterwerbszweig	*2B*
gaming industry	Glücksspielbranche	*2B*
tax revenue	Steueraufkommen	*2B*
resort	Freizeitkomplex	*2B*
currently	zurzeit	*2B*
under construction	im Bau	*2B*
to near completion	kurz vor der Fertigstellung stehen	*2B*
inventory	Bestand	*2B*
room total	Gesamtbestand an Zimmern	*2B*
on the move	in Bewegung, im Umbruch	*2B*
regardless of	gleichgültig ob	*2B*
to measure	messen	*2B*

17

contribution	Beitrag	*2.7*
engineering product	Maschinenbauerzeugnis	*2.7*
transport equipment	Transportausrüstung	*2.7*
industrial raw material	Industrierohstoff	*2.7*
consumer goods	Verbrauchsgüter, Konsumgüter	*2.7*
vehicle	Fahrzeug, Kraftfahrzeug	*2.7*
capital goods	Investitionsgüter, Kapitalgüter	*2.7*
related equipment	Zubehör	*2.7*
crude oil	Rohöl	*2.7*
export destination	Zielland der Ausfuhren	*2.7*
country of origin	Herkunftsland	*2.7*

18

respectively	beziehungsweise	*2.8*
major	groß, bedeutend	*2.8*
in percentage terms	prozentual, in Prozent ausgedrückt	*2.8*
despite	trotz	*2.8*
petroleum	Rohöl	*2.8*
in volume terms	mengenmäßig	*2.8*
to take up	ausmachen, abnehmen	*2.8*
to head the list	die Liste anführen	*2.8*
employment level	Beschäftigungsniveau	*2.9*
to cover	umfassen, abdecken	*2.9*

19

trading partner	Handelspartner	*2.10*
employer	Arbeitgeber	*2.10*

Unit 3 Tourism and business travel

20

flying temper	Wutausbruch	*3A*
overcrowded	überfüllt	*3A*
resort	Urlaubsort	*3A*
sunbed	Sonnenliege	*3A*

patch	Stück	*3A*
prospect	Aussicht	*3A*
package company	Veranstalter von Pauschalreisen	*3A*
market domination	Marktbeherrschung	*3A*
shake-up	Neuordnung	*3A*
peak	Höhepunkt	*3A*
corporate name	Unternehmensname	*3A*
to dominate	beherrschen	*3A*
market leader	Marktführer	*3A*
high street	Hauptgeschäftsstraße	*3A*
chain	(Laden)Kette	*3A*
consolidation	Zusammenschluss	*3A*
shortage	Mangel	*3A*
accommodation	Unterkunft, Unterbringung	*3A*
diversification	Produkterweiterung	*3A*
Mediterranean	Mittelmeer	*3A*
package	Pauschalreise	*3A*
long haul	Fernreise	*3A*
(to) cruise	Kreuzfahrt (machen)	*3A*
in vogue	aktuell	*3A*
21		
bucket	Eimer	*3A*
spade	Spaten	*3A*
director	Vorstandsmitglied	*3A*
federation	Bund	*3A*
tour operator	Reiseveranstalter	*3A*
destination	Reiseziel	*3A*
regulation	Vorschrift	*3A*
to expand	expandieren, erweitern	*3A*
to flock back	zurück strömen	*3A*
planning restriction	Planungsbeschränkung	*3A*
to prevent	behindern	*3A*
to fall over oneself to do sth	sich drängen, etwas zu tun	*3A*
long-term	langfristig	*3A*
counterpart	Gegenstück	*3A*
ownership structure	Besitzverhältnis	*3A*
to involve	mit einbeziehen	*3A*
state-owned bank	öffentlich-rechtliche Bank	*3A*
takeover	Übernahme	*3A*
to convey	vermitteln	*3.2*
to take over	übernehmen	*3.2*
22		
to devote	widmen	*3.4*
to proceed with	fortfahren mit	*3.4*
to bear	ertragen	*3.4*
overseas	ausländisch	*3.4*
to attribute to	zurückführen auf	*3.4*
advertising effort	Werbekampagne	*3.4*
second-rate	zweitklassig	*3.4*
earnings	Einnahmen	*3.4*
to be short of	Mangel haben an	*3.4*
to postpone	verschieben	*3.4*
holidaymaker	Urlauber(in)	*3.4*
overtime	Überstunden	*3.4*
23		
to click to go	auf Start klicken	*3B*

globe	Welt	*3B*
conservative	vorsichtig	*3B*
e-commerce	elektronischer Handel	*3B*
via	per	*3B*
electronic ticketing	elektronischer Fahrkartenverkauf	*3B*
in advance	im Voraus	*3B*
at a rate of	um	*3B*
distribution channel	Vertriebsweg	*3B*
managing director	etwa: Vorstandsvorsitzende(r), Generaldirektor(in)	*3B*
travel spending	Reiseausgaben	*3B*
to utilize	ausnutzen	*3B*
to capture	erfassen	*3B*
to control	bereit haben	*3B*
data	Daten	*3B*
car rental company	Autoverleihfirma	*3B*
to pose a threat	Drohung darstellen	*3B*
travel agency	Reisebüro	*3B*
vice-president	etwa: stellvertretender Vorstandsvorsitzender	*3B*
leisure traveller	Urlaubsreisende(r)	*3B*
in the years ahead	in den nächsten Jahren	*3B*
virtually	so gut wie	*3B*
executive	leitende(r) Angestellte(r)	*3B*
to download	herunterladen	*3B*
flight schedule	Flugplan	*3B*
to beam at	richten auf	*3B*
24		
issue	Ausgabe	*3.5*
vacancy	freies Zimmer	*3.5*
route	Weg	*3.5*
to lend itself to	sich eignen für	*3.6*
annual	jährlich	*3.6*
to rely on	sich verlassen auf	*3.6*
convenient	bequem	*3.7*
supplier	Lieferant	*3.7*
not-too-distant	nicht zu fern	*3.7*
booking form	Buchungsformular	*3.8*
departure	Abfahrt	*3.8*
room rate	Zimmerpreis	*3.8*
confirmation	Bestätigung	*3.8*
25		
reservations manager	Reservierungsbearbeiter(in)	*3.9*
on behalf of	im Namen von	*3.9*
sales manager	Verkaufsleiter(in)	*3.9*
requirement	Bedarf, Bedürfnis	*3.9*
refreshment	Erfrischung	*3.9*
equipment	Ausstattung	*3.9*
occurrence	Begebenheit	*3 Gr*
habit	Gewohnheit	*3 Gr*
decreasing	abnehmend	*3 Gr*
momentum	Schwung	*3 Gr*
bargain holiday	preisgünstiger Urlaub	*3.10*
city break	Städtereise	*3.10*
access	Zugang	*3.10*
refurbishment	Modernisierung	*3.10*
announcement	Bekanntmachung	*3.10*

26

fashion fair	Modemesse	*3.11*
liable	haftbar	*3.11*
business trip	Geschäftsreise	*3.11*

Unit 4 Personal banking

27

banking services	Bankdienstleistungen	*4A*
current account	Girokonto, laufendes Konto	*4A*
debit card	Abbuchungskarte	*4A*
instant access	direkter Zugang	*4A*
cashpoint	Geldautomat	*4A*
free of charge	kostenlos	*4A*
direct debit	Abbuchung(sverfahren), Lastschrift(verfahren)	*4A*
to manage	verwalten	*4A*
overdraft facility	Überziehungskredit, Dispositionskredit	*4A*
safety net	Sicherheitsnetz	*4A*
emergency spending	ganz dringende Ausgaben	*4A*
cheque	Scheck	*4A*
deposit	Einlage, Einzahlung	*4A*
transfer	Überweisung	*4A*
account statement	Kontoauszug	*4A*

28

branch	Zweigstelle, Filiale	*4A*
to credit	gutschreiben	*4A*
day-to-day	tagtäglich	*4A*
DIY store	Baumarkt, Heimwerkermarkt	*4A*
to give access to	Zugang ermöglichen	*4A*
withdrawal	Abhebung	*4A*
varying	sich ändernd	*4A*
standing order	Dauerauftrag	*4A*
to set up	einrichten	*4A*
cheque book	Scheckheft	*4A*
to keep track of	nachhalten, überwachen	*4A*
to sign up for	sich entscheiden für, teilnehmen an	*4A*
balance	Saldo	*4A*
savings account	Sparkonto	*4A*
electronic banking facility	Online-Banking(-Dienst)	*4A*
transaction	Bankauftrag	*4A*
to apply	beantragen	*4A*
overdraft	Kontoüberziehung	*4A*
personal loan	persönliches Darlehen, Kleinkredit	*4A*
to approve	genehmigen, zustimmen, gewähren	*4A*
application	Antrag	*4A*
arrangement	Vereinbarung; Möglichkeit	*4A*
to borrow	Kredit aufnehmen	*4A*
to waive	verzichten auf	*4A*
interest	Zinsen; Berechnung von Zinsen	*4A*
to charge	berechnen, belasten mit	*4A*
fee	Gebühr	*4A*
charges	Gebühren	*4A*
in credit	im Plus	*4A*
smooth	glatt; bequem, einfach	*4A*
welcome pack	Begrüßungspaket	*4A*
to authorize	bevollmächtigen	*4.1*
to debit	(Konto) belasten	*4.1*
in excess of	über ... hinaus	*4.1*

29

favourable	günstig	*4.4*
terms	Bedingungen	*4.4*
to contact	sich in Verbindung setzen mit	*4.4*
interest earned	Guthabenzinsen	*4.4*
WAP	internetfähiges Handy	*4.4*
33% off	Ermäßigung von 33%	*4.4*
Young Person's Railcard	Bahncard für Jugendliche	*4.4*
travel insurance	Reiseversicherung	*4.4*

30

instruction	Anweisung	*4.4*
specified	bestimmt	*4.4*
to present	vorlegen	*4.4*
open cheque	Barscheck	*4.4*
crossed cheque	Verrechnungsscheck	*4.4*
cheque counterfoil	Scheckleiste	*4.5*
cheque crossing	Scheckkreuzung	*4.5*
payee	Zahlungsempfänger(in)	*4.5*
sort code	Bankleitzahl (BLZ)	*4.5*
to remit	überweisen	*4.7*

31

commercial bank	Geschäftsbank	*4B*
consolidation	Konzentration	*4B*
complaint	Klage, Beschwerde	*4B*
to change ownership	Besitzer wechseln	*4B*
community bank	örtliche Bank	*4B*
to prevent	nicht zulassen, nicht erlauben	*4B*
to operate	aktiv/tätig sein	*4B*
to push around	herumschubsen, sagen, wo es lang geht	*4B*
to be fragmented	mit vielen kleinen Banken	*4B*
pre-historic	vorsintflutlich	*4B*
across the state border	jenseits der Staatsgrenze	*4B*
head of research	Leiter(in) der Forschungsabteilung	*4B*
renowned	berühmt	*4B*
financial analyst	Finanzexperte, -expertin	*4B*
to cut back	beschneiden, zurücknehmen	*4B*
to restrict	beschränken	*4B*
federal law	Bundesgesetz(gebung)	*4B*
to reckon that	rechnen (da)mit, davon ausgehen, dass	*4B*
deal	Vereinbarung	*4B*
process	Verfahren	*4B*
brand name	Markenname	*4B*
cash machine	Geldautomat	*4B*

widespread	weit verbreitet	*4B*
hard-to-satisfy	schwer zufriedenzustellen	*4B*
concern	Vorbehalt	*4B*
Congress	Abgeordnetenhaus und Senat	*4B*
to process	bearbeiten	*4B*
to bounce	(Scheck) platzen lassen	*4B*

32

competitiveness	Wettbewerbsfähigkeit	*4.8*
financial institution	Finanzinstitut, Bank	*4.8*
outlet	Geschäftsstelle	*4.9*
progressive	fortschrittlich	*4.9*
restructuring	Umstrukturierung, Neuordnung	*4.9*
legislation	Gesetzgebung	*4.9*
to apply to	gelten für	*4.9*
to comply with	erfüllen, einhalten	*4.9*

33

inconvenient	lästig, schwierig	*4.10*
significant	bedeutend; bezeichnend	*4.10*
obstacle	Hindernis	*4.10*
dissatisfied	unzufrieden	*4.10*
efficient	rationell	*4.10*
to gather momentum	Fahrt gewinnen	*4.10*
to put through	durchsetzen, durchbringen	*4.10*
to bring into line	angleichen	*4.10*
consumer-friendly	verbraucherfreundlich	*4.10*

Unit 5 Recruitment

35

• **work placement**	(Betriebs)Praktikum	*5*
trade journal	Fachzeitschrift	*5*
trade fair	Handelsmesse, Fachmesse	*5*
agency	Agentur	*5*
army careers office	Stellenvermittlung der brit. Armee	*5*
job centre	Arbeitsamt	*5*
commercial	(Radio, Fernsehen) Werbesendung	*5*
• **job opportunity**	freie Stelle	*5*
edition	Ausgabe	*5*
recruitment website	Webseite für freie Stellen	*5*
commercial recruitment agency	private Stellenvermittlungs-agentur	*5*
to find employment	Stelle finden	*5*
to be on offer	angeboten werden	*5*
prospective	potenziell, möglich	*5*
• **expert advice**	fachliche Beratung	*5*

36

• **small and medium-sized enterprises**	mittelständische Unternehmen	*5A*
• **staff**	Mitarbeiter, Personal	*5A*
• **to take on a new role**	in eine neue Rolle schlüpfen	*5A*
• **to interview sb**	Vorstellungsgespräch mit jdm. führen	*5A*
• **to select**	auswählen	*5A*
pile	Stapel	*5A*
• **CV (curriculum vitae)**	Lebenslauf	*5A*
• **cautious**	vorsichtig; unverbindlich	*5A*
• **reference**	Empfehlungsschreiben, Gutachten, Referenz	*5A*
to come down to	hinauslaufen auf	*5A*
guesswork	Ratespiel	*5A*
recruitment	Personalbeschaffung, Einstellung	*5A*
• **obvious**	offenkundig	*5A*
to outsource	fremdvergeben, an Dritte vergeben	*5A*
recruitment process	Einstellungsverfahren	*5A*
ill-judged idea	falsche Vorstellung	*5A*
attribute	Eigenschaft	*5A*
recruitment industry	Personalvermittlungs-branche	*5A*
• **to argue**	die Meinung vertreten	*5A*
professionals	Fachleute, Profis	*5A*
• **to come into one's own**	zeigen können/müssen, was man kann	*5A*
human resources manager	Personalleiter(in)	*5A*
recruiter	Personalvermittler(in)	*5A*
• **skill**	Fertigkeit, Kompetenz	*5A*
• **essential**	wichtig	*5A*
to check a reference	Referenz einholen	*5A*
snapshot	oberflächlicher Eindruck	*5A*
to narrow the field	das Bewerberfeld einschränken	*5A*
screen-to-client technology	Methode der Vorauswahl per Video	*5A*
objective	Ziel	*5A*
to provide	zur Verfügung stellen	*5A*
shortlist	(Vor)Auswahl	*5A*
state-of-the-art	modernst, allerneuest	*5A*
IT (information technology)	Informationstechnologie	*5A*
recruitment assignment	(Tätigkeit in der) Personalbeschaffung	*5A*
• **to ensure**	sicherstellen	*5A*
rate of success	Erfolgsquote	*5A*
recruitment consultant	Personalberater(in)	*5A*
position on offer	freie/ausgeschriebene Stelle	*5A*
• **face-to-face interview**	persönliches Vorstellungsgespräch	*5A*
issue	Problem	5A

37

flow chart	Ablauf-, Flussdiagramm	*5.3*
agency interview	Auswahlgespräch in der Stellenvermittlungsagentur	*5.3*
candidate profile	Bewerberprofil	*5.3*
company magazine	Firmenzeitschrift	*5.3*
in-house	firmenintern	*5.3*
noticeboard	Schwarzes Brett	*5.3*
personnel department	Personalabteilung	*5.3*
• **job description**	Stellenbeschreibung	*5.3*
unsolicited application	Initiativbewerbung, Blindbewerbung	*5.3*

media advertising	Auschreibung in den Medien	5.3

38

mobile	Handy	5B
• **personal profile**	Persönlichkeitsbild	5B
• **reliable**	zuverlässig	5B
• **to take charge**	Verantwortung übernehmen	5B
• **pressure situation**	Stresssituation	5B
social sciences	Sozialwissenschaften	5B
assistant courier	Mitarbeiter(in) in der Reiseleitung	5B
travel arrangements	Reiseplanung	5B
• **to promote**	organisieren	5B
accounts dept	Buchhaltung(sabteilung)	5B
in charge of	verantwortlich für	5B
administration	Verwaltungsarbeiten	5B
goods-in dept	Warenannahme	5B
to keep records	Belege bearbeiten	5B
delivery	Wareneingang, Warenanlieferung	5B
reviewing	Überwachung	5B
stock level	Lagerbestand	5B
fluent	fließend	5B
• **fair**	ziemlich gut(e Kenntnisse)	5B
parachuting	Fallschirmspringen	5B
references available on request	Referenzen können auf Wunsch beigebracht werden	5B

39

cover letter	Begleitschreiben	5.7
graduate training programme	Traineeprogramm für Hochschulabsolventen (innen)	5.7
honours degree	brit. Hochschulabschluss	5.7
• **to apply for**	sich bewerben um	5.7
finance management	Finanzwirtschaft	5.7
risk management	Risikomanagement	5.7
• **traineeship**	Ausbildungsplatz	5.7
• **career**	Berufsweg, Berufslaufbahn	5.7

40

to announce	ankündigen	5.8
to publicize	veröffentlichen, bekannt geben	5.8
after-sales complaint	Reklamation	5.8
human resources officer	Personalsachbearbeiter(in)	5.8
sales executive	Sachbearbeiter(in) im Verkauf, Verkäufer(in)	5.8
• **request**	Bitte, Wunsch	5.8
personnel officer	Personalsachbearbeiter(in)	
to interrogate	befragen	5.8
part-time	Teilzeit-	5.9
temporary work	Zeitarbeit	5.9
to graduate	Hochschulabschluss/Examen machen	5.9
keyboarding skills	Fähigkeiten in der Texterfassung	5.9
insight	Einblick	5.9
export manager	Exportleiter(in)	5.10
benefits	Sozialleistungen	5.10
prospects	Beförderungsmöglichkeiten	5.10
ASAP (as soon as possible)	sofort	5.10
to forward	senden	5.10
people-based	mit Menschen zu tun haben	5.10
to beat deadlines	Termine einhalten	5.10
junior	Nachwuchs-	5.10
telesales marketing	Telefonverkauf	5.10
customer database	Kundenstamm	5.10
telesales people	Telefonverkäufer(innen)	5.10
• **proven track record**	nachweislicher Erfolg	5.10
• **communicative skills**	kommunikative Kompetenz	5.10
• **computer-literate**	mit EDV-Kenntnissen	5.10
salary details	Gehaltsvorstellungen	5.10

41

fringe benefit	freiwillige Sozialleistung	5.12
flexitime	Gleitzeit, flexible Arbeitszeit	5.12
working hours	Arbeitszeit	5.12
• **relevant experience**	einschlägige Erfahrung	5.12
pay package	Vergütung(spaket)	5.12
job content	Arbeitsinhalt	5.12
holiday entitlement	Urlaubsanspruch	5.12
career prospects	Aufstiegschancen	5.12
promotion	Beförderung	5.12

42

secondary school	Gesamtschule, Gymnasium usw.	5.14
internship	(Betriebs)Praktikum	5.14
PR (public relations)	Öffentlichkeitsarbeit	5.14
business administration	Betriebswirtschaft	5.14

Unit 6 Modern forms of work

43

telecommuting	Telearbeit	6A
piece worker	Akkordarbeiter(in)	6A
freelancer	Freiberufler(in)	6A
chief technology officer	technische(r) Leiter(in)	6A
giant	Großunternehmen	6A
prime	herausragend	6A
to negotiate oneself into	durch Verhandlungen erreichen, dass	6A
to rise through the ranks	Karriere machen, aufsteigen	6A
to pursue a lifestyle	Leben führen	6A
non-negotiable	unabdingbar, nicht verhandelbar	6A
to go on to become	sogar ... werden	6A
living proof	sichtbarer Beweis	6A
senior executive	Führungskraft, leitende(r) Mitarbeiter(in)	6A

corn mill	(Getreide)Mühle	*6A*
headquarters	Hauptverwaltung	*6A*
chief economist	Chef-Ökonom(in)	*6A*
Institute of Directors	brit. Arbeitgeberverband	*6A*
outdated	nicht mehr zeitgemäß	*6A*
virtual corporation	virtuelles Unternehmen	*6A*
Labour Force Survey	Arbeitsmarktstudie	*6A*
telephone link	Telefonverbindung	*6A*
previous year	Vorjahr, Jahr zuvor	*6A*
to render obsolete	überflüssig machen	*6A*
debatable	fraglich, umstritten	*6A*

44

corporate culture	Unternehmenskultur	*6A*
staff supervision	Überwachung der Mitarbeiter	*6A*
on-the-job training	Ausbildung am Arbeitsplatz	*6A*
security	Sicherheit	*6A*
sensitive data	wichtige/geheime Daten	*6A*
to cope with	bewältigen	*6A*
data flow volume	Datenflussmenge	*6A*
off-site	extern	*6A*
teleworker	Telearbeiter(in)	*6A*
conscientiously	gewissenhaft	*6A*
benefit	Nutzen	*6A*
conclusion	Schluss(folgerung)	*6A*
to fall into the trap	dazu verleitet werden	*6A*
piece of equipment	Ausrüstungsgegenstand	*6.1*
contract	Vertrag	*6.1*
to advance	aufsteigen	*6.1*
steady	stetig	*6.1*
unalterable	unveränderbar	*6.1*
arts programme	Kulturprogramm	*6.1*
building site	Baustelle	*6.1*
consistent	beständig	*6.1*
self-conscious	gehemmt, befangen	*6.1*
confidential	vertraulich	*6.1*

45

to prevent	hindern an	*6.2*
to experience	erleben, erfahren	*6.3*
working environment	Arbeitsumfeld	*6.3*
to be stuck	festsitzen	*6.3*
time management	Zeitplanung	*6.3*

46

pros and cons	Vor- und Nachteile	*6.5*
valued	wichtig	*6.5*
trainee	Auszubildende(r)	*6.5*

47

to take care	sich kümmern	*6B*
computer maker	Computerhersteller	*6B*
to fix	reparieren	*6B*
native tongue	Muttersprache	*6B*
tech-support staff	technische Kundenberater(innen)	*6B*
perk	Vergünstigung	*6B*
to envy	beneiden	*6B*
gym	Fitnesstudio	*6B*
split-level	auf zwei Ebenen	*6B*
panorama view	Rundumsicht	*6B*
national day	Nationalfeiertag	*6B*
payroll	Gehaltsliste, Belegschaft	*6B*
sponsored	gefördert	*6B*
business degree	Abschluss/Diplom in Wirtschaftswissen-schaften	*6B*
pampering	Verhätschelung	*6B*
multinational	Multi, multinationales Unternehmen	*6B*
to look set to hit	höchstwahrscheinlich erreichen	*6B*
flight	Flug	*6B*
to route	(Telefonat) leiten	*6B*
high-tech skills	Kompetenz in moderner Technologie	*6B*
command	Beherrschung	*6B*
to staff	(personell) besetzen, mit Personal ausstatten	*6B*
to meet the demand	Nachfrage befriedigen	*6B*
training course	Ausbildungskurs	*6B*
to trawl	absuchen	*6B*
to land	finden, anwerben	*6B*
recruit	Kandidat(in), neue(r) Mitarbeiter(in)	*6B*
charm	Reiz	*6B*
computer-savvy	etwas von Computern verstehend	*6B*
to lure	anlocken	*6B*
scores	zig	*6B*
hyperhip	voll angesagt	*6B*
draw	Anziehungskraft	*6B*
to outstrip	übertreffen, größer sein als	*6B*
prosperity	Wohlstand	*6B*
to clog	verstopfen	*6B*
housing	Wohnraum	*6B*
to soar	steil ansteigen	*6B*
in line with	parallel zu	*6B*
rival	Konkurrent(in)	*6B*
to serve a market	Markt versorgen	*6B*
Low Countries	die Niederlande, Belgien und Luxemburg	*6B*
criss-crossing	kreuz und quer verlaufend	*6B*
linguistic	Sprach-	*6B*
frontier	Grenze	*6B*
mastery	Beherrschung	*6B*
commonplace	alltäglich	*6B*
lifestyle draw	Attraktivität der Lebensqualität	*6B*
managerial capacity	Leitungsfunktion	*6.6*

48

economies	Einsparungen	*6.8*
to exceed	übersteigen, übertreffen	*6.8*
hiring	Anwerbung, Einstellung	*6.8*
maintenance engineer	Kundendiensttechniker(in)	*6.8*
vacancy	freie Stelle	*6.10*

Unit 7 Retailing

50

mall	Einkaufszentrum	*7A*
twin	Zwilling	*7A*
Viking	Wikinger(in)	*7A*
downtown	Innenstadt-	*7A*
acre	0,4 Hektar	*7A*
to intersect	durchkreuzen	*7A*
to be under-retailed	zu wenig Einzelhandelsgeschäfte haben	*7A*
research	Forschung, Untersuchung	*7A*
square foot	0,09 m^2	*7A*
to lease	pachten, verpachten	*7A*
department store	Kaufhaus	*7A*

51

variety	Vielzahl	*7A*
retail pie	Einzelhandelskuchen	*7A*
to account for	der Grund sein für	*7A*
gas	Benzin	*7A*
lodging	Unterkunft	*7A*
proximity	Nähe	*7A*
enclosed	überdacht	*7A*
to thrive	gedeihen	*7A*

52

scarcity	Mangel	*7.2*
retail outlet	Einzelhandelsverkaufsstelle	*7.2*
adverse	widrig	*7.2*
market stall	Marktstand	*7.3*
corner shop	Laden an der Ecke, Tante-Emma-Laden	*7.3*
convenience store	Nachbarschaftsladen	*7.3*
cooperative	Konsum	*7.3*
mail order house	Versandhaus	*7.3*
superstore	Verbrauchermarkt	*7.3*
vending machine	Verkaufsautomat	*7.3*
chain store	Kettenladen	*7.3*
soft drink	alkoholfreies Getränk	*7.4*
to comprise	umfassen	*7.4*
furnishing	Einrichtung	*7.4*

53

cosy	gemütlich	*7.5*
layout	Anlage, Aufmachung	*7.6*
to lay out	anlagen	*7.6*
to encourage	ermutigen	*7.6*
impulse buy	Spontankauf	*7.6*
to prompt	veranlassen	*7.6*
hot spot	auffälliger Ort	*7.6*
at eye level	in Augenhöhe	*7.6*
own brand	Eigenmarke	*7.6*
profit margin	Gewinnspanne	*7.6*
aisle	Gang	*7.6*
high-profit	gewinnträchtig	*7.6*
to design	planen	*7.6*
to space out	räumlich verteilen	*7.6*

54

sweets	Süßigkeiten	*7.7*
lottery	Lotto	*7.7*
spirits	Spirituosen	*7.7*
toiletries	Toilettenartikel	*7.7*
detergent	Waschmittel	*7.7*
checkout	(Supermarkt)Kasse	*7.7*
cereal	Frühstückskost (aus Getreide)	*7.7*
counter	Theke	*7.7*
tinned food	Dosennahrung	*7.7*
pie	Pastete	*7.7*
bacon	Speck	*7.7*
dairy product	Molkereiprodukt	*7.7*
pet food	Haustierfutter	*7.7*
in-store	ladeneigen	*7.7*
to position	anordnen	*7.7*
product range	Sortiment	*7.7*

55

forecast	Vorhersage	*7B*
to release	veröffentlichen	*7B*
retail consultancy	Einzelhandelsberatungs-unternehmen	*7B*
to fuel	antreiben	*7B*
groceries	Lebensmittel	*7B*
mobile telephone	Handy	*7B*
turnover	Umsatz	*7B*
to cannibalize	wegnehmen, ausschlachten	*7B*
to launch	einrichten	*7B*
bricks and mortar	Stein und Mörtel	*7B*
physical presence	tatsächlicher Laden	*7B*
brand	Marke	*7B*
to fail	scheitern	*7B*
flight	Flucht	*7B*
merger	Zusammenschluss	*7B*
acquisition	Erwerb	*7B*
dotcom	Internetfirma	*7B*
established	etabliert, alteingesessen	*7B*
scale	Maßstab	*7B*
muscle	Stärke	*7B*
brand differentiation	Markendifferenzierung	*7B*
upmarket	hochwertig	*7.8*
make	Marke	*7.8*

56

to yield	abwerfen	*7.9*
sales volume	Verkaufsvolumen	*7.9*
to boost	fördern, steigern	*7.9*
to be affected	beeinträchtigt werden	*7.9*
speciality shop	Fachgeschäft	*7.10*
wholesale	massiv, generell	*7.10*
turkey	Truthahn	*7.10*
in next to no time	im Handumdrehen	*7.10*
pint	0,57 Liter	*7.10*
chore	lästige Arbeit	*7.10*
virtual	virtuell	*7.10*

57

gift hamper	Geschenkkorb	*7.12*
answerphone	Anrufbeantworter	*7.12*
to log onto	einloggen	*7 Gr*
to make it	schaffen	*7 Gr*

to take for granted	als selbstverständlich hinnehmen	*7 Gr*
in progress	im Gang	*7 Gr*
wholesale trade	Großhandel	*7.13*
to decrease	abnehmen	*7.13*
to bother	sich die Mühe machen	*7.13*
to run out of	nicht mehr haben, ausgehen	*7.13*
sales seminar	Verkaufsseminar	*7.13*

Unit 8 Marketing

59

night-cap	Absacker	*8*
target group	Zielgruppe	*8*

60

set	Reihe, Satz	*8A*
to be involved in	beteiligt sein bei	*8A*
to anticipate	vorwegnehmen	*8A*
market research	Marktforschung, Markterhebung	*8A*
home decoration	Wohnungsausstattung	*8A*
ongoing	fortdauernd	*8A*
to respond to	reagieren auf	*8A*
range	Sortiment	*8A*
office furniture	Büromöbel	*8A*
design	Entwurf, Design	*8A*
to target	als Zielgruppe wählen	*8A*
facility	Räumlichkeit	*8A*
pricing	Preisfestsetzung	*8A*
consumer preference	Verbrauchervorliebe	*8A*
promotion	Werbekampagne	*8A*
free gift	Werbegeschenk	*8A*
sponsorship	Fördertätigkeit	*8A*
charity	wohltätige Vereinigung	*8A*
public-sector organization	öffentlich-rechtliche Organisation	*8A*
to adapt	sich anpassen	*8A*
image-building	zur Verbesserung des Ansehens	*8A*
famine	Hunger(snot)	*8A*
relief	Hilfe	*8A*
to persuade	überreden	*8.1*
investigation	Untersuchung	*8.1*
event	Veranstaltung	*8.1*

61

to market	vermarkten	*8.2*
one-off	einmalig	*8.2*
sound	stattlich	*8.2*
to confuse	verwechseln	*8.3*
so-called	so genannt	*8.3*
marketing mix	Marketinginstrumentarium	*8.3*
packaging	Verpackung(smaterial)	*8.3*
to make available	bereit stellen	*8.3*
to opt	wählen	*8.3*
appropriate	passend	*8.4*
motorist	Autofahrer(in)	*8.4*
to break down	Panne haben	*8.4*
rescue organization	Rettungsdienst	*8.4*
hard-hitting	zupackend, drastisch	*8.4*
advertising campaign	Werbekampagne	*8.4*
emergency service	Notdienst	*8.4*
apathy	Gleichgültigkeit	*8.4*
benefit	Leistung, Dienst	*8.4*
memorable	einprägsam	*8.4*
to bring home	klar machen	*8.4*
breakdown cover	Pannenschutz	*8.4*
launch	Markteinführung	*8.4*
ambulance	Krankentransport	*8.4*
mistaken	irrtümlich	*8.4*
competitive edge	Wettbewerbsvorsprung	*8.4*

62

billboard	Plakatwand	*8.5*
flyer	Prospekt	*8.5*
leaflet	Flugblatt	*8.5*
mailshot	Postwurfsendung	*8.5*
newspaper ad	Zeitungsanzeige	*8.5*
point of sale advertising	Werbung an der Kasse	*8.5*
press release	Presseveröffentlichung	*8.5*
product placement	Produktplatzierung	*8.5*
sample	Muster, Stichprobe	*8.5*
showroom	Ausstellungsraum	*8.5*
word of mouth	Mund-zu-Mund	*8.5*
to make a start	anfangen	*8 UPh*
to rephrase	umformulieren	*8 UPh*
concise	präzise, knapp	*8 UPh*
specific	besonders	*8 UPh*
to focus on	sich konzentrieren auf	*8 UPh*
visual aid	Anschauungsmaterial	*8 UPh*
overhead	Folie	*8 UPh*
screen	Leinwand	*8 UPh*
transparency	Folie	*8 UPh*

63

faced by	ausgesetzt sein	*8 Info*
in-house presentation	betriebsinterne Präsentation	*8.6*
recipe	Rezept	*8.6*
device	Vorrichtung	*8.6*
to redefine	sich neu definieren	*8B*
consumer electronics	Konsumelektronik	*8B*
urban clothing	Kleidung für die Stadt	*8B*
trainers	Turnschuhe	*8B*
record store	Plattenladen	*8B*
to stretch into	ausdehnen auf	*8B*
better off	besser gestellt	*8B*
sophisticated	anspruchsvoll	*8B*
rare	selten	*8B*
to stand out	sich auszeichnen	*8B*

64

old-established	alt eingesessen	*8B*
legacy	Geschichte	*8B*
revenue	Einnahme	*8B*
exposure	Aussetzung	*8B*
lifespan	Lebensdauer	*8B*
branding consultancy	Markenberatungs-unternehmen	*8B*
elasticity	Bandbreite	*8B*
tangible asset	materieller Vermögenswert	*8B*

intangible	immateriell	*8B*
to position oneself	sich positionieren	*8B*
chairman	Aufsichtsratsvorsitzender	*8B*
fizzy	sprudelnd	*8B*
to deny	leugnen	*8B*
to extend	weiter verbreiten	*8B*
licensing programme	Lizensierungsprogramm	*8B*
licensee	Lizenznehmer(in)	*8B*
trademark	Markenname	*8B*
to overwhelm	überwältigen	*8B*
response	Reaktion	*8B*
appealing	anziehend	*8B*
heritage	Erbe	*8B*
authenticity	Echtheit	*8B*
global appeal	weltweite Attraktivität	*8B*
retro flavour	Atmosphäre der Vergangenheit	*8B*
flavour	Atmosphäre, Anflug	*8B*
distinct	getrennt	*8.7*
enterprise	Unternehmen	*8.7*
link	Verbindung	*8.8*

65

to regain	wiedergewinnen	*8.8*
departure	Abkehr	*8.8*
to herald	einläuten	*8.8*
to induce	veranlassen	*8.8*
engineering	Maschinenbau	*8.9*
food retail	Lebensmitteleinzelhandel	*8.9*

Unit 9 International trade

68

to push for	drängen auf	*9*
trade ties	Handelsbeziehungen	*9*
to fly the flag	patriotisch denken	*9*
WTO (World Trade Organization)	Welthandelsorganisation	*9*

69

beverage	Getränk	*9A*
domestic	Binnen-, inländisch	*9A*
decline	Verringerung	*9A*
expenditure	Ausgaben(volumen)	*9A*
commodity	Rohstoff	*9A*
external market	Außenmarkt	*9A*
to top	anführen	*9A*
composition	Zusammensetzung	*9A*
visible exports	Warenausfuhr(en), Warenexport(e)	*9A*
aerospace	Luft- und Raumfahrt	*9A*
electronics	Elektronikerzeugnisse	*9A*
stockbroking	Börsenhandel	*9A*
aviation	Luftfahrt	*9A*
engineering consultancy	technische Beratung	*9A*
invisible exports	Dienstleistungsausfuhr(en)	*9A*
balance of payments	Zahlungsbilanz	*9A*
to be equivalent to	entsprechen	*9A*
surplus	Überschuss	*9A*
ultimately	letztlich	*9A*
non-inflationary	nicht-inflationär	*9A*

70

advisory	beratend	*9.2*
vital	sehr wichtig	*9.3*
to coincide with	zusammenfallen mit	*9.3*
interdependent	wechselseitig abhängig	*9.3*
trade pattern	Außenhandelsstruktur	*9.3*
cross-border	grenzüberschreitend	*9.3*
trade barrier	Handelsschranke	*9.3*

71

to impose	verhängen	*9.4*
quota	Mengenbegrenzung, Kontingent	*9.4*
to obtain	beschaffen	*9.4*
customs clearance	Zollabfertigung	*9.4*
bonded warehouse	Zoll(verschluss)lager	*9.4*
customs duty	Zoll(gebühr)	*9.4*
payable	zahlbar	*9.4*
preferential	Vorzugs-	*9.4*
most-favoured	meistbegünstigt	*9.4*

72

to adopt	einführen	*9B*
policy	Strategie, Politik	*9B*
self-sufficiency	Autarkie, Selbstversorgung	*9B*
to dispense with	verzichten auf	*9B*
to pursue	verfolgen	*9B*
tariff barrier	Zollschranke	*9B*
non-tariff	nicht-tarifär	*9B*
inward investment	Ausländeranlage, Investitionen durch Ausländer	*9B*
outward investment	Investition(en) im Ausland, Auslandsinvestition(en) durch Inländer	*9B*
to exploit	nutzen	*9B*
manufacturing facility	Produktionseinrichtung, Fabrik(anlage)	*9B*
subsidiary	Tochterunternehmen	*9B*
group	Konzern, Gruppe	*9B*
billion (bn)	Milliarde	*9B*
saturation	Sättigung	*9B*
to seek	bestrebt sein	*9B*
economies of scale	Kostendegression durch optimale Betriebsvergrößerung, Skalenerträge	*9B*
negotiation	Verhandlung	*9B*
overcapacity	Überkapazität	*9B*
emerging-market	mit aufstrebendem Markt	*9B*
environmental concern	Sorge hinsichtlich der Umwelt	*9B*
footing	Basis	*9B*
production-related	produktionsbezogen	*9B*
component	Zubehörteil	*9B*
abolition	Abschaffung	*9B*
high-cost	teuer, kostenintensiv	*9B*
joint venture	Gemeinschaftsunternehmen	*9B*
distinction	Unterscheidung	*9B*

73

hurdle	Hürde	*9.6*
outside	Fremd-	*9.6*
corporate	unternehmerisch, Unternehmens-	*9.6*
capital expenditure	Kapitalaufwand	*9.6*
Common Market	Gemeinsamer Markt	*9.7*
to pool	zusammenfassen	*9.7*
resources	Mittel, Ressourcen	*9.7*
semi-finished	Halbfertig-	*9.8*

74

balance on current account	Leistungsbilanz	*9 Info*
balance of visible trade	Handelsbilanz	*9 Info*
balance of invisible trade	Dienstleistungsbilanz	*9 Info*
raw material	Rohstoff	*9 Info*
balance on financial and capital account	Kapitalbilanz	*9 Info*
loan	Kredit, Darlehen	*9 Info*
license fee	Lizenzgebühr	*9 Info*
corporation	Kapitalgesellschaft	*9 Info*
premium	Prämie	*9 Info*
income receipt	Einnahme	*9 Info*
unilateral	einseitig	*9 Info*
grant	Beihilfe	*9 Info*
remittance	Überweisung	*9 Info*
asset	Vermögenswert	*9 Info*
farm labourer	Landarbeiter(in)	*9.9*
aircraft	Flugzeug	*9.9*
UNESCO (United Nations Educational, Scientific and Cultural Organization)		*9.9*

75

exceeding	äußerst	*9.11*
vast	riesig	*9.11*
performance	Leistung	*9.11*
on receipt	bei Erhalt	*9.11*

Unit 10 Logistics

78

supply chain management	Warenwirtschaftslogistik, Prozesskettenmanagement	*10A*
inbound	eingehend	*10A*
outbound	ausgehend	*10A*
supplies	Nachschub, Warenlieferung	*10A*
production location	Produktionsstandort	*10A*
plant	Werk, Fabrik	*10A*
to involve	beinhalten	*10A*
warehousing	Lagerung, Lagerhaltung	*10A*
stock management	Bestandsverwaltung, Lagerhaltung	*10A*
supply chain	Lieferkette	*10A*
economic output	Wirtschaftsleistung; Güterproduktion	*10A*
to earn	beziehen	*10A*
revenues	Einnahmen	*10A*
overseas sales	Absatz im Ausland	*10A*
part	(Zuliefer)Teil	*10A*
to complicate	erschweren, schwierig gestalten	*10A*
on-time delivery	zeitgenaue/pünktliche (An)Lieferung	*10A*
freight	Fracht	*10A*
shipper	Versender, Verlader	*10A*
cost savings	Kosteneinsparungen	*10A*
transport mode	Transportart, Beförderungsart	*10A*
competitive	wettbewerbsfähig, kostengünstig	*10A*
carrier	Transportunternehmen, Beförderer	*10A*
third-party supplier	Drittanbieter; Lieferant	*10A*
shipment	(Waren)Sendung, Versandpartie	*10A*
to maximize	bestmögliche/ günstigste ... wählen	*10A*
direct routing opportunity	Möglichkeit des Direktversands	*10A*
to cut out	vermeiden	*10A*
intermediate distribution centre	Warenverteilzentrum auf der Strecke	*10A*
delivery service	Anlieferung, Lieferdienst	*10A*
high-value	hochwertig	*10A*
electronic equipment	elektronische Geräte	*10A*
automotive part(s)	Automobilzubehör, Autozulieferteil(e)	*10A*
consignment	(Waren)Sendung	*10A*
departure	Versand, Abgang	*10A*
to delay	verzögern	*10A*
to deliver late	verspätet anliefern/ausliefern	*10A*
purchasing	Beschaffung, Einkauf	*10A*
optimum balance	bestmögliches Verhältnis	*10A*
production scheduling	Produktionsplanung	*10A*
load planning	Ladungsdisposition; Kapazitätsplanung	*10A*
inventory holding	Lagerhaltung, Vorratshaltung	*10A*
to claim	behaupten	*10A*
to locate	orten, ausfindig machen	*10A*
cause	Ursache	*10A*
safety stocks	Sicherheitsbestand	*10A*
to meet a need	Bedürfnis befriedigen	*10A*
forwarder	Spediteur, Versender	*10A*
customs broker	Zollagent	*10A*
to handle	verantwortlich sein für, sich kümmern um	*10A*
door-to-door visibility	vollständige Sendungsverfolgung	*10A*
reliability	Zuverlässigkeit	*10A*
satellite-based	satellitengestützt	*10A*
tracking and tracing	Sendungsverfolgung	*10A*
to monitor	überwachen	*10A*
freight forwarder	Frachtführer(in), Speditionsunternehmen	*10A*
to broaden	ausweiten	*10A*
ocean freight	Hochseefracht	*10A*
customs brokerage	Zollagententätigkeit	*10A*

ocean carrier	Seefrachtunternehmen, Seefrachtspediteur, Hochseereederei	*10A*
range of services	Leistungsangebot	*10A*
forwarding service	Speditionsleistung(en)	*10A*
to complement	ergänzen, vervollständigen	*10A*
ocean shipping	Seefrachtgeschäft	*10A*
freight consolidation (operation)	Frachtbündelung, Erstellung von Sammelladungen	*10A*
one-stop freight service	Frachtdienstleistungen aus einer Hand	*10A*

79

transport facility	Transportausrüstung, Transportgerät	*10.2*
premium	Höchst-	*10.2*
freight rate	Frachtsatz, Frachttarif	*10.2*
whereabouts	Verbleib	*10.2*
operation	Aktivität, Betrieb	*10.2*
cargo airline	Luftfrachtgesellschaft	10.3
consignee	(Sendungs)Empfänger	*10.3*
consignor	Absender	*10.3*
forwarding agent	Spediteur	*10.3*
freight agent	Frachtenmakler, Spediteur	*10.3*
shipping company	Reederei, Schifffahrtsgesellschaft	*10.3*
shipping agent	Reedereivertreter, Spediteur	*10.3*
haulier	Spedition(sfirma)	*10.3*
haulage company	Spedition(sfirma)	*10.3*
recipient	Empfänger	*10.3*

80

consolidator	Sammelladungsspediteur	*10.4*
draft	(gezogener) Wechsel, Zahlungsanweisung	*10.4*
franchisor, franchiser	Franchisegeber(in)	*10.4*
to license	Lizenz/Konzession vergeben	*10.4*
operator	Betreiber(gesellschaft)	*10.4*
general cargo	Stückgut, gemischte Fracht	*10.5*
full container load (FCL)	Container-Komplettladung	*10.5*
FOB (free on board)	FOB (frei an Bord)	*10.5*
seaport	Seehafen	*10.5*
fresh	neu	*10.5*
sensible	vernünftig, zweckmäßig	*10.5*
in commercial terms	wirtschaftlich gesehen	*10.5*
environmentally unacceptable	aus Umweltschutzgründen nicht vertretbar	*10.5*
fleet	(Fahrzeug)Flotte, Fuhrpark	*10.5*
truck	LKW	*10.5*
freight note	Frachtbrief, LKW-Ladeschein	*10.5*
proof of delivery	Nachweis der Lieferung	*10.5*
buffer stocks	Ausgleichsvorräte, Reservelager	*10.6*
containerization	Versand in Containern	*10.6*
groupage consignment	Sammelladung	*10.6*
high-bay warehouse	Hochregallager	*10.6*
just-in-time (JIT) delivery	einsatzsynchrone Anlieferung	*10.6*
palletizing	Verpackung/Versand auf Paletten	*10.6*
to pick	kommissionieren	*10.6*
storage	(Ein)Lagerung	*10.6*
retrieval	(Produkt)Entnahme	*10.6*
transshipment	Umladung	*10.6*
to break bulk	Sammelladung auflösen, umpacken	*10.6*
forklift truck	Gabelstapler	*10.6*
container crane	Containerladebrücke, Containerkran	*10.6*
goods storage	Güterlagerung	*10.6*
to change beyond recognition	sich grundlegend ändern	*10.6*

81

pallet	Palette	*10.6*
fully mechanized	vollautomatisiert	*10.6*
to dispatch	versenden	*10.6*
within a matter of	innerhalb von	*10.6*
assembly line	Montageband	*10.6*
emergency	Notfall	*10.6*
end-user	Endverbraucher	*10.7*
wheat	Weizen	*10.7*
timber	(Nutz)Holz	*10.7*
combine harvester	Mähdrescher	*10.7*
bulk carrier	Massengutfrachter	*10.7*
mill	(Getreide)Mühle	*10.7*
iron ore	Eisenerz	*10.7*
inland waterway	Binnenwasserstraße	*10.7*
vessel	Schiff	*10.7*
seaborne transport	Seetransport	*10.7*
on-carriage	Weitertransport	*10.7*
processing plant	Weiterverarbeitungsanlage	*10.7*
processing	Weiterverarbeitung, Veredlung	*10.7*
steel plant	Stahlwerk	*10.7*
carmaker	Automobilhersteller	*10.7*
engineering company	Maschinenbauunternehmen	*10.7*
toolmaker	Werkzeugmaschinenhersteller	*10.7*
storage depot	Lager(haus)	*10.7*
await	bis zu(r, m)	*10.7*
service package	Dienstleistungsangebot	*10.8*

82

shipshape	blitzblank, tipptopp (sauber)	*10B*
to face	sich gegenübersehen	*10B*
immediate	drängend	*10B*
to retain business	Kunden halten	*10B*
to meet the demands	den Anforderungen entsprechen	*10B*
shipowner user	Reedereikunde	*10B*

jumbo container vessel	Riesencontainerschiff	*10B*
to overlap	sich teilweise decken, sich überschneiden	*10B*
quay	Kai(anlage)	*10B*
marshalling yard	Rangierbahnhof	*10B*
support service	Nebenleistung; Nebenbetrieb	*10B*
container facility	Containeranlage	*10B*
port authority	Hafenbehörde	*10B*
stevedore	Schauermann; Verladegesellschaft	*10B*
to drive down costs	Kosten senken	*10B*
operational performance	Wirtschaftlichkeit, Rentabilität	*10B*
turnaround time	Umschlagszeit, Verweildauer	*10B*
to upgrade	verbessern, modernisieren	*10B*
security system	Sicherheitsanlage	*10B*
to acknowledge	zugestehen, anerkennen	*10B*
fierce competition	scharfer/harter Wettbewerb	*10B*
increased productivity	Produktivitätssteigerung	*10B*
impetus	Anstoß	*10B*
intermodal service/ operation	kombinierter Ladungsverkehr (KLV)	*10B*
environmental benefit	Umweltnutzen	*10B*
to enhance	erhöhen, verbessern	*10B*
regulatory standards	staatlich festgelegte Normen	*10B*
value-added service	Mehrwert schaffende Dienstleistung	*10B*
further processing	Weiterverarbeitung, Veredelung	*10B*
pre-delivery inspection	Warenkontrolle vor Auslieferung	*10B*
distribution park	(Güter)Verteilzentrum	*10B*
focus	Blick	*10B*
interface	Schnittstelle	*10B*
transport chain	Transportkette	*10B*
to transfer	umladen	*10B*
mode of transport	Transportart	*10B*
environmental sensitivity	Umweltbewusstsein	*10B*
to translate	umsetzen	*10B*
grain	Getreide	*10B*
animal feedstock	Futtermittel	*10B*
bulk commodity	Massengut, Schüttgut	*10B*
stringent	streng	*10B*
inland navigation	Binnenschifffahrt	*10B*
eco-friendly	umweltfreundlich	*10B*
transport volume	Transportaufkommen	*10B*
container-carrying barge	Binnenschiff für Containertransporte	*10B*
integral part	integraler/fester Bestandteil	*10B*
inland distribution	Inlandsvertrieb	*10B*
blast furnace	Hochofen	*10B*
to transship	umladen	*10B*
push vessel	Schubschiff	*10B*
car-carrying barge	Binnenschiff für den Autotransport	*10B*
familiar	vertraut	*10B*
terminal	Be- und Entladeanlage, Verladeanlage	*10B*
approach channel	Zufahrt	*10B*
drawing	mit einem Tiefgang von	*10B*
seaborne trade	Seehandel	*10B*

83

intermodal transport	kombinierter Ladungsverkehr	*10.9*
consideration	Erwägung	*10.9*
to attract traffic	Kunden gewinnen	*10.9*
to refine	raffinieren	*10.10*
environmentalist	Umweltschützer(in)	*10.10*
sensitive	empfindlich	*10.10*
express parcels delivery	Eilpaketauslieferung	*10.12*
milestone	Meilenstein	*10.12*
parcel carrier	Paketdienst	*10.12*
volume	(Paket)Aufkommen	*10.12*
vulnerable to	ausgesetzt	*10.12*
competitive pressure	Wettbewerbsdruck	*10.12*
hub	Warenverteilzentrum, Logistikzentrum	*10.12*
truck fleet	LKW-Fuhrpark	*10.12*
to allocate	aufwenden	*10.12*
to incorporate	umfassen, einschließen	*10.12*
sorting capability	Sortieranlagen	*10.12*

84

seaborne freight	Seefracht	*10 Info*
roll-on/roll-off (RoRo) facility	RoRo-Rampe, Verladerampe für Straßen- und Schienenfahrzeuge	*10 Info*
cargo liner	Linienfrachter	*10 Info*
container vessel	Containerschiff	*10 Info*
scheduled service	fahrplanmäßiger Dienst	*10 Info*
tramp	Trampschiff	*10 Info*
voyage	(Schiffs)Reise	*10 Info*
tanker	Tankschiff	*10 Info*
commodity	Produkt	*10 Info*
bulk cargo	Massengut	*10 Info*
bulky	sperrig	*10 Info*
transformer	Transformator	*10 Info*
road haulage	Straßengüterverkehr	*10 Info*
truck and trailer	Zugmaschine und Hänger	*10 Info*
articulated vehicle	Gelenkfahrzeug, Sattelschlepper	*10 Info*
multimodal transport	kombinierter Ladungsverkehr (KLV)	*10 Info*
to equip	ausstatten, ausrüsten	*10 Info*
swapbody	Wechselaufbau	*10 Info*
flatbed wagon	Flachwagen	*10 Info*
piggyback service	Huckepackverkehr	*10 Info*
trainload	Zugladung	*10 Info*

box wagon	Kastenwagen	*10 Info*
tank wagon	Tankwagen	*10 Info*
palletized load	Palettenladung	*10 Info*
airborne freight	Luftfracht	*10 Info*
parcel	Paket	*10 Info*
air container	Luftfrachtcontainer	*10 Info*
liquid	Flüssigkeit, Flüssigstoff	*10 Info*
medical supplies	medizinische Güter	*10.13*
destination	Zielort, Bestimmungsort	*10.13*
toxic	giftig	*10.13*

85

port facilities	Hafenanlagen	*10.14*
non-bulk	Stückgut-	*10.14*
freight package	Frachtangebot	*10.14*
storage facility	Lager(haus)	*10.14*
dock area	Hafengebiet	*10.14*

Unit 11 Insurance

87

personal insurance	Personenversicherung	*11A*
non-personal insurance	Sachversicherung	*11A*
to evolve	sich entwickeln	*11A*
supplier	Anbieter(in)	*11A*
creditor	Gläubiger(in)	*11A*
premium	Aufgeld	*11A*
theft	Diebstahl	*11A*
underwriting	(Risiko)Absicherung	*11A*
moneylender	Geldverleiher	*11A*
risk-sharing scheme	Risikostreuung	*11A*
to devise	entwickeln	*11A*
to survive	überleben	*11A*
underwriter	Versicherungsgeber(in)	*11A*
percentage	Prozentsatz	*11A*
in return for	(im Gegenzug) für	*11A*
party	(Vertrags)Partei	*11A*
insurer	Versicherungsgeber(in)	*11A*
to provide cover	Deckung/Versicherungsschutz gewähren	*11A*
the insured	Versicherungsnehmer(in), Versicherte(r)	*11A*
uninsured	unversichert, ungedeckt	*11A*
to lay down	niederlegen	*11A*
policy	(Versicherungs)Police	*11A*
to require	voraussetzen	*11A*
likelihood	Wahrscheinlichkeit	*11A*
policyholder	Versicherungsnehmer(in)	*11A*
to make a claim	Anspruch geltend machen	*11A*
actuary	Versicherungsmathematiker(in)	*11A*
probability	Wahrscheinlichkeit	*11A*
appropriate	angemessen, angebracht	*11A*
personal risk	Personenrisiko	*11A*
disability	Behinderung	*11A*
unemployment	Arbeitslosigkeit	*11A*
property risk	Sachschadenrisiko, Vermögensrisiko	*11A*
riot	Aufruhr	*11A*
civil commotion	bürgerliche Unruhe	*11A*
flooding	Überschwemmung	*11A*
air crash	Flugzeugabsturz	*11A*
loss at sea	Schiffsunglück, Havarie	*11A*
rail disaster	Eisenbahnunglück	*11A*
road traffic accident	Verkehrsunfall	*11A*
economic unit	Wirtschaftssubjekt	*11A*
to be subject to	ausgesetzt sein	*11A*
family business	Familienbetrieb	*11A*
small business	kleines/mittelständiges Unternehmen	*11A*
loan to customer	Kundenkredit	*11A*
credit insurance	Kreditausfallversicherung	*11A*
damage to property	Vermögensschaden, Sachbeschädigung	*11A*
loss of property	Vermögensverlust	*11A*
all-inclusive	Pauschal-, Global-	*11A*
business policy	Gewerbeversicherung	*11A*
health insurance	Krankenversicherung	*11A*
statutory	gesetzlich (vorgeschrieben)	*11A*
life insurance	Lebensversicherung	*11A*
term insurance	Risiko-Lebensversicherung, Kurzversicherung	*11A*
endowment insurance	Kapitallebensversicherung, Versicherung auf den Todes- und Erlebensfall	*11A*
savings component	Sparkomponente	*11A*
in the event of	im Falle	*11A*
dependant	Unterhaltsberechtigte(r)	*11A*
to stipulate	vertraglich vereinbaren/festlegen; fordern, verlangen	*11A*
investment returns	Kapitalerträge	*11A*
self-employed	selbstständig (tätig)	*11A*
to supplement	ergänzen	*11A*
pension	Rente, Pension	*11A*
automobile insurance	Kfz-Versicherung	*11A*
bodily injury	Personenschaden	*11A*
property damage liability	Haftpflicht für Vermögensschäden	*11A*
third-party policy	Haftpflichtversicherung	*11A*
required	vorgeschrieben	*11A*
to register	zulassen	*11A*
comprehensive policy	Vollkaskoversicherung	*11A*
coverage	Versicherungsschutz, Deckung	*11A*
to be at fault	schuld sein, verschuldet haben	*11A*
excess	Selbstbeteiligung	*11A*
motor insurer	Kfz-Versicherungsgeber(in)	*11A*
uninsured motorist coverage	Deckung bei Unfällen mit nicht versicherten Autofahrern	*11A*
safe driver plan	Schadenfreiheitstarif	*11A*
in accordance with	je nach	*11A*
driving record	Schadensverlauf	*11A*
equivalent	Entsprechung	*11A*
safe driver	unfallfreie(r) Autofahrer(in)	*11A*
no-claims bonus/discount	Schadenfreiheitsrabatt	*11A*

88

hooligan	Randalierer	*11.1*
to classify	einstufen	*11.1*
to reward	belohnen	*11.1*
indispensable	unverzichtbar	*11.2*
to operate at a loss	mit Verlust arbeiten	*11.2*
proposal form	Versicherungsantrag	*11.2*
intermediary	Mittelsperson, Vermittler(in)	*11.2*
goal	Ziel	*11.2*
occupation	Beruf	*11.2*
accidental damage	Unfallschaden	*11.2*
accessories	Zubehör	*11.2*
to tow	abschleppen	*11.2*
recommended garage	Vertragswerkstatt	*11.2*
to attempt	versuchen	*11.2*
windscreen	Windschutzscheibe	*11.2*
to relate to	sich beziehen auf, betreffen	*11.2*
rug	(kleiner) Teppich	*11.2*
personal belongings	persönliche Habe	*11.2*
personal injury	Personenschaden	*11.2*
liability	Haftpflicht	*11.2*
passenger negligence	Fahrlässigkeit von Insassen	*11.2*
hire purchase	Mietkauf	*11.2*
legal defence	Rechtsschutz	*11.2*
personal accident cover	Unfallversicherung	*11.2*
irrespective of	unabhängig von, gleichgültig, ungeachtet	*11.2*
spouse	Ehegatte, Ehegattin	*11.2*
loss of limb	Verlust eines Glieds	*11.2*
medical expenses	Kosten für ärztliche Versorgung	*11.2*
incurred	entstanden	*11.2*

89

joint venture	gemeinsames Projekt	*11B*
insurance group	Versicherungskonzern	*11B*
to result in	zur Folge haben	*11B*
agent	(Versicherungs)Vertreter(in)	*11B*
to convince	überzeugen	*11B*
efficiency gain	Rationalisierungserfolg	*11B*
due to	wegen	*11B*
life policy	Lebensversicherungspolice	*11B*
prospective	angehend	*11B*
to undergo a test	sich untersuchen lassen	*11B*
blood test	Blutuntersuchung	*11B*
approval	Annahme	*11B*
life policy proposal	Antrag auf Lebensversicherung	*11B*
executive	Mitarbeiter(in), Sachbearbeiter(in)	*11B*
applicant	Antragsteller(in)	*11B*
to complete a deal	Vertrag abschließen	*11B*
medical record	ärztliche Unterlagen, Krankenakte	*11B*
confident	zuversichtlich	*11B*
privacy concern	Vorbehalt aus Datenschutzgründen	*11B*
wholesale	Gruppenversicherung	*11B*
insurance broker	Versicherungsbüro, Versicherungsmakler(in)	*11B*
simplicity	einfache Struktur	*11B*
background check	Kontrolluntersuchung	*11B*
regulatory approval	staatliche Genehmigung	*11B*
permission	Genehmigung	*11B*

90

to speed up	beschleunigen	*11.7*
burglary	Einbruchdiebstahl	*11.8*
discount	Rabatt, Nachlass	*11.8*

91

in conjunction with	in Verbindung mit, wegen	*11.9*
renewal	Verlängerung	*11.9*
to maintain	aufrechterhalten	*11.9*
to make payable to	(Scheck) ausstellen auf	*11.9*
renewal premium	Prämie bei Vertragsverlängerung	*11.9*
rate increase	Tariferhöhung	*11.9*
survey	Vergleich der Konditionen	*11.9*
to enclose	beifügen	*11.9*
renewal papers	Unterlagen für die Policenverlängerung	*11.9*
sum insured	Versicherungssumme	*11.9*
adjustment	Korrektur, Anpassung	*11.9*
item	(Wert)Gegenstand	*11.9*
adequate	ausreichend	*11.9*
service charge	Bearbeitungsgebühr	*11.9*

92

to acknowledge	bestätigen	*11.10*
to purchase	kaufen, erwerben	*11.10*
the deceased	verstorben	*11 Gr*
unemployment benefit	Arbeitslosengeld	*11.11*
to contribute	Beiträge entrichten	*11.11*
social security	Sozialversicherung	*11.11*
to be entitled to	Anspruch haben auf	*11.11*
sum assured	Versicherungssumme	*11.11*
to opt for	sich entscheiden für, wählen	*11.11*
ultimately	letztlich	*11.11*
relief	Fürsorge, Unterstützung	*11.11*
cover note	Deckungsbestätigung	*11.11*
eventuality	Eventualfall	*11.11*

Unit 12 Forms of business organization

93

business organization	Unternehmensform	*12*
abbreviation	Abkürzung	*12*
survey	Übersicht	*12A*
sole trader	Einzelunternehmer(in), Einzelkaufmann/-frau	*12A*
sole proprietor	Einzelunternehmer(in), Einzelkaufmann/-frau	*12A*
partnership	(Personen)Gesellschaft	*12A*
general partnership	offene Handelsgesellschaft (OHG)	*12A*
deed of partnership	Gesellschaftsvertrag	*12A*

allocation	Verteilung	*12A*

94

unincorporated	nicht eingetragen	*12A*
incorporated	eingetragen	*12A*
private limited company (Ltd)	Gesellschaft mit beschränkter Haftung (GmbH)	*12A*
shareholder	Anteilseigner, Aktionär(in), Gesellschafter(in)	*12A*
public limited company (plc)	Aktiengesellschaft (AG)	*12A*
limited partnership	Kommanditgesellschaft (KG)	*12A*
consent	Zustimmung	*12A*
respective	jeweilig	*12A*
stake	Anteil	*12A*
Registrar of Companies [GB]	Handelsregister	*12A*
certificate of incorporation	handelsregistergerichtliche Eintragungsurkunde	*12A*
distinct legal entity	juristische Person	*12A*
to sue	klagen, gerichtlich verfolgen	*12A*
chairperson	Vorsitzende(r)	*12A*
non-executive	ohne Geschäftsbereich, Aufsichts-	*12A*
chief executive	Vorstandsvorsitzende(r)	*12A*
to file with	hinterlegen bei	*12A*
listed	(börsen)notiert	*12A*
stock exchange	Börse	*12A*
prospectus	Börsen(zulassungs)prospekt, Subskriptionsanzeige	*12A*
to subscribe	zeichnen	*12A*
official list	Verzeichnis börsengängiger Wertpapiere	*12A*
bidder	Bieter	*12A*
cooperative society	Genossenschaft	*12A*
friendly society	Unterstützungskasse, gemeinnütziger Verein	*12A*
non-profit-making	nicht gewinnorientiert	*12A*
mutual organization	Organisation auf Gegenseitigkeit	*12A*
building society	Bausparkasse	*12A*
public-sector	öffentlich, Staats-	*12A*
NHS (National Health Service)	Nationaler Gesundheitsdienst	*12A*
BBC (British Broadcasting Corporation)	öffentlich-rechtliche britische Rundfunkgesellschaft	*12A*

95

body	Körperschaft	*12.1*
to inherit	erben	*12.2*
construction business	Bauunternehmen	*12.2*
redundant	arbeitslos	12.2

96

annual general meeting (AGM)	(Jahres)Hauptversammlung (HV)	*12.3*
board	Vorstand und Aufsichtsrat	*12.3*
chairwoman	Aufsichtsratsvorsitzende	*12.3*
close corporation	Gesellschaft mit beschränkter Haftung (GmbH)	*12.3*
supervisory board	Aufsichtsrat	*12.3*
quoted	(börsen)notiert	*12.3*
open corporation	Aktiengesellschaftt (AG)	*12.3*
to discharge	entlasten	*12.3*

97

notice	Ankündigung	*12.5*
resolution	Entschließung, Beschluss	*12.5*
auditor	Buchprüfungsunternehmen, Wirtschaftsprüfer(in), Wirtschaftsprüfungsgesellschaft	*12.5*
ordinary share	Stammaktie	*12.5*
provision	Bestimmung	*12.5*
Companies Act	Aktiengesetz	*12.5*
remuneration	Vergütung	*12.5*
company secretary	Justitiar(in) und Generalbevollmächtigte(r)	*12.5*
entitled to	berechtigt zu	*12.5*
proxy	Stellvertreter(in)	*12.5*

98

estimate	Schätzung	*12B*
troubled	in Schwierigkeiten befindlich	*12B*
to inspire	auslösen, hervorrufen	*12B*
leap	Sprung	*12B*
quarter	Quartal	*12B*
stock	Aktie	*12B*
operating performance	Betriebsleistung	*12B*
ahead of	vor	*12B*
schedule	Plan, Programm	*12B*
to gain ground	Fortschritte machen	*12B*
operating income	Betriebsergebnis	*12B*
first-quarter	im ersten Quartal	*12B*
execution	Durchführung	*12B*
to slacken	nachlassen	*12B*
to use up	aufbrauchen, aufzehren	*12B*
to undermine	untergraben	*12B*
chief operating officer	technischer Vorstand	*12B*
to stick by	festhalten an	*12B*
gross	brutto	*12B*
operating margin	Gewinnspanne	*12B*
high-end	hochwertig, im oberen Marktsegment	*12B*
to concede	zugeben, eingestehen	*12B*
challenging	anspruchsvoll, schwierig	*12B*
to prevent	abwehren, verhindern	*12B*
disposal	Verkauf	*12B*
stock in hand	Warenlager, Warenbestand	*12.6*

99

to edge up/down	leicht steigen/fallen	*12 V*
to weaken	sich abschwächen	*12 V*
gradual	allmählich	*12 V*
moderate	mäßig	*12 V*

100

factual	tatsächlich	*12 Gr*
unlikely	unwahrscheinlich	*12 Gr*
improbability	Unwahrscheinlichkeit	*12 Gr*
to reject	ablehnen	*12 Gr*
to propose	vorschlagen	*12 Gr*
irregularity	Unregelmäßigkeit	*12.10*
bankruptcy	Bankrott	*12.10*
sufficiently	genügend	*12.10*
to file for	beantragen	*12.10*
to step down	zurücktreten	*12.10*
to dismiss	entlassen	*12.10*
competitor	Konkurrent(in), Wettbewerber(in)	*12.10*

Unit 13 Money and markets

102

stock market	(Aktien)Börse	*13A*
mystique	etw. Mystisches/ Geheimnisvolles	*13A*
high-powered	anspruchsvoll	*13A*
marketmaker	Marktmacher(in)	*13A*
stallholder	Standinhaber(in)	*13A*
stockbroker	Börsenmakler(in)	*13A*
security	Wertpapier	*13A*
equity	Aktie	*13A*
bond	Anleihe, Obligation	*13A*
share dealer	Aktienhändler(in)	*13A*
debts	Schulden, Verschuldung	*13A*
shareholding	Aktienbesitz	*13A*
part-owner	Teilinhaber(in)	*13A*
to exercise a right	Recht ausüben	*13A*
to share in	beteiligt sein an	*13A*
dividend	Dividende	*13A*

103

bull	Haussespekulant, Haussier, Bulle	*13A*
bear	Baissespekulant, Baissier, Bär	*13A*
price	(Aktien)Kurs	*13A*
bull market	haussierender Markt, Markt mit steigenden Kursen	*13A*
to anticipate	erwarten	*13A*
bear market	Markt mit fallenden Kursen	*13A*
floor trading	Parketthandel	*13A*
to be a thing of the past	der Vergangenheit angehören	*13A*
fraction of what it costs	Bruchteil der Kosten	*13A*
technology stock market	Technologiebörse	*13A*
to serve as	fungieren als, die Rolle einnehmen von	*13A*
middleman	Mittelsperson, Mittler	*13A*
trading room	Börsensaal	*13A*
drive	Offensive, Aktion	*13A*
inconceivable	unvorstellbar	*13A*
virtual trading	virtueller Handel	*13A*
volatility	Kursschwankungen, Kursausschläge	*13A*
dealing	(Börsen)Handel	*13A*
margin	Handelsspanne, Gewinnspanne	*13A*
expertise	Sachkenntnis, Fachwissen	*13A*
online trading	Internet-Handel	*13A*
blue chip	Standardwert, Standardaktie	*13.4*
futures market	Terminmarkt	*13.4*
gilt	Staatsanleihe	*13.4*
hedging	Kurssicherung	*13.4*
initial public offering (IPO)	Börsengang, Erstemission	*13.4*
price-earnings ratio (p/e)	Kurs-Gewinnverhältnis (KGV)	*13.4*
unit trust	Investmentfonds	*13.4*
yield	Rendite	*13.4*
to glitter	glänzen, funkeln	*13.4*
going public	Börsengang	*13.4*

104

for once	ausnahmsweise	*13.4*
slice	Stück, Scheibe	*13.4*
fund manager	Fondsmanager(in), Fondsverwalter(in)	*13.4*
contract	(Termin)Kontrakt	*13.4*
indication	Hinweis, Anzeichen	*13.6*
uptrend	Aufwärtstrend	*13.6*
corporate bond	Unternehmensanleihe	*13.6*
government bond	Staatsanleihe	*13.6*
speculative investment	spekulative Anlage (form)	*13.6*
unit price	Preis pro Anteil, Anteilspreis	*13.6*
oil future	Ölterminkontrakt	*13.6*
stockpile	Vorrat, Lagerbestand	13.6
to rocket	stark ansteigen	*13 V*
to shoot up	in die Höhe schnellen	*13 V*
to surge	steil ansteigen	*13 V*
to peak	höchsten Punkt erreichen	*13 V*

105

to plummet	stark fallen	*13 V*
to plunge	stark fallen	*13 V*
to (nose)dive	abstürzen	*13 V*
to slump	stark fallen	*13 V*
to slip	leicht nachgeben	*13 V*
to dip	leicht nachgeben	*13 V*
to slide	nachgeben	*13 V*
to bottom out	tiefsten Punkt erreichen	*13 V*
at midsession	nach der ersten Hälfte des Handelstages	*13.7*

106

volatile	(stark) schwankend	*13 V*
erratic movement	Schwankung(en) nach beiden Seiten	*13 V*
modest/good gains	leichter/beträchtlicher Anstieg, leichter/ ansehnlicher Gewinn	*13 V*

short-lived	von kurzer Dauer, kurzlebig	*13 V*
to stage a rally	(Kurs) sich erholen	*13 V*
underlying trend	Grundtendenz	*13 V*
to go about one's business	seinen Pflichten nachgehen, sich um seine Geschäfte kümmern	*13B*
to bring down	unter Kontrolle bringen	*13B*
to earn sb's respect	jdm Achtung/Anerkennung einbringen	*13B*
Federal Reserve Board	US-Zentralbank	*13B*
European Central Bank (ECB)	Europäische Zentralbank (EZB)	*13B*
money supply	Geldmenge	*13B*
recession	Rezession, Konjunkturrückgang	*13B*
monetary policy	Geldpolitik	*13B*
statutory goal	gesetzlich verankertes Ziel	*13B*
economic growth	Wirtschaftswachstum, konjunkturelles Wachstum	*13B*
to pursue a policy	Politik verfolgen	*13B*
interest rate	Zinssatz	*13B*
discount rate	Diskontsatz	*13B*
commercial paper	Handelspapier, Finanzwechsel	*13B*

107

bill of exchange	Wechsel	*13B*
government security	Staatsanleihe	*13B*
vice versa	umgekehrt	*13B*
customer deposits	Kundeneinlagen, Kundengelder	*13B*
to engage in	sich beteiligen an	*13B*
open market operation	Offenmarkt-Geschäft	*13B*
top priority	wichtigstes Ziel	*13.10*
to secure	gewährleisten	*13.10*
monetary policy goal	geldpolitisches Ziel	*13.10*
corporate investment	Investitionen der Firmen	*13.10*

108

corporate earnings	Unternehmensgewinne	*13.11*
to weigh down	drücken, belasten	*13.11*
dotcom sector	Markt für Internetunternehmen	*13.11*
IPO market collapse	Zusammenbruch des Marktes für Börsenneulinge	*13.11*
at the close of trading	zum Ende der Börsensitzung	*13.11*
to recede	nachlassen	*13.11*
inflationary pressure	Inflationsdruck	*13.11*

109

core rate	Kern(zins)satz	*13.12*
rate cut	Zinssenkung	*13.12*
monetary easing	kreditpolitische Lockerung	*13.12*
underlying rate of inflation	Kerninflationsrate	*13.12*
retail price inflation	Inflationsrate der Einzelhandelspreise	*13.12*
mortgage interest payment	Hypothekenzins(zahlung)	*13.12*
Office for National Statistics	Zentrales Amt für Statistik, Statistisches (Bundes)Amt	*13.12*
quarter-point	um einen Viertelpunkt	*13.12*
mortgage lender	Hypothekenbank	*13.12*
to be set to be sth	auf dem besten Weg sein, etwas zu werden	*13.12*
core inflation	Kerninflation	*13.12*

Unit 14 Taxation

110

to levy	erheben	*14A*
to fund	finanzieren	*14A*
welfare	Sozialfürsorge	*14A*
to bring about	hervorbringen	*14A*
income tax	Einkommenssteuer	*14A*
corporation tax	Körperschaftssteuer	*14A*
sales tax	Umsatzsteuer	*14A*
value-added tax (VAT)	Mehrwertsteuer (MwSt.)	*14A*
to cite	anführen, nennen	*14A*
to be required to	verpflichtet sein	*14A*
burden	Last	*14A*
to shift	abwälzen	*14A*
pump price	Tankstellenpreis	*14A*
fuel tax	Treibstoffsteuer	*14A*
to be subject to	(Steuer) unterliegen	*14A*
exemption	Befreiung	*14A*
deduction	(Steuer)Abzug	*14A*
effectively	faktisch, effektiv	*14A*
taxable	zu versteuernd, steuerpflichtig	*14A*
rate structure	(Steuer)Tarifstruktur	*14A*
tax band	Tarifstufe	*14A*
income bracket	Einkommenssteuerstufe, Einkommenshöhe	*14A*
by way of	als, durch	*14A*
tax liability	Steuerschuld	*14A*
to file	einreichen	*14A*
joint return	gemeinsame Steuererklärung	*14A*
retirement income	Ruhestandsbezüge	*14A*
tax-exempted	steuerbefreit	*14A*
threshold	Schwelle	*14A*

111

tax base	Besteuerungsgrundlage	*14A*
expense	Kosten	*14A*
to incur	(Kosten) entstehen	*14A*
to be liable for	(Steuer) pflichtig sein, unterliegen	*14A*
tax regime	Steuersystem	*14A*
depreciation	Abschreibung, Wertminderung	*14A*
deductible	abzugsfähig, absetzbar	*14A*
to write off	(vollständig) abschreiben	*14A*
excise duty	Verbrauchssteuer	*14A*

revenue-raising	Einnahmen einbringend	*14A*
to facilitate	erleichtern, ermöglichen	*14A*
cascading tax	Allphasenumsatzsteuer	*14A*
to operate	funktionieren	*14A*
commercial rate	Gewerbesteuer	*14A*
inheritance tax	Erbschaftssteuer	*14A*
capital transfer tax [GB]	Erbschafts- und Schenkungssteuer	*14A*
spread	Verteilung	*14.1*
tax take	Steueraufkommen	*14.1*
to set off	absetzen	*14.1*
real estate	Immobilien	*14.1*
local authority	Kommunalbehörde	*14.1*

112

nursery school	Kindergarten	*14.2*
fire service	Feuerwehr	*14.2*
allowance	Freibetrag	*14.3*
joint income	gemeinsames Einkommen	*14.3*
way below	erheblich unter	*14 Info*
bottling machine	Abfüllmaschine	*14 Info*
input tax	Vorsteuer	*14 Info*
sole	einzig	*14 Info*
output tax	Umsatzsteuer	*14 Info*
accounting department	Buchhaltungsabteilung	*14 Info*

113

to sell up	(alles) verkaufen	*14B*
non-resident	Nichtansässige(r)	*14B*
exempt from	befreit von	*14B*
to undertake	leisten	*14B*
to rent out	vermieten	*14B*
expatriate	im Ausland lebende(r) Staatsbürger(in)	*14B*
maintenance expense	Unterhaltungskosten	*14B*
consecutive	aufeinander folgend	*14B*
Revenue	Steuerbehörde	*14B*
to be domiciled	Wohnsitz haben	*14B*
double taxation agreement	Doppelbesteuerungs-abkommen	*14B*
to forfeit	verlieren, verlustig gehen	*14B*
pension contribution	Rentenbeitrag	*14B*
eligibility	Berechtigung, Anspruch	*14B*
tax-saving scheme	Steuersparplan, Steuersparmodell	*14B*

114

Inland Revenue [GB]	Steuerbehörde	*14.6*
earned income	Einkommen aus nicht-selbstständiger Arbeit	*14.6*
rental income	Mieteinkünfte	*14.6*
to stand to do sth	wohl etwas tun	*14.6*
mere	bloß	*14 V*

115

council tax [GB]	Kommunalsteuer	*14.7*
National Insurance [GB]	Sozialversicherung	*14.7*
income security [US]	Ruhegeldsicherung	*14.8*
Medicare [US]	staatliche Krankenversicherung für Bürger über 65 Jahre	*14.8*
national defence	Landesverteidigung	*14.8*
countable	zählbar	*14 Gr*
tax adviser	Steuerberater(in)	*14 Gr*
to foot the bill	die Zeche bezahlen	*14 Gr*
to collect	einnehmen	*14 Gr*
hooked	gefangen	*14.9*
to complete	ausfüllen	*14.9*
tax evasion	Steuerhinterziehung	*14.9*

116

tax haven	Steuerparadies	*14.9*
tax dodge	Trick zur Steuerumgehung	*14.9*
tax shelter	Steueroase	*14.9*
tax loophole	Steuerschlupfloch	*14.9*

Unit 15 The environment

117

carbon dioxide	Kohlendioxid	*15*
climate change	Klimawandel	*15*
global warming	Erderwärmung	*15*
ozone layer	Ozonschicht	*15*
emission	Ausstoß	*15*
fossil fuel	nicht erneuerbarer Brennstoff	*15*
greenhouse effect	Treibhauseffekt	*15*

118

business	Wirtschaft	*15A*
environmental issue	Umweltfrage, Umweltproblem	*15A*
permanent part	fester Bestandteil	*15A*
agenda	Tagesordnung	*15A*
build-up	Anstieg	*15A*
atmospheric	in der Erdatmosphäre	*15A*
implication	Auswirkung	*15A*
diminution	Verringerung, Abbau	*15A*
protective	Schutz-	*15A*
CFC gas	FCKW-Gas	*15A*
chlorofluorocarbon	Fluorchlorkohlenwasserstoff	*15A*
aerosol	Spraydose	*15A*
to phase out	auslaufen lassen	*15A*
habitat	Lebensraum	*15A*
logging	Holzeinschlag, Holzernte	*15A*
extinction	Auslöschung	*15A*
species	Tier- und Pflanzenart	*15A*
scientist	Wissenschaftler(in), Experte, Expertin	*15A*
harmful	schädlich, umweltschädigend	*15A*
to minimize	minimieren, auf ein Minimum reduzieren	*15A*
mankind	Menschheit	*15A*
footprint	Spur, Einwirkung	*15A*
environmental audit	Umweltanalyse	*15A*

to interact with	wechselseitig einwirken auf	*15A*
review	Bestandsaufnahme	*15A*
life cycle	Lebenszyklus(dauer)	*15A*
to research	erforschen	*15A*
component	Bestandteil	*15A*
waste	Abfall, Müll	*15A*
waste disposal	Abfallentsorgung	*15A*
profit opportunity	Gewinnchance	*15A*
waste product	Abfallprodukt	*15A*
savings on materials	Materialeinsparung	*15A*
waste reduction	Abfallreduzierung, Abfallminimierung	*15A*
recycling	Recycling, Wiederverwertung	*15A*
profit potential	Gewinnchance, Gewinnmöglichkeit	*15A*
to recycle	recyceln, wieder verwerten	*15A*
to reuse	wieder verwenden	*15A*
environmental image	Ansehen wegen umweltgerechten Verhaltens	*15A*
energy source	Energiequelle	*15A*
power source	Energiequelle, Treibstoffquelle	*15A*
emphasis	Gewicht, Betonung	*15A*
environmental footprint	Umweltfolgen	*15A*
to shape strategies	Strategien beeinflussen	*15A*
constraint	Zwang	*15A*
to impose	auferlegen	*15A*
dependence	Abhängigkeit	*15A*
to uncover	entdecken, aufdecken	*15A*
by-product	Nebenerzeugnis, Nebenprodukt	*15A*

119

non-labour costs	nicht lohnbezogene Kosten	*15.2*
to eliminate	ausschalten, beseitigen	*15.4*
corporate decision-making	unternehmerische Entscheidungsprozesse	*15.4*
vehicle emissions	Fahrzeugemissionen	*15.4*
energy efficiency	bestmögliche Energienutzung	*15.4*
non-renewable	nicht erneuerbar	*15.4*
pollutant	Schadstoff	*15.4*
refrigeration plant	Kühlanlage	*15.4*

120

heap	Haufen	*15B*
rubbish	Abfall	*15B*
trash	Abfall, Müll	*15B*
topsy-turvy	auf den Kopf gestellt	*15B*
economics of waste	Theorie der Abfallwirtschaft	*15B*
roundabout	Karussell	*15B*
phenomenal	sagenhaft, unglaublich	*15B*
wasteful	verschwenderisch	*15B*
trashing	Abfallproduktion	*15B*
consumption	Verbrauch	*15B*
pollution	Umweltverschmutzung	*15B*
tremendous	riesig, enorm	*15B*
landfill site	(Abfall)Deponie, Deponiestandort	*15B*
plastic-seeming	plastikähnlich	*15B*
in their backyard	vor der Haustür	*15B*
to emit	abgeben	*15B*
methane	Methan(gas)	*15B*
to leak	Flüssigkeit abgeben, nicht dicht sein	*15B*
ominous	bedrohlich	*15B*
to dump	abkippen, abladen	*15B*
to incinerate	verbrennen	*15B*
air pollution	Luftverschmutzung	*15B*
to release	freisetzen	*15B*
toxin	Giftstoff	*15B*
to raise the alert	Alarm schlagen	*15B*
to respond	reagieren	*15B*
to alter	(ver)ändern	*15B*
to creep up	langsam ansteigen	*15B*
household waste	Haushaltsmüll	*15B*
mindshift	Sinneswandel	*15B*
to take the lid off	Deckel abnehmen	*15B*
rubbish bin	Mülltonne	*15B*
to tackle a problem	Problem angehen	*15B*
beast	(wildes) Tier	*15B*
bin	Tonne, Abfalleimer	*15B*

121

beneficial	vorteilhaft, nützlich	*15.5*
residues	Rückstände, Reststoffe	*15.5*
stench	Gestank	*15.5*
layer	Schicht	*15.5*
to dispose of	entsorgen	*15.5*
irresponsible	unverantwortlich	*15.5*
domestic waste	Haushaltsabfälle	*15.5*
incinerator	Verbrennungsanlage	*15.7*
garbage	Abfall, Müll	*15.7*

122

to expel	ausstoßen, verstoßen	*15.8*
suitability	Eignung	*15.9*

123

nuisance	Belästigung, Ärgernis	*15.10*
to mend one's way	sich bessern	*15.10*
noxious	(umwelt)schädlich	*15.10*
to assess	messen, bewerten	*15.11*
depletion	Ausschöpfung, Verringerung	*15.11*
natural resources	natürliche Rohstoffe	*15.11*
competitive advantage	Wettbewerbsvorteil	*15.11*
to name and shame	öffentlich brandmarken	*15.11*

124

smelting plant	(Schmelz)Hütte	*15.12*
deadly toxic	hochgiftig	*15.12*
smelter	(Schmelz)Hütte	*15.12*
versus	gegen	*15.12*
credible	glaubwürdig	*15.12*
federation of car dealers	Verband der Autohändler	*15.12*

airports authority	Flughafenbehörde	*15.12*
road haulage association	Straßengüterverkehrsverband	*15.12*
railway transport group	Interessenvertretung der Bahn	*15.12*
association of bus companies	Verband der Busunternehmer	*15.12*

Unit 16 The European Union

125

customs union	Zollunion	*16A*
common external tariff	gemeinsamer Außenzoll(tarif)	*16A*
transit country	Transitland, Durchgangsland	*16A*

126

based	ansässig	*16A*
to shelter	schützen	*16A*
incentive	Anreiz	*16A*
market share	Marktanteil	*16A*
to outweigh	aufwiegen	*16A*
dispatch	Versand	*16.1*

127

European Coal and Steel Community (ECSC)	Montanunion, Europäische Gemeinschaft für Kohle und Stahl (EGKS)	*16.3*
Treaty of Rome	römische Verträge	*16.3*
European Economic Community (EEC)	Europäische Wirtschaftsgemeinschaft (EWG)	*16.3*
Common Agricultural Policy	gemeinsame Agrarpolitik	*16.3*
Eire	Irland	*16.3*
to take a turn	eine Wendung nehmen	*16.3*
accession	Beitritt	*16.3*
Single Market	einheitlicher Markt	*16.3*
border control	Grenzkontrolle	*16.3*
agreement	Vertrag, Übereinkunft	*16.3*
to materialize	sich bewahrheiten	*16.3*
to envisage	planen, beabsichtigen	*16.3*
persuasion	Überzeugung, Ausrichtung	*16.3*

128

budget	Haushalt	*16.4*
to draft	entwerfen	*16.4*
to implement	(Gesetz) umsetzen	*16.4*
co-decision	Mitbestimmung	*16.4*
to legislate	Gesetze verabschieden	*16.4*
operation	Funktionieren	*16.4*
suffrage	Wahlrecht	*16.4*
budgetary	Haushalts-	*16.4*
Council of the European Union	Europarat	*16.4*
Council of Ministers	Ministerrat	*16.4*
decision-making	entscheidungsfindend, Entscheidungs-	*16.4*
to conclude	(Verträge) abschließen	*16.4*
foreign affairs	Außenpolitik	*16.4*
executive body	Exekutive, Exekutivorgan	*16.4*
Court of Justice	Gerichtshof	*16.4*
uniformly	einheitlich	*16.4*
Court of Auditors	Rechnungshof	*16.4*
sound	solide	*16.4*

130

way ahead	weit voraus	*16.6*

131

mobility	Mobilität, Flexibilität	*16B*
to be in place	gültig sein, vorhanden sein	*16B*
to rally behind	unterstützen	*16B*
to dismantle	abbauen	*16B*
compatible	vereinbar, kompatibel	*16B*
new-economy	neu, hochmodern	*16B*
skills gap	Facharbeitermangel	*16B*
divergence	Unterschied	*16B*
one-size-fits-all	Einheits-, Standard-	*16B*
to exacerbate	verschärfen	*16B*
builder	Bauunternehmer, Bauunternehmen	*16B*
to flock	in Scharen reisen	*16B*
reversal	Umkehrung	*16B*
flow	(Wanderungs)Strom	*16B*
bilateral	zweiseitig, bilateral	*16B*
to smooth out	beseitigen, glätten	*16B*
tax barrier	Steuerhemmnis	*16B*
supplementary	Zusatz-, zusätzlich	*16B*
portable	übertragbar	*16B*
recognition	Anerkennung	*16B*
deterrent	Abschreckung	*16B*
bother	Unannehmlichkeit	*16B*
selective	wählerisch	*16B*
onus	Last, Verpflichtung	*16B*
adaptable	anpassungsfähig	*16B*
rootlessness	Wurzellosigkeit	*16B*
dependency	Abhängigkeit	*16B*

132

transferable	übertragbar	*16.8*
unique	einzigartig	*16.12*
treaty-based	auf Verträgen basierend	*16.12*
to establish	einrichten, etablieren	*16.12*
novel	neuartig	*16.12*
sovereignty	Souveränität	*16.12*

Alphabetical word list

A

abbreviation *Abkürzung* 12 ■ **93**
abolition *Abschaffung* 9B ■ **72**
access *Zugang* 3.10 ■ **25**
accessible *zugänglich* 1B ■ **10**
accession *Beitritt* 16.3 ■ **127**
accessories *Zubehör* 11.2 ■ **88**
accidental damage *Unfallschaden* 11.2 ■ **88**
accommodation *Unterkunft, Unterbringung* 3A ■ **20**
accordance: in accordance with *je nach* 11A ■ **87**; *entsprechend* 12.5 ■ **97**
to account for *ausmachen, auf … entfallen* 2A ■ **14**; *der Grund sein für* 7A ■ **51**
account statement *Kontoauszug* 4A ■ **27**
accounting department *Buchhaltungsabteilung* 14 Info ■ **112**
accounts dept *Buchhaltung(sabteilung)* 5B ■ **38**
to accumulate *ansammeln* 1 Info ■ **9**
to achieve *erreichen* 1.2 ■ **8**
to acknowledge *zugestehen, anerkennen* 10B ■ **82**; *bestätigen* 11.10 ■ **92**
to acquire *erwerben* 1B ■ **10**
acquisition *Erwerb* 7B ■ **55**
acre *0,4 Hektar* 7A ■ **50**
across the state border *jenseits der Staatsgrenze* 4B ■ **31**
actuary *Versicherungsmathematiker(in)* 11A ■ **87**
to adapt *sich anpassen* 8A ■ **60**
adaptable *anpassungsfähig* 16B ■ **131**
adequate *ausreichend* 11.9 ■ **91**
adjustment *Korrektur, Anpassung* 11.9 ■ **91**
administration *Verwaltungsarbeiten* 5B ■ **38**
to adopt *einführen* 9B ■ **72**
to advance *aufsteigen* 6.1 ■ **44**
advance: in advance *im Voraus* 3B ■ **23**
adverse *widrig* 7.2. ■ **52**
advertising campaign *Werbekampagne* 8.4 ■ **61**
advertising effort *Werbekampagne* 3.4 ■ **22**
advertising space *Werbefläche* 1B ■ **10**
advisory *beratend* 9.2 ■ **70**
aerosol *Spraydose* 15A ■ **118**
aerospace *Luft- und Raumfahrt* 9A ■ **69**
aerospace equipment *Erzeugnisse der Luft- und Raumfahrtindustrie* 2A ■ **14**
to affect *beeinflussen* 1.1 ■ **8**
affected: to be affected *beeinträchtigt werden* 7.9 ■ **56**
after-sales complaint *Reklamation* 5.8 ■ **40**
agency *Agentur* 5 ■ **35**
agency interview *Auswahlgespräch in der Stellenvermittlungsagentur* 5.3 ■ **37**
agenda *Tagesordnung* 15A ■ **118**
agent *(Versicherungs)Vertreter(in)* 11B ■ **89**
agrarian society *Agrargesellschaft* 1A ■ **8**
agreement *Vertrag, Übereinkunft* 16.3 ■ **127**
agriculture *Landwirtschaft* 1.2 ■ **8**
ahead of *vor* 12B ■ **98; in the years ahead** *in den nächsten Jahren* 3B ■ **23**
aid to trade *kommerzielle Dienstleistung* 1.3 ■ **9**
air container *Luftfrachtcontainer* 10 Info ■ **84**
air crash *Flugzeugabsturz* 11A ■ **87**
air pollution *Luftverschmutzung* 15B ■ **120**
airborne freight *Luftfracht* 10 Info ■ **84**
aircraft *Flugzeug* 9.9 ■ **74**
airports authority *Flughafenbehörde* 15.12 ■ **124**
aisle *Gang* 7.6 ■ **53**
alert: to raise the alert *Alarm schlagen* 15B ■ **120**
all-inclusive *Pauschal-, Global-* 11A ■ **87**
to allocate *aufwenden* 10.12 ■ **83**
allocation *Verteilung* 12A ■ **93**
allowance *Freibetrag* 14.3 ■ **112**
to alter *(ver)ändern* 15B ■ **120**
ambitious *ehrgeizig; gewagt* 2B ■ **16**
ambulance *Krankentransport* 8.4 ■ **61**
analyst *Analyst(in)* 2B ■ **16**
animal feedstock *Futtermittel* 10B ■ **82**
to announce *ankündigen* 5.8 ■ **40**
announcement *Bekanntmachung* 3.10 ■ **25**
annual *jährlich* 3.6 ■ **24**
annual general meeting (AGM) *(Jahres)Hauptversammlung (HV)* 12.3 ■ **96**
answerphone *Anrufbeantworter* 7.12 ■ **57**
to anticipate *vorwegnehmen* 8A ■ **60**; *erwarten* 13A ■ **103**
apathy *Gleichgültigkeit* 8.4 ■ **61**
appealing *anziehend* 8B ■ **64**
applicant *Bewerber(in)* 1 Gr ■ **12**; *Antragsteller(in)* 11B ■ **89**
application *Antrag* 4A ■ **28**
to apply *beantragen* 4A ■ **28**
to apply for *sich bewerben um* 5.7 ■ **39**
to apply to *gelten für* 4.9 ■ **32**
approach *Methode* 1.7 ■ **11**
approach channel *Zufahrt* 10B ■ **82**
appropriate *passend* 8.4 ■ **61**; *angemessen, angebracht* 11A ■ **87**
approval *Annahme* 11B ■ **89**
to approve *genehmigen, zustimmen, gewähren* 4A ■ **28**
approximately *ungefähr, annähernd* 2A ■ **14**
to argue *die Meinung vertreten* 5A ■ **36**
army careers office *Stellenvermittlung der brit. Armee* 5 ■ **35**
arrangement *Vereinbarung; Möglichkeit* 4A ■ **28**
articulated vehicle *Gelenkfahrzeug, Sattelschlepper* 10 Info 2 ■ **84**

arts programme *Kulturprogramm* 6.1 ■ **44**
ASAP (as soon as possible) *sofort* 5.10 ■ **40**
aside from *neben, außer* 2B ■ **16**
assembly line *Montageband* 10.6 ■ **81**
assembly-line worker *Fließbandarbeiter(in)* 1.3 ■ **9**
to assess *messen, bewerten* 15.11 ■ **123**
asset *Vermögenswert* 9 Info ■ **74**
to assist *unterstützen, helfen* 2B ■ **16**
assistant courier *Mitarbeiter(in) in der Reiseleitung* 5B ■ **38**
associate *verbinden, assoziieren* 1.7 ■ **11**
association of bus companies *Verband der Busunternehmer* 15.12 ■ **124**
atmospheric *in der Erdatmosphäre* 15A ■ **118**
to attempt *versuchen* 11.2 ■ **88**
attitude *Haltung* 2B ■ **16**
to attract traffic *Kunden gewinnen* 10.9 ■ **83**
attribute *Eigenschaft* 5A ■ **36**
to attribute to *zurückführen auf* 3.4 ■ **22**
auditor *Buchprüfungsunternehmen, Wirtschaftsprüfer(in), Wirtschaftsprüfungsgesellschaft* 12.5 ■ **97**
authenticity *Echtheit* 8B ■ **64**
to authorize *bevollmächtigen* 4.1 ■ **28**
automaking *Automobilherstellung* 1.3 ■ **9**
automobile insurance *Kfz-Versicherung* 11A ■ **87**
automotive part(s) *Automobilzubehör, Autozulieferteil(e)* 10A ■ **78**
availability *Verfügbarkeit* 1 Info ■ **9**
available *verfügbar* 1A ■ **8**; **to make available** *bereit stellen* 8.3 ■ **61**
aviation *Luftfahrt* 9A ■ **69**
to await *bis zu(r, m)* 10.7 ■ **81**

B

background check *Kontrolluntersuchung* 11B ■ **89**
backyard: in their backyard *vor der Haustür* 15B ■ **120**
bacon *Speck* 7.7 ■ **54**
balance *Saldo* 4A ■ **28**
balance of invisible trade *Dienstleistungsbilanz* 9 Info ■ **74**
balance of payments *Zahlungsbilanz* 9A ■ **69**
balance of visible trade *Handelsbilanz* 9 Info ■ **74**
balance on current account *Leistungsbilanz* 9 Info ■ **74**
balance on financial and capital account *Kapitalbilanz* 9 Info ■ **74**
to balance out *ausgleichen* 2.1 ■ **15**
banking services *Bankdienstleistungen* 4A ■ **27**
bankruptcy *Bankrott* 12.10 ■ **100**
bargain holiday *preisgünstiger Urlaub* 3.10 ■ **25**
barter *Tauschhandel* 1A ■ **7**
based *ansässig* 16A ■ **126**
basic need *Grundbedürfnis* 1A ■ **7**
BBC (British Broadcasting Corporation) *öffentlich-rechtliche britische Rundfunkgesellschaft* 12A ■ **94**
to beam at *richten auf* 3B ■ **23**
to bear *ertragen* 3.4 ■ **22**
bear *Baissespekulant, Baissier, Bär* 13A ■ **103**
bear market *Markt mit fallenden Kursen* 13A ■ **103**
beast *Biest, (wildes) Tier* 15B ■ **120**
behalf: on behalf of *im Namen von* 3.9 ■ **25**
beneficial *vorteilhaft, nützlich* 15.5 ■ **121**
benefit *Nutzen* 6A ■ **44**; *Leistung, Dienst* 8.4 ■ **61**
to benefit *Nutzen ziehen aus, profitieren von* 2A ■ **14**
benefits *Sozialleistungen* 5.10 ■ **40**
better off *besser gestellt* 8B ■ **63**
beverage *Getränk* 9A ■ **69**
bidder *Bieter* 12A ■ **94**
bidding *Angebot(sangabe)* 1B ■ **10**
bilateral *zweiseitig, bilateral* 16.B ■ **131**
bill of exchange *Wechsel* 13B ■ **107**
billboard *Plakatwand* 8.5 ■ **62**
billion (bn) *Milliarde* 9B ■ **72**
bin *Tonne, Abfalleimer* 15B ■ **120**
black market *Schwarzmarkt* 1B ■ **10**
blast furnace *Hochofen* 10B ■ **82**
blood test *Blutuntersuchung* 11B ■ **89**
blue chip *Standardwert, Standardaktie* 13.4 ■ **103**
board *Behörde, Ausschuss* 1 Gr ■ **12**; *Vorstand und Aufsichtsrat* 12.3 ■ **96**
bodily injury *Personenschaden* 11A ■ **87**
body *Körperschaft* 12.1 ■ **95**
bond *Anleihe, Obligation* 13A ■ **102**
bonded warehouse *Zoll(verschluss)lager* 9.4 ■ **71**
booking form *Buchungsformular* 3.8 ■ **24**
to boost *fördern, steigern* 7.9 ■ **56**
border control *Grenzkontrolle* 16.3 ■ **127**
to borrow *Kredit aufnehmen* 4A ■ **28**
to bother *sich die Mühe machen* 7.13 ■ **57**
bother *Unannehmlichkeit* 16B ■ **131**
bottling machine *Abfüllmaschine* 14 Info ■ **112**
to bottom out *tiefsten Punkt erreichen* 13 V ■ **105**
to bounce *(Scheck) platzen lassen* 4B ■ **31**
box wagon *Kastenwagen* 10 Info ■ **84**
branch *Zweigstelle, Filiale* 4A ■ **28**
brand *Marke* 7B ■ **55**
brand differentiation *Markendifferenzierung* 7B ■ **55**
brand name *Markenname* 4B ■ **31**
branding consultancy *Markenberatungsunternehmen* 8B ■ **64**
to break bulk *Sammelladung auflösen, umpacken* 10.6 ■ **80**
to break down *Panne haben* 8.4 ■ **61**
breakdown cover *Pannenschutz* 8.4 ■ **61**
bricklayer *Maurer* 1.3 ■ **9**
bricks and mortar *Stein und Mörtel* 7B ■ **55**
to bring about *hervorbringen* 14A ■ **110**
to bring down *unter Kontrolle bringen* 13B ■ **106**
to bring home *klar machen* 8.4 ■ **61**
to bring into line *angleichen* 4.10 ■ **33**
to broaden *ausweiten* 10A ■ **78**
brochure *Prospekt, Broschüre* 1B ■ **10**
bucket *Eimer* 3A ■ **21**
budget *Haushalt* 16.4 ■ **128**
budgetary *Haushalts-* 16.4 ■ **128**
buffer stocks *Ausgleichsvorräte, Reservelager* 10.6 ■ **80**
builder *Bauunternehmer, Bauunternehmen* 16B ■ **131**

building site *Baustelle* 6.1 ■ **44**
building society *Bausparkasse* 12A ■ **94**
build-up *Anstieg* 15A ■ **118**
bulk cargo *Massengut,* 10 Info ■ **84**
bulk carrier *Massengutfrachter* 10.7 ■ **81**
bulk commodity *Massengut* 10B ■ **82**
bulky *sperrig* 10 Info ■ **84**
bull *Haussespekulant, Haussier, Bulle* 13A ■ **103**
bull market *haussierender Markt, Markt mit steigenden Kursen* 13A ■ **103**
burden *Last* 14A ■ **110**
burglary *Einbruchdiebstahl* 11.8 ■ **90**
business *Wirtschaft* 15A ■ **118**; **to retain business** *Kunden halten* 10B ■ **82**; **to go about one's business** *seinen Pflichten nachgehen, sich um seine Geschäfte kümmern* 13B ■ **106**
business administration *Betriebswirtschaft* 5.14 ■ **42**
business degree *Abschluss/Diplom in Wirtschaftswissenschaften* 6B ■ **47**
business organization *Unternehmensform* 12 ■ **93**
business park *Gewerbepark* 2B ■ **16**
business policy *Gewerbeversicherung* 11A ■ **87**
business transaction *Geschäft(svorgang)* 1A ■ **7**
business trip *Geschäftsreise* 3.11 ■ **26**
by way of *als, durch* 14A ■ **110**
by-product *Nebenerzeugnis, Nebenprodukt* 15A ■ **118**

C

candidate profile *Bewerberprofil* 5.3 ■ **37**
to cannibalize *wegnehmen, ausschlachten* 7B ■ **55**
capital expenditure *Kapitalaufwand* 9.6 ■ **73**
capital goods *Investitionsgüter, Kapitalgüter* 2.7 ■ **17**
capital transfer tax [GB] *Erbschafts- und Schenkungssteuer* 14A ■ **117**
to capture *erfassen* 3B ■ **23**
car rental company *Autoverleihfirma* 3B ■ **23**
carbon dioxide *Kohlendioxid* 15A ■ **117**
car-carrying barge *Binnenschiff für den Autotransport* 10B ■ **82**
care: to take care *sich kümmern* 6B ■ **47**
career *Berufsweg, Berufslaufbahn* 5.7 ■ **39**
career prospects *Aufstiegschancen* 5.12 ■ **41**
cargo airline *Luftfrachtgesellschaft* 10.3 ■ **79**
cargo liner *Linienfrachter* 10 Info ■ **84**
carmaker *Automobilhersteller* 10 Info ■ **81**
carrier *Transportunternehmen, Beförderer* 10A ■ **78**
cascading tax *Allphasenumsatzsteuer* 14A ■ **111**
cash machine *Geldautomat* 4B ■ **31**
cashpoint *Geldautomat* 4A ■ **27**
cattle *Rinder* 2A ■ **14**
cause *Ursache* 10A ■ **78**
cautious *vorsichtig; unverbindlich* 5A ■ **36**
cereal *Frühstückskost (aus Getreide)* 7.7 ■ **54**
certificate of incorporation *handelsregister-gerichtliche Eintragungsurkunde* 12A ■ **94**
CFC gas *FCKW-Gas* 15A ■ **118**
chain *(Laden)Kette* 3A ■ **20**
chain store *Kettenladen* 7.3 ■ **52**
chairman *Aufsichtsratsvorsitzender* 8B ■ **64**
chairperson *Vorsitzende(r)* 12A ■ **94**
chairwoman *Aufsichtsratsvorsitzende* 12.3 ■ **96**
challenge *Herausforderung* 1B ■ **10**
challenging *anspruchsvoll, schwierig* 12B ■ **98**
to change beyond recognition *sich grundlegend ändern* 10.6 ■ **80**
to change ownership *Besitzer wechseln* 4B ■ **31**
to charge *berechnen, belasten mit* 4A ■ **28**
charge: to take charge *Verantwortung übernehmen* 5B ■ **38**
charges *Gebühren* 4A ■ **28**
charity *wohltätige Vereinigung* 8A ■ **60**
charm *Reiz* 6B ■ **47**
to check a reference *Referenz einholen* 5A ■ **36**
checkout *(Supermarkt)Kasse* 7.7 ■ **54**
chemicals *Chemieerzeugnisse* 1.3 ■ **9**
cheque *Scheck* 4A ■ **27**
cheque book *Scheckheft* 4A ■ **28**
cheque counterfoil *Scheckleiste* 4.5 ■ **30**
cheque crossing *Scheckkreuzung* 4.5 ■ **30**
chief economist *Chef-Ökonom(in)* 6A ■ **43**
chief executive *Vorstandsvorsitzende(r)* 12A ■ **94**
chief operating officer *technischer Vorstand* 12B ■ **98**
chief technology officer *technische(r) Leiter(in)* 6A ■ **43**
chlorofluorocarbon (CFC) *Fluorchlorkohlenwasserstoff (FCKW)* 15A ■ **118**
chore *lästige Arbeit* 7.10 ■ **56**
to cite *anführen, nennen* 14A ■ **110**
city break *Städtereise* 3.10 ■ **25**
civil commotion *bürgerliche Unruhe* 11A ■ **87**
claim: to make a claim *Anspruch geltend machen* 11A ■ **87**
to claim *behaupten* 10A ■ **78**
to classify *einstufen* 11.1 ■ **88**
to click to go *auf Start klicken* 3B ■ **23**
client *Kunde, Kundin, Klient(in)* 1B ■ **10**
climate change *Klimawandel* 15A ■ **117**
to clog *verstopfen* 6B ■ **47**
close: at the close of trading *zum Ende der Börsensitzung* 13.11 ■ **108**
close corporation *Gesellschaft mit beschränkter Haftung (GmbH)* 12.3 ■ **96**
co-decision *Mitbestimmung* 16.4 ■ **128**
to coincide with *zusammenfallen mit* 9.3 ■ **70**
to collect *einnehmen* 14 Gr ■ **115**
combine harvester *Mähdrescher* 10.7 ■ **81**
to come down to *hinauslaufen auf* 5A ■ **36**
to come into one's own *Zeigen können/müssen, was man kann* 5A ■ **36**
command *Beherrschung* 6B ■ **47**
commercial *(Radio, Fernsehen) Werbesendung* 5 ■ **35**
commercial: in commercial terms *wirtschaftlich gesehen* 10.5 ■ **80**
commercial bank *Geschäftsbank* 4B ■ **31**
commercial land *Gewerbefläche, Industriegrundstück* 2B ■ **16**
commercial paper *Handelspapier, Finanzwechsel* 13B ■ **106**
commercial rate *Gewerbesteuer* 14A ■ **111**

commercial recruitment agency *private Stellenvermittlungsagentur* 5 ■ **35**
commodity *Rohstoff* 9A ■ **69**; *Produkt* 10 Info ■ **84**
Common Agricultural Policy *Gemeinsame Agrarpolitik* 16.3 ■ **127**
common external tariff *gemeinsamer Außenzoll(tarif)* 16A ■ **125**
Common Market *Gemeinsamer Markt* 9.7 ■ **73**
commonplace *alltäglich* 6B ■ **47**
communicative skills *kommunikative Kompetenz* 5.10 ■ **40**
community bank *örtliche Bank* 4B ■ **31**
Companies Act *Aktiengesetz* 12.5 ■ **97**
company magazine *Firmenzeitschrift* 5.3 ■ **37**
company secretary *Justitiar(in) und Generalbevollmächtigte(r)* 12.5 ■ **97**
compatible *vereinbar, kompatibel* 16.B ■ **131**
competition *Wettbewerb, Konkurrenz* 1 Info ■ **9**
competitive *wettbewerbsfähig, kostengünstig* 10A ■ **78**
competitive advantage *Wettbewerbsvorteil* 15.11 ■ **123**
competitive edge *Wettbewerbsvorsprung* 8.4 ■ **61**
competitive pressure *Wettbewerbsdruck* 10.12 ■ **83**
competitiveness *Wettbewerbsfähigkeit* 4.8 ■ **32**
competitor *Konkurrent(in), Wettbewerber(in)* 12.10 ■ **100**
complaint *Klage, Beschwerde* 4B ■ **31**
to complement *ergänzen, vervollständigen* 10A ■ **78**
complementary *sich ergänzend* 1 Info ■ **9**
to complete *ausfüllen* 14.9 ■ **115**
to complete a deal *Vertrag abschließen* 11B ■ **89**
to complicate *erschweren, schwierig gestalten* 10A ■ **78**
to comply with *erfüllen, einhalten* 4.9 ■ **32**
component *Zubehörteil* 9B ■ **72**; *Bestandteil* 15A ■ **118**
composition *Zusammensetzung* 9A ■ **69**
comprehensive policy *Vollkaskoversicherung* 11A ■ **87**
to comprise *umfassen* 7.4 ■ **52**
computer-literate *mit EDV-Kenntnissen* 5.10 ■ **40**
computer maker *Computerhersteller* 6B ■ **47**
computer-savvy *etwas von Computern verstehend* 6B ■ **47**
to concede *zugeben, eingestehen* 12B ■ **98**
concern *Vorbehalt* 4B ■ **31**
concise *präzise, knapp* 8P ■ **62**
to conclude *(Verträge) abschließen* 16.4 ■ **128**
conclusion *Schluss(folgerung)* 6A ■ **44**
to conduct *durchführen* 1A ■ **7**
confident *zuversichtlich* 11B ■ **89**
confidential *vertraulich* 6.1 ■ **44**
confirmation *Bestätigung* 3.8 ■ **24**
to confuse *verwechseln* 8.3 ■ **61**
Congress *Abgeordnetenhaus und Senat* 4B ■ **31**
conjunction: in conjunction with *in Verbindung mit, wegen* 11.9 ■ **91**
conscientiously *gewissenhaft* 6A ■ **44**
consecutive *aufeinander folgend* 14B ■ **113**
consent *Zustimmung* 12A ■ **94**
conservative *vorsichtig* 3B ■ **23**
consideration *Erwägung* 10.9 ■ **83**
consignee *(Sendungs)Empfänger* 10.3 ■ **79**
consignment *(Waren)Sendung* 10A ■ **78**
consignor *Absender* 10.3 ■ **79**
consistent *beständig* 6.1 ■ **44**
consolidated *gemeinsam, konzertiert* 2B ■ **16**
consolidation *Zusammenschluss* 3A ■ **20**; *Konzentration* 4B ■ **31**
consolidator *Sammelladungsspediteur* 10.4 ■ **80**
constraint *Zwang* 15A ■ **118**
construction *Bauwirtschaft* 1.3 ■ **9**; **under construction** *im Bau* 2B ■ **16**
construction business *Bauunternehmen* 12.2 ■ **95**
consumer electronics *Konsumelektronik* 8B ■ **63**
consumer goods *Verbrauchsgüter, Konsumgüter* 2.7 ■ **17**
consumer preference *Verbrauchervorliebe* 8A ■ **60**
consumer-friendly *verbraucherfreundlich* 4.10 ■ **33**
consumption *Verbrauch* 15B ■ **120**
to contact *sich in Verbindung setzen mit* 4.4 ■ **29**
container crane *Containerladebrücke, Containerkran* 10.6 ■ **80**
container facility *Containeranlage* 10B ■ **82**
container vessel *Containerschiff* 10 Info ■ **84**
container-carrying barge *Binnenschiff für Containertransporte* 10B ■ **82**
containerization *Versand in Containern* 10.6 ■ **80**
contract *Vertrag* 6.1 ■ **44**; *(Termin)Kontrakt* 13.4 ■ **104**
to contribute *beisteuern, beitragen* 2A ■ **14**; *Beiträge entrichten* 11.11 ■ **92**
contribution *Beitrag* 2.7 ■ **17**
to control *bereit haben* 3B ■ **23**
convenience store *Nachbarschaftsladen* 7.3 ■ **52**
convenient *bequem* 3.7 ■ **24**
conversion *Umwandlung* 1A ■ **7**
to convey *vermitteln* 3.2 ■ **21**
to convince *überzeugen* 11B ■ **89**
cooperative *Konsum* 7.3 ■ **52**
cooperative society *Genossenschaft* 12A ■ **94**
to cope with *bewältigen* 6A ■ **44**
core inflation *Kerninflation* 13.12 ■ **109**
core rate *Kern(zins)satz* 13.12 ■ **109**
corn mill *(Getreide)Mühle* 6A ■ **43**
corner shop *Laden an der Ecke, Tante-Emma-Laden* 7.3 ■ **52**
corporate *unternehmerisch, Unternehmens-* 9.6 ■ **73**
corporate bond *Unternehmensanleihe* 13.6 ■ **104**
corporate culture *Unternehmenskultur* 6A ■ **44**
corporate decision-making *unternehmerische Entscheidungsprozesse* 15.4 ■ **119**
corporate earnings *Unternehmensgewinne* 13.11 ■ **108**
corporate investment *Investitionen der Firmen* 13.10 ■ **107**
corporate name *Unternehmensname* 3A ■ **20**
corporation *Kapitalgesellschaft* 9 Info ■ **74**
corporation tax *Körperschaftssteuer* 14A ■ **110**

D

F

federation *Bund* 3A ■ **21**
federation of car dealers *Verband der Autohändler* 15.12 ■ **124**
fee *Gebühr* 4A ■ **28**
field: to narrow the field *das Bewerberfeld einschränken* 5A ■ **36**
fierce competition *scharfer/harter Wettbewerb* 10B ■ **82**
to file *einreichen* 14A ■ **110**
to file for *beantragen* 12.10 ■ **100**
to file with *hinterlegen bei* 12A ■ **94**
finance management *Finanzwirtschaft* 5.7 ■ **39**
financial analyst *Finanzexperte* 4B ■ **31**
financial institution *Finanzinstitut, Bank* 4.8 ■ **32**
finished product *Fertigerzeugnis* 1A ■ **7**
fire service *Feuerwehr* 14.2 ■ **112**
first-quarter *im ersten Quartal* 12B ■ **98**
to fix *reparieren* 6B ■ **47**
fizzy *sprudelnd* 8B ■ **64**
flag: to fly the flag *patriotisch denken* 9 ■ **68**
flatbed wagon *Flachwagen* 10 Info ■ **84**
flavour *Atmosphäre, Anflug* 8B ■ **64**
fleet *(Fahrzeug)Flotte, Fuhrpark* 10.5 ■ **80**
flexitime *Gleitzeit, flexible Arbeitszeit* 5.12 ■ **41**
flight *Flug* 6B ■ **47**; *Flucht* 7B ■ **55**
flight schedule *Flugplan* 3B ■ **23**
to flock *in Scharen reisen* 16B ■ **131**
to flock back *zurückströmen* 3A ■ **21**
flooding *Überschwemmung* 11A ■ **87**
floor trading *Parketthandel* 13A ■ **103**
flow *(Wanderungs)Strom* 16B ■ **131**
flow chart *Ablauf-, Flussdiagramm* 5.3 ■ **37**
fluent *fließend* 5B ■ **38**
flyer *Prospekt* 8.5 ■ **62**
flying temper *Wutausbruch* 3A ■ **20**
FOB (free on board) *FOB (frei an Bord)* 10.5 ■ **80**
focus *Blick* 10B ■ **82**
to focus on *sich konzentrieren auf* 8 UPh ■ **62**
food requirements *Nahrungsmittelbedarf* 2A ■ **14**
food retail *Lebensmitteleinzelhandel* 8.9 ■ **65**
to foot the bill *die Zeche bezahlen* 14 Gr ■ **115**
footing *Basis* 9B ■ **72**
footprint *Spur, Einwirkung* 15A ■ **118**
for once *ausnahmsweise einmal* 13.4 ■ **104**
forecast *Vorhersage* 7B ■ **55**
foreign affairs *Außenpolitik* 16.4 ■ **128**
foreign trade *Außenhandel* 1.3 ■ **9**
forestry *Forstwirtschaft* 1.3 ■ **9**
to forfeit *verlieren, verlustig gehen* 14B ■ **113**
forklift truck *Gabelstapler* 10.6 ■ **80**
to forward *senden* 5.10 ■ **40**
forwarder *Spediteur, Versender* 10A ■ **78**
forwarding agent *Spediteur* 10.3 ■ **79**
forwarding service *Speditionsleistung(en)* 10A ■ **78**
fossil fuel *nicht erneuerbarer Brennstoff* 15 ■ **117**
to found *gründen* 1 Gr ■ **12**
fraction: a fraction of what it costs *ein Bruchteil der Kosten* 13A ■ **103**
fragmented: to be fragmented *mit vielen kleinen Banken* 4B ■ **31**
franchisor, franchiser *Franchisegeber,* 10.4 ■ **80**
free gift *Werbegeschenk* 8A ■ **60**
free of charge *kostenlos* 4A ■ **27**
freelancer *Freiberufler(in)* 6A ■ **43**
free-market economy *freie Marktwirtschaft* 1 Info ■ **9**
freight *Fracht* 10A ■ **78**
freight agent *Frachtenmakler, Spediteur* 10.3 ■ **79**
freight consolidation (operation) *Frachtbündelung, Erstellung von Sammelladungen* 10A ■ **78**
freight forwarder *Frachtführer(in), Speditionsunternehmen* 10A ■ **78**
freight note *Frachtbrief, LKW-Ladeschein* 10.5 ■ **80**
freight package *Frachtangebot* 10.14 ■ **85**
freight rate *Frachtsatz, Frachttarif* 10.2 ■ **79**
fresh *neu* 10.5 ■ **80**
friendly society *Unterstützungskasse, gemeinnütziger Verein* 12A ■ **94**
fringe benefit *freiwillige Sozialleistung* 5.12 ■ **41**
frontier *Grenze* 6B ■ **47**
fuel *Brennstoff* 2A ■ **14**
to fuel *antreiben* 7B ■ **55**
fuel tax *Treibstoffsteuer* 14A ■ **110**
full container load (FCL) *Container-Komplettladung* 10.5 ■ **80**
fully mechanized *vollautomatisiert* 10.6 ■ **81**
to fund *finanzieren* 14A ■ **110**
fund manager *Fondsmanager(in), Fondsverwalter(in)* 13.4 ■ **104**
furnishing *Einrichtung* 7.4 ■ **52**
further processing *Weiterverarbeitung, Veredelung* 10B ■ **82**
futures market *Terminmarkt* 13.4 ■ **103**

G

gaming industry *Glücksspielbranche* 2B ■ **16**
garbage *Abfall, Müll* 15.7 ■ **121**
gas *Benzin* 7A ■ **51**
general cargo *Stückgut, gemischte Fracht* 10.5 ■ **80**
general partnership *offene Handelsgesellschaft (OHG)* 12A ■ **93**
to generate *entstehen* 2B ■ **16**
giant *Großunternehmen* 6A ■ **43**
gift hamper *Geschenkkorb* 7.12 ■ **57**
gilt *Staatsanleihe* 13.4 ■ **103**
to give access to *Zugang ermöglichen* 4A ■ **28**
to glitter *glänzen, funkeln* 13.4 ■ **103**
global appeal *weltweite Attraktivität* 8B ■ **64**
global warming *Erderwärmung* 15 ■ **117**
globe *Welt* 3B ■ **23**
to go on to become *sogar ... werden* 6A ■ **43**
goal *Ziel* 11.2 ■ **88**
going public *Börsengang* 13.4 ■ **103**
goods storage *Güterlagerung* 10.6 ■ **80**
goods-in dept *Warenannahme* 5B ■ **38**
government bond *Staatsanleihe* 13.6 ■ **104**
government security *Staatsanleihe* 13B ■ **107**
gradual *allmählich* 12 V ■ **99**
graduate *Hochschulabschluss/Examen machen* 5.9 ■ **40**

graduate training programme *Traineeprogramm für Hochschulabsolventen(innen)* 5.7 ■ **39**
grain *Getreide* 10B ■ **82**
grain farming *Getreideanbau* 2A ■ **14**
grant *Beihilfe* 9 Info ■ **74**
greenhouse effect *Treibhauseffekt* 15 ■ **117**
groceries *Lebensmittel* 7B ■ **55**
gross *brutto* 12B ■ **98**
gross national income (GNI) *Bruttosozialprodukt (BSP)* 2A ■ **14**
gross national product (GNP) *Bruttosozialprodukt (BSP)* 2A ■ **14**
gross revenue *Bruttoeinnahmen* 2B ■ **16**
ground: to gain ground *Fortschritte machen* 12B ■ **98**
group *Konzern, Gruppe* 9B ■ **72**
groupage consignment *Sammelladung* 10.6 ■ **80**
growth industry *Wachstumsindustrie, Wachstumsbranche* 1A ■ **8**
guesswork *Ratespiel* 5A ■ **36**
gym *Fitnessstudio* 6B ■ **47**

H

habit *Gewohnheit* 3 Gr ■ **25**
habitat *Lebensraum* 15A ■ **118**
to handle *verantwortlich sein für, sich kümmern um* 10A ■ **78**
hard sell *schwer zu verkaufen* 1B ■ **10**
hard-hitting *zupackend, drastisch* 8.4 ■ **61**
hard-to-satisfy *schwer zufriedenzustellen* 4B ■ **31**
harmful *schädlich, umweltschädigend* 15A ■ **118**
haulage company *Spedition(sfirma)* 10.3 ■ **79**
haulier *Spedition(sfirma)* 10.3 ■ **79**
head of research *Leiter(in) der Forschungsabteilung* 4B ■ **31**
to head the list *die Liste anführen* 2.8 ■ **18**
headquarters *Hauptverwaltung* 6A ■ **43**
health care *Gesundheitsfürsorge* 1A ■ **8**
health insurance *Krankenversicherung* 11A ■ **87**
heap *Haufen* 15B ■ **120**
hedging *Kurssicherung* 13.4 ■ **103**
to herald *einläuten* 8.8 ■ **65**
heritage *Erbe* 8B ■ **64**
high street *Hauptgeschäftsstraße* 3A ■ **20**
high-bay warehouse *Hochregallager* 10.6 ■ **80**
high-cost *teuer, kostenintensiv* 9B ■ **72**
high-end *hochwertig, im oberen Marktsegment* 12B ■ **98**
high-powered *anspruchsvoll* 13A ■ **102**
high-profit *gewinnträchtig* 7.6 ■ **53**
high-tech industry *Hochtechnologieindustrie* 2A ■ **14**
high-tech skills *Kompetenz in moderner Technologie* 6B ■ **47**
high-value *hochwertig* 10A ■ **78**
hire purchase *Mietkauf* 11.2 ■ **88**
hiring *Anwerbung, Einstellung* 6.8 ■ **48**
holiday entitlement *Urlaubsanspruch* 5.12 ■ **41**
holidaymaker *Urlauber(in)* 3.4 ■ **22**
home decoration *Wohnungsausstattung* 8A ■ **60**
home sales *Verkauf von Wohnungen/Eigenheimen* 2B ■ **16**
honours degree *brit. Hochschulabschluss* 5.7 ■ **39**
hooked *gefangen* 14.9 ■ **115**
hooligan *Randalierer* 11.1 ■ **88**
hot spot *auffälliger Ort* 7.6 ■ **53**
household waste *Haushaltsmüll* 15B ■ **120**
housing *Wohnraum* 6B ■ **47**
hub *Zentrum* 2B ■ **16**
hub *Warenverteil-, Logistikzentrum* 10.12 ■ **83**
human resources manager *Personalleiter(in)* 5A ■ **36**
human resources officer *Personalsachbearbeiter(in)* 5.8 ■ **40**
hurdle *Hürde* 9.6 ■ **73**
hyperhip *voll angesagt* 6B ■ **47**

I

ill-judged idea *falsche Vorstellung* 5A ■ **36**
image-building *zur Verbesserung des Ansehens* 8A ■ **60**
immediate *drängend* 10B ■ **82**
impact *Auswirkung* 1.9 ■ **11**
impetus *Anstoß* 10B ■ **82**
to implement *(Gesetz) umsetzen* 16.4 ■ **128**
implication *Auswirkung* 15A ■ **118**
to impose *verhängen* 9.4 ■ **71**; *auferlegen* 15A ■ **118**
improbability *Unwahrscheinlichkeit* 12 Gr ■ **100**
impulse buy *Spontankauf* 7.6 ■ **53**
inbound *eingehend* 10A ■ **78**
incentive *Anreiz* 16A ■ **126**
to incinerate *verbrennen* 15B ■ **120**
incinerator *Verbrennungsanlage* 15.7 ■ **121**
income bracket *Einkommenssteuerstufe, Einkommenshöhe* ■ 14A ■ **110**
income receipt *Einnahme* 9 Info ■ **74**
income security [US] *Ruhegeldsicherung* 14.8 ■ **115**
income tax *Einkommenssteuer* 14A ■ **110**
inconceivable *unvorstellbar* 13A ■ **103**
inconvenient *lästig, schwierig* 4.10 ■ **33**
to incorporate *umfassen, einschließen* 10.12 ■ **83**
incorporated *eingetragen* 12A ■ **94**
increased productivity *Produktivitätssteigerung* 10B ■ **82**
to incur *(Kosten) entstehen* 14A ■ **111**
incurred *entstanden* 11.2 ■ **88**
to indicate *darauf hindeuten, erkennen lassen, anzeigen* 2B ■ **16**
indication *Hinweis, Anzeichen* 13.6 ■ **104**
indicator *Anzeichen* 2B ■ **16**
indispensable *unverzichtbar* 11.2 ■ **88**
to induce *veranlassen* 8.8 ■ **65**
industrial raw material *Industrierohstoff* 2.7 ■ **17**
inflationary pressure *Inflationsdruck* 13.11 ■ **108**
information technology (IT) *Informationstechnologie* 2A ■ **14**
to inherit *erben* 12.2 ■ **95**
inheritance tax *Erbschaftssteuer* 14A ■ **111**
in-house *firmenintern* 5.3 ■ **37**
in-house presentation *betriebsinterne Präsentation* 8.6 ■ **63**
initial public offering (IPO) *Börsengang, Erstemission* 13.4 ■ **103**

inland distribution *Inlandsvertrieb* 10B ■ **82**
inland navigation *Binnenschifffahrt* 10B ■ **82**
Inland Revenue [GB] *Steuerbehörde* 14.6 ■ **114**
inland waterway *Binnenwasserstraße* 10.7 ■ **81**
input tax *Vorsteuer* 14 Info ■ **112**
insight *Einblick* 5.9 ■ **40**
to inspire *auslösen, hervorrufen* 12B ■ **98**
instant access *direkter Zugang* 4A ■ **27**
Institute of Directors *brit. Arbeitgeberverband* 6A ■ **43**
in-store *ladeneigen* 7.7 ■ **54**
instruction *Anweisung* 4.4 ■ **30**
insurance *Versicherung* 1.3 ■ **9**
insurance agent *Versicherungsvertreter(in)* 1.3 ■ **9**
insurance broker *Versicherungsbüro, Versicherungsmakler(in)* 11B ■ **89**
insurance group *Versicherungskonzern* 11B ■ **89**
to insure *versichern* 1.10 ■ **12**
insured: the insured *Versicherungsnehmer(in), Versicherte(r)* 11A ■ **87**
insurer *Versicherungsgeber(in)* 11A ■ **87**
intangible *immateriell* 8B ■ **64**
integral part *integraler/fester Bestandteil* 10B ■ **82**
to interact with *wechselseitig einwirken auf* 15A ■ **118**
interdependent *wechselseitig abhängig* 9.3 ■ **70**
interest *Zinsen; Berechnung von Zinsen* 4A ■ **28**
interest earned *Guthabenzinsen* 4.4 ■ **29**
interest rate *Zinssatz* 13B ■ **106**
interface *Schnittstelle* 10B ■ **82**
interference *Einmischung* 1 Info ■ **9**
intermediary *Mittelsperson, Vermittler(in)* 11.2 ■ **88**
intermediate distribution centre *Warenverteilzentrum auf der Strecke* 10A ■ **78**
intermodal service/operation *kombinierter Ladungsverkehr (KLV)* 10B ■ **82**
intermodal transport *kombinierter Ladungsverkehr (KLV)* 10.9 ■ **83**
internship *(Betriebs)Praktikum* 5.14 ■ **42**
to interrogate *befragen* 5.8 ■ **40**
to intersect *durchkreuzen* 7A ■ **50**
to interview sb *Vorstellungsgespräch mit jdm. führen* 5A ■ **36**
inventory *Bestand* 2B ■ **16**
inventory holding *Lagerhaltung, Vorratshaltung* 10A ■ **78**
investigation *Untersuchung* 8.1 ■ **60**
investment returns *Kapitalerträge* 11A ■ **87**
invisible exports *Dienstleistungsausfuhr(en)* 9A ■ **69**
to involve *mit einbeziehen* 3A ■ **21**; *beinhalten* 10A ■ **78**
involved: to be involved in *beteiligt sein bei* 8A ■ **60**
inward investment *Ausländeranlage, Investitionen durch Ausländer* 9B ■ **72**
IPO market collapse *Zusammenbruch des Marktes für Börsenneulinge* 13.11 ■ **108**
iron ore *Eisenerz* 10.7 ■ **81**
irregularity *Unregelmäßigkeit* 12.10 ■ **100**
irrespective of *unabhängig von, gleichgültig* 11.2 ■ **88**
irresponsible *unverantwortlich* 15.5 ■ **121**
issue *Ausgabe* 3.5 ■ **24**; *Problem* 5A ■ **36**
IT (information technology) *Informationstechnologie* 5A ■ **36**
item *Posten, Stück, Artikel* 1 Gr ■ **12**; *(Wert)Gegenstand* 11.9 ■ **91**

J

job centre *Arbeitsamt* 5 ■ **35**
job content *Arbeitsinhalt* 5.12 ■ **41**
job description *Stellenbeschreibung* 5.3. ■ **37**
job loss *Arbeitsplatzverlust* 2A ■ **14**
job opportunity *freie Stelle* 5 ■ **35**
joint income *gemeinsames Einkommen* 14.3 ■ **112**
joint return *gemeinsame Steuererklärung* 14A ■ **110**
joint venture *Gemeinschaftsunternehmen* 9B ■ **72**; *gemeinsames Projekt* 11B ■ **89**
jumbo container vessel *Riesencontainerschiff* 10B ■ **82**
junior *Nachwuchs-* 5.10 ■ **40**
just-in-time (JIT) delivery *einsatzsynchrone Anlieferung* 10.6 ■ **80**

K

keyboarding skills *Fähigkeiten in der Texterfassung* 5.9 ■ **40**

L

labour costs *Arbeitskosten* 1 Gr ■ **12**
labour force *Arbeitskräfte* 2B ■ **16**
Labour Force Survey *Arbeitsmarktstudie* 6A ■ **43**
to lag behind *hinterher hinken* 2A ■ **14**
to land *finden, anwerben* 6B ■ **47**
landfill site *(Abfall)Deponie, Deponiestandort* 15B ■ **120**
launch *Markteinführung* 8.4 ■ **61**
to launch *einrichten* 7B ■ **55**
to lay down *niederlegen* 11A ■ **87**
to lay out *anlagen, planen* 7.6 ■ **53**
layer *Schicht* 15.5 ■ **121**
layout *Anlage, Aufmachung* 7.6 ■ **53**
leaflet *Flugblatt* 8.5 ■ **62**
to leak *Flüssigkeit abgeben, nicht dicht sein* 15B ■ **120**
leap *Sprung* 12B ■ **98**
to lease *pachten, verpachten* 7A ■ **50**
legacy *Geschichte* 8B ■ **64**
legal defence *Rechtsschutz* 11.2 ■ **88**
to legislate *Gesetze verabschieden* 16.4 ■ **128**
legislation *Gesetzgebung* 4.9 ■ **32**
leisure traveller *Urlaubsreisende(r)* 3B ■ **23**
to lend itself to *sich eignen für* 3.6 ■ **24**
level: to scale to new levels *zu neuen Höhen bringen* 1B ■ **10**
to levy *erheben* 14A ■ **110**
liability *Haftpflicht* 11.2 ■ **88**
liable *haftbar* 3.11 ■ **26**; **to be liable for** *(Steuer) unterliegen* 14A ■ **111**
to license *Lizenz/Konzession vergeben* 10.4 ■ **80**
license fee *Lizenzgebühr* 9 Info ■ **74**
licensee *Lizenznehmer(in)* 8B ■ **64**
licensing programme *Lizensierungsprogramm* 8B ■ **64**

lid: to take the lid off *Deckel abnehmen* 15B ■ **120**
life cycle *Lebenszyklus(dauer)* 15A ■ **118**
life insurance *Lebensversicherung* 11A ■ **87**
life policy *Lebensversicherungspolice* 11B ■ **89**
life policy proposal *Antrag auf Lebensversicherung* 11B ■ **89**
lifeblood *Lebensnerv; Haupterwerbszweig* 2B ■ **16**
lifespan *Lebensdauer* 8B ■ **64**
lifestyle: to pursue a lifestyle *Leben führen* 6A ■ **43**
lifestyle draw *Attraktivität der Lebensqualität* 6B ■ **47**
likelihood *Wahrscheinlichkeit* 11A ■ **87**
limited partnership *Kommanditgesellschaft (KG)* 12A ■ **94**
line: in line with *parallel zu* 6B ■ **47**
linguistic *Sprach-* 6B ■ **47**
link *Verbindung* 8.8 ■ **64**
liquid *Flüssigkeit, Flüssigstoff* 10 Info ■ **84**
listed *(börsen)notiert* 12A ■ **94**
livestock farming *Viehzucht, Viehwirtschaft* 2A ■ **14**
living proof *sichtbarer Beweis* 6A ■ **43**
load planning *Ladungsdisposition; Kapazitätsplanung* 10A ■ **78**
loan *Kredit, Darlehen* 9 Info ■ **74**
loan to customer *Kundenkredit* 11A ■ **87**
local authority *Kommunalbehörde* 14.1 ■ **111**
to locate *(sich) ansiedeln; errichten* 2A ■ **14**; *orten, ausfindig machen* 10A ■ **78**
location *Standort, Lage* 1A ■ **8**
to lock up *(Kapital) binden* 1B ■ **10**
lodging *Unterkunft* 7A ■ **51**
to log onto *einloggen* 7 Gr ■ **57**
logging *Holzeinschlag, Holzernte* 15A ■ **118**
long haul *Fernreise* 3A ■ **20**
long-term *langfristig* 3A ■ **21**
to look set to hit *höchstwahrscheinlich erreichen* 6B ■ **47**
loss: to operate at a loss *mit Verlust arbeiten* 11.2 ■ **88**
loss at sea *Schiffsunglück, Havarie* 11A ■ **87**
loss of limb *Verlust eines Glieds* 11.2 ■ **88**
loss of property *Vermögensverlust* 11A ■ **87**
lottery *Lotto* 7.7 ■ **54**
Low Countries *die Niederlande, Belgien und Luxemburg* 6B ■ **47**
to lure *anlocken* 6B ■ **47**

M

mail order house *Versandhaus* 7.3 ■ **52**
mailshot *Postwurfsendung* 8.5 ■ **62**
to maintain *aufrechterhalten* 11.9 ■ **91**
maintenance engineer *Kundendiensttechniker(in)* 6.8 ■ **48**
maintenance expense *Unterhaltungskosten* 14B ■ **113**
major *groß, bedeutend* 2.8 ■ **18**
majority *Mehrheit* 1 Gr ■ **12**
make *Marke* 7.8 ■ **55**
to make it *schaffen* 7 Gr ■ **57**
to make up *ausmachen, bilden* 1 Gr ■ **12**
mall *Einkaufszentrum* 7A ■ **50**
to manage *verwalten* 4A ■ **27**
managerial capacity *Leitungsfunktion* 6.6 ■ **47**
managing director *etwa: Vorstandsvorsitzende(r), Generaldirektor(in)* 3B ■ **23**
mankind *Menschheit* 15A ■ **118**
manufacture *Produkt/Erzeugnis* 2A ■ **14**
manufacturing *Fertigung, Produktion; gewerbliche Industrie* 1.3 ■ **9**
manufacturing facility *Produktionseinrichtung, Fabrik(anlage)* 9B ■ **72**
manufacturing sector *gewerblicher Sektor* 1A ■ **7**
margin *Handelsspanne, Gewinnspanne* 13A ■ **103**
market: to serve a market *Markt versorgen* 6B ■ **47**
to market *vermarkten* 8.2 ■ **61**
market domination *Marktbeherrschung* 3A ■ **20**
market leader *Marktführer* 3A ■ **20**
market research *Marktforschung, Markterhebung* 8A ■ **60**
market share *Marktanteil* 16A ■ **126**
market stall *Marktstand* 7.3 ■ **52**
marketing mix *Marketinginstrumentarium* 8.3 ■ **61**
marketmaker *Marktmacher(in)* 13A ■ **102**
marshalling yard *Rangierbahnhof* 10B ■ **82**
mastery *Beherrschung* 6B ■ **47**
to materialize *sich bewahrheiten* 16.3 ■ **127**
mathematics *Mathematik* 1 Gr ■ **12**
to maximize *bestmögliche/günstigste ... wählen* 10A ■ **78**
means of production *Produktionsmittel* 1 Info ■ **9**
to measure *messen* 2B ■ **16**
media advertising *Auschreibung in den Medien* 5.3 ■ **37**
medical expenses *Kosten für ärztliche Versorgung* 11.2 ■ **88**
medical record *ärztliche Unterlagen, Krankenakte* 11B ■ **89**
medical supplies *medizinische Güter* 10.13 ■ **84**
Medicare [US] *staatliche Krankenversicherung für Bürger über 65 Jahre* 14.8 ■ **115**
Mediterranean *Mittelmeer* 3A ■ **20**
medium of exchange *Tauschmittel* 1A ■ **7**
mega resort *Riesen-Freizeitanlage* 2B ■ **16**
memorable *einprägsam* 8.4 ■ **61**
merchandise *(Handels)Ware* 1 Gr ■ **12**
mere *bloß* 14 V ■ **115**
merger *Zusammenschluss* 7B ■ **55**
methane *Methan(gas)* 15B ■ **120**
Metropolitan Police *Londoner Polizei* 1 Gr ■ **12**
middleman *Mittelsperson, Mittler* 13A ■ **103**
midsession: at midsession *nach der ersten Hälfte des Handelstages* 13.7 ■ **105**
milestone *Meilenstein* 10.12 ■ **83**
mill *(Getreide)Mühle* 10.7 ■ **81**
mindshift *Sinneswandel* 15B ■ **120**
to minimize *minimieren, auf ein Minimum reduzieren* 15A ■ **118**
mistaken *irrtümlich* 8.4 ■ **61**
mixed-use *für gemischte Nutzung* 2B ■ **16**
mobile *Handy* 5B ■ **38**
mobile telephone *Handy* 7B ■ **55**

open market operation *Offenmarkt-Geschäft* 13B ▪ **107**
to operate *aktiv/tätig sein* 4B ▪ **31**; *funktionieren* 14A ▪ **111**
operating income *Betriebsergebnis* 12B ▪ **98**
operating margin *Gewinnspanne* 12B ▪ **98**
operating performance *Betriebsleistung* 12B ▪ **98**
operation *Aktivität, Betrieb* 10.2 ▪ **79**; *Funktionieren* 16.4 ▪ **128**
operational performance *Wirtschaftlichkeit, Rentabilität* 10B ▪ **82**
operator *Betreiber(gesellschaft)* 10.4 ▪ **80**
to opt *wählen* 8.3 ▪ **61**
to opt for *sich entscheiden für, wählen* 11.11 ▪ **92**
optimum balance *bestmögliches Verhältnis* 10A ▪ **78**
ordinary share *Stammaktie* 12.5 ▪ **97**
outbound *ausgehend* 10A ▪ **78**
outdated *nicht mehr zeitgemäß* 6A ▪ **43**
outlet *Geschäftsstelle* 4.9 ▪ **32**
to outpace *übertreffen, übersteigen* 2B ▪ **16**
output tax *Umsatzsteuer* 14 Info ▪ **112**
outside *Fremd-* 9.6 ▪ **73**
to outsource *fremdvergeben, an Dritte vergeben* 5A ▪ **36**
to outstrip *übertreffen, größer sein als* 6B ▪ **47**
outward investment *Investition(en) im Ausland, Auslandsinvestition(en) durch Inländer 9B* ▪ **72**
to outweigh *aufwiegen* 16A ▪ **126**
overcapacity *Überkapazität* 9B ▪ **72**
to overcome *überwinden, ausräumen* 1B ▪ **10**
overcrowded *überfüllt* 3A ▪ **20**
overdraft *Kontoüberziehung* 4A ▪ **28**
overdraft facility *Überziehungskredit, Dispositionskredit* 4A ▪ **27**
overhead *Folie* 8 UPh ▪ **62**
to overlap *sich teilweise decken, sich überschneiden* 10B ▪ **82**
overseas *ausländisch* 3.4 ▪ **22**
overseas sales *Absatz im Ausland* 10A ▪ **78**
to overtake *überholen* 1A ▪ **8**
overtime *Überstunden* 3.4 ▪ **22**
to overwhelm *überwältigen* 8B ▪ **64**
own brand *Eigenmarke* 7.6 ▪ **53**
ownership structure *Besitzverhältnis* 3A ▪ **21**
ozone layer *Ozonschicht* 15A ▪ **117**

P

package *Pauschalreise* 3A ▪ **20**
package company *Veranstalter von Pauschalreisen* 3A ▪ **20**
packaging *Verpackung(smaterial)* 8.3 ▪ **61**
pallet *Palette* 10.6 ▪ **81**
palletized load *Palettenladung* 10 Info ▪ **84**
palletizing *Verpackung/Versand auf Paletten* 10.6 ▪ **80**
pampering *Verhätschelung* 6B ▪ **47**
panorama view *Rundumsicht* 6B ▪ **47**
parachuting *Fallschirmspringen* 5B ▪ **38**
parcel *Paket* 10 Info ▪ **84**
parcel carrier *Paketdienst* 10.12 ▪ **83**
part *(Zuliefer)Teil* 10A ▪ **78**
partnership *(Personen)Gesellschaft* 12A ▪ **93**
part-owner *Teilinhaber(in)* 13A ▪ **102**
part-time *Teilzeit-* 5.9 ▪ **40**
party *(Vertrags)Partei* 11A ▪ **87**
passenger negligence *Fahrlässigkeit von Insassen* 11.2 ▪ **88**
patch *Stück* 3A ▪ **20**
pay package *Vergütung(spaket)* 5.12 ▪ **41**
payable *zahlbar* 9.4 ▪ **71**; **to make payable to** *(Scheck) ausstellen auf* 11.9 ▪ **91**
payee *Zahlungsempfänger(in)* 4.5 ▪ **30**
payroll *Gehaltsliste, Belegschaft* 6B ▪ **47**
peak *Höhepunkt* 3A ▪ **20**
to peak *höchsten Punkt erreichen* 13 V ▪ **104**
pension *Rente, Pension* 11A ▪ **87**
pension contribution *Rentenbeitrag* 14B ▪ **113**
people-based *mit Menschen zu tun haben* 5.10 ▪ **40**
per capita *pro Kopf* 2A ▪ **14**
percentage *Prozentsatz* 11A ▪ **87**; **in percentage terms** *prozentual, in Prozent ausgedrückt* 2.8 ▪ **18**
performance *Leistung* 9.11 ▪ **75**
perk *Vergünstigung* 6B ▪ **47**
permanent part *fester Bestandteil* 15A ▪ **118**
permission *Genehmigung* 11B ▪ **89**
personal accident cover *Unfallversicherung* 11.2 ▪ **88**
personal belongings *persönliche Habe* 11.2 ▪ **88**
personal injury *Personenschaden* 11.2 ▪ **88**
personal insurance *Personenversicherung* 11A ▪ **87**
personal loan *persönliches Darlehen, Kleinkredit* 4A ▪ **28**
personal profile *Persönlichkeitsbild* 5B ▪ **38**
personal risk *Personenrisiko* 11A ▪ **87**
personnel department *Personalabteilung* 5.3 ▪ **37**
personnel officer *Personalsachbearbeiter(in)* 5.8 ▪ **40**
to persuade *überreden* 8.1 ▪ **60**
persuasion *Überzeugung, Ausrichtung* 16.3 ▪ **127**
pet food *Haustierfutter* 7.7 ▪ **54**
petroleum *Rohöl* 2.8 ▪ **18**
pharmaceuticals *Arzneimittel, Pharmaprodukte* 1.3 ▪ **9**
to phase out *auslaufen lassen* 15A ▪ **118**
phenomenal *sagenhaft, unglaublich* 15B ▪ **120**
physical presence *tatsächlicher Laden* 7B ▪ **55**
to pick *kommissionieren* 10.6 ▪ **80**
pie *Pastete* 7.7 ▪ **54**
piece of equipment *Ausrüstungsgegenstand* 6.1 ▪ **44**
piece worker *Akkordarbeiter(in)* 6A ▪ **43**
piggyback service *Huckepackverkehr* 10 Info ▪ **84**
pile *Stapel* 5A ▪ **36**
pint *0,57 Liter* 7.10 ▪ **56**
place: to be in place *gültig sein, vorhanden sein* 16B ▪ **131**
planned economy *Planwirtschaft* 1 Info ▪ **9**
planning restriction *Planungsbeschränkung* 3A ▪ **21**
plant *Werk, Fabrik* 10A ▪ **78**
plastic-seeming *plastikähnlich* 15B ▪ **120**
player *Anbieter* 1B ▪ **10**
to plummet *stark fallen* 13 V ▪ **105**
to plunge *stark fallen* 13 V ▪ **105**

respective *jeweilig* 12A ■ **94**
respectively *beziehungsweise* 2.8 ■ **18**
to respond (to) *reagieren (auf)* 8A ■ **60**
response *Reaktion* 8B ■ **64**
to restrict *beschränken* 4B ■ **31**
restructuring *Umstrukturierung, Neuordnung* 4.9 ■ **32**
to result in *zur Folge haben* 11B ■ **89**
retail *Einzelhandel* 2B ■ **16**
retail consultancy *Einzelhandelsberatungsunternehmen* 7B ■ **55**
retail outlet *Einzelhandelsverkaufsstelle* 7.2 ■ **52**
retail pie *Einzelhandelskuchen* 7A ■ **51**
retail price inflation *Inflationsrate der Einzelhandelspreise* 13.12 ■ **109**
retail store *Einzelhandelsgeschäft* 2B ■ **16**
retailing *Einzelhandel* 1.3 ■ **9**
to retain *beibehalten* 1 Gr ■ **12**
retirement income *Ruhestandsbezüge* 14A ■ **110**
retrieval *(Produkt)Entnahme* 10.6 ■ **80**
retro flavour *Atmosphäre der Vergangenheit* 8B ■ **64**
return: in return *im Gegenzug* 1B ■ **10**
to reuse *wieder verwenden* 15A ■ **118**
revenue *Einnahme* 8B ■ **64**
Revenue *Steuerbehörde* 14B ■ **113**
revenue-raising *Einnahmen einbringend* 14A ■ **111**
revenues *Einnahmen* 10A ■ **78**
reversal *Umkehrung* 16B ■ **131**
review *Bestandsaufnahme* 15A ■ **118**
reviewing *Überwachung* 5B ■ **38**
revival *Wiederbelebung* 1B ■ **10**
to reward *belohnen* 11.1 ■ **88**
riot *Aufruhr* 11A ■ **87**
risk management *Risikomanagement* 5.7 ■ **39**
risk-sharing scheme *Risikostreuung* 11A ■ **87**
rival *Konkurrent(in)* 6B ■ **47**
road haulage *Straßengüterverkehr* 10 Info ■ **84**
road haulage association *Straßengüterverkehrsverband* 15.12 ■ **124**
road traffic accident *Verkehrsunfall* 11A ■ **87**
roadbuilding *Straßenbau* 1.3 ■ **9**
to rocket *stark ansteigen* 13 V ■ **104**
role: to take on a new role *in eine neue Rolle schlüpfen* 5A ■ **36**
roll-on/roll-off (RoRo) facility *RoRo-Rampe, Verladerampe für Straßen- und Schienenfahrzeuge* 10 Info ■ **84**
room rate *Zimmerpreis* 3.8 ■ **24**
room total *Gesamtbestand an Zimmern* 2B ■ **16**
rootlessness *Wurzellosigkeit* 16B ■ **131**
roundabout *Karussell* 15B ■ **120**
route *Weg* 3.5 ■ **24**
to route *(Telefonat) leiten* 6B ■ **47**
rubbish *Abfall* 15B ■ **120**
rubbish bin *Mülltonne* 15B ■ **120**
rug *(kleiner) Teppich* 11.2 ■ **88**
to run out of *nicht mehr haben, ausgehen* 7.13 ■ **57**

S

safe driver *unfallfreie(r) Autofahrer(in)* 11A ■ **87**
safe driver plan *Schadenfreiheitstarif* 11A ■ **87**
safety net *Sicherheitsnetz* 4A ■ **27**
safety stocks *Sicherheitsbestand* 10A ■ **78**
salary details *Gehaltsvorstellungen* 5.10 ■ **40**
sales executive *Sachbearbeiter(in) im Verkauf, Verkäufer(in)* 5.8 ■ **40**
sales manager *Verkaufsleiter(in)* 3.9 ■ **25**
sales seminar *Verkaufsseminar* 7.13 ■ **57**
sales tax *Umsatzsteuer* 14A ■ **110**
sales volume *Verkaufsvolumen* 7.9 ■ **56**
sample *Muster, Stichprobe* 8.5 ■ **62**
satellite-based *satellitengestützt* 10A ■ **78**
satisfactory *zufriedenstellend* 1.2 ■ **8**
saturation *Sättigung* 9B ■ **72**
savings *Ersparnisse; Einsparungen* 1 Gr ■ **12**
savings account *Sparkonto* 4A ■ **28**
savings component *Sparkomponente* 11A ■ **87**
savings on materials *Materialeinsparung* 15A ■ **118**
scale *Maßstab* 7B ■ **55**
scale: on a large scale *in großem Umfang* 2A ■ **14**
scarcity *Mangel* 7.2 ■ **52**
schedule *Plan, Programm* 12B ■ **98**
scheduled service *fahrplanmäßiger Dienst* 10 Info ■ **84**
scientist *Wissenschaftler(in), Experte, Expertin* 15A ■ **118**
scores *zig* 6B ■ **47**
screen *Leinwand* 8 UPh ■ **62**
screen-to-client technology *Methode der Vorauswahl per Video* 5A ■ **36**
seaborne freight *Seefracht* 10 Info ■ **84**
seaborne trade *Seehandel* 10B ■ **82**
seaborne transport *Seetransport* 10.7 ■ **81**
seaport *Seehafen* 10.5 ■ **80**
secondary production *Sekundärgüterproduktion, gewerbliche Erzeugung* 1A ■ **7**
secondary school *Gesamtschule, Gymnasium, Realschule, Hauptschule* 5.14 ■ **42**
second-rate *zweitklassig* 3.4 ■ **22**
sector *(Industrie)Branche, Industriezweig* 2A ■ **14**
to secure *gewährleisten* 13.10 ■ **107**
security *Sicherheit* 6A ■ **44**; *Wertpapier* 13A ■ **102**
security system *Sicherheitsanlage* 10B ■ **82**
to seek *bestrebt sein* 9B ■ **72**
to select *auswählen* 5A ■ **36**
selective *wählerisch* 16.B ■ **131**
self-conscious *selbstbewusst* 6.1 ■ **44**
self-employed *selbstständig (tätig)* 11A ■ **87**
self-sufficiency *Autarkie, Selbstversorgung* 9B ■ **72**
self-sufficient *autark, selbstversorgend* 1A ■ **7**
to sell up *(alles) verkaufen* 14B ■ **113**
semi-finished *Halbfertig-* 9.8 ■ **73**
senior executive *Führungskraft, leitende(r) Mitarbeiter(in)* 6A ■ **43**
sensible *vernünftig, zweckmäßig* 10.5 ■ **80**
sensitive *empfindlich* 10.10 ■ **83**
sensitive data *wichtige/geheime Daten* 6A ■ **44**
to serve as *fungieren als, die Rolle einnehmen von* 13A ■ **103**
service charge *Bearbeitungsgebühr* 11.9 ■ **91**

service package *Dienstleistungsangebot* 10.8 ■ **81**
set *Reihe, Satz* 8A ■ **60**
set: to be set to be *werden* 13.12 ■ **109**
set of figures *Statistik* Info ■ **15**
to set off *absetzen* 14.1 ■ **111**
to set up *einrichten* 4A ■ **28**
shake-up *Neuordnung* 3A ■ **20**
share dealer *Aktienhändler(in)* 13A ■ **102**
to share in *beteiligt sein an* 13A ■ **102**
shareholder *Anteilseigne(r), Aktionä(r), Gesellschafte(r)* 12A ■ **94**
shareholding *Aktienbesitz* 13A ■ **102**
to shelter *schützen* 16A ■ **126**
shift *Verschiebung* 1A ■ **8**
to shift *abwälzen* 14A ■ **110**
shipment *(Waren)Sendung, Versandpartie* 10A ■ **78**
shipowner user *Reedereikunde* 10B ■ **82**
shipper *Versender, Verlader* 10A ■ **78**
shipping agent *Reedereivertreter, Spediteur* 10.3 ■ **79**
shipping company *Reederei, Schifffahrtsgesellschaft* 10.3 ■ **79**
shipshape *blitzblank, tipptopp (sauber)* 10B ■ **82**
to shoot up *in die Höhe schnellen* 13 V ■ **104**
short: to be short of *Mangel haben an* 3.4 ■ **22**
shortage *Mangel* 3A ■ **20**
shortlist *(Vor)Auswahl* 5A ■ **36**
short-lived *von kurzer Dauer, kurzlebig* 13 V ■ **106**
showroom *Ausstellungsraum* 8.5 ■ **62**
to sign up *beitreten* 1B ■ **10**
to sign up for *sich entscheiden für, teilnehmen an* 4A ■ **28**
significant *bedeutend; bezeichnend* 4.10 ■ **33**
simplicity *einfache Struktur* 11B ■ **89**
Single Market *einheitlicher Markt* 16.3 ■ **127**
site *Webseite* 1B ■ **10**
skill *Fertigkeit, Kompetenz* 5A ■ **36**
skills gap *Facharbeitermangel* 16B ■ **131**
to slacken *nachlassen* 12B ■ **98**
slice *Stück, Scheibe* 13.4 ■ **104**
to slide *nachgeben* 13 V ■ **105**
to slip *leicht nachgeben* 13 V ■ **105**
to slump *stark fallen* 13 V ■ **105**
small and medium-sized enterprises *mittelständische Unternehmen* 5A ■ **36**
small business *kleines/mittelständiges Unternehmen* 11A ■ **87**
small-business *Kleinunternehmens-, mittelständisch* 1B ■ **10**
smelter *(Schmelz)Hütte* 15.12 ■ **124**
smelting plant *(Schmelz)Hütte* 15.12 ■ **124**
smokestack industry *alte Industrie* 2A ■ **14**
smooth *glatt; bequem, einfach* 4A ■ **28**
to smooth out *beseitigen, glätten* 16B ■ **131**
snapshot *oberflächlicher Eindruck* 5A ■ **36**
to soar *steil ansteigen* 6B ■ **47**
so-called *so genannt* 8.3 ■ **61**
social sciences *Sozialwissenschaften* 5B ■ **38**
social security *Sozialversicherung* 11.11 ■ **92**
soft drink *alkoholfreies Getränk* 7.4 ■ **52**
sole *einzig* 14 Info ■ **112**
sole proprietor *Einzelunternehmer(in), Einzelkaufmann/-frau* 12A ■ **93**
sole trader *Einzelunternehmer(in), Einzelkaufmann/-frau* 12A ■ **93**
sophisticated *anspruchsvoll* 8B ■ **63**
sort code *Bankleitzahl (BLZ)* 4.5 ■ **30**
sorting capability *Sortieranlagen* 10.12 ■ **83**
sound *stattlich* 8.2 ■ **61**; *solide* 16.4 ■ **128**
sovereignty *Souveränität* 16.12 ■ **132**
to space out *räumlich verteilen* 7.6 ■ **53**
spade *Spaten* 3A ■ **21**
speciality shop *Fachgeschäft* 7.10 ■ **56**
species *Tier- und Pflanzenart* 15A ■ **118**
specific *besonders* 8 UPh ■ **62**
specified *bestimmt* 4.4 ■ **30**
speculative investment *spekulative Anlage(form)* 13.6 ■ **104**
to speed up *beschleunigen* 11.7 ■ **90**
spirits *Spirituosen* 7.7 ■ **54**
split-level *auf zwei Ebenen* 6B ■ **47**
sponsored *gefördert* 6B ■ **47**
sponsorship *Fördertätigkeit* 8A ■ **60**
spouse *Ehegatte, Ehegattin* 11.2 ■ **88**
spread *Verteilung* 14.1 ■ **111**
square foot *0,09* m^2 ■ 7A ■ **50**
staff *Mitarbeiter, Personal* 5A ■ **36**
to staff *(personell) besetzen, mit Personal ausstatten* 6B ■ **47**
staff supervision *Überwachung der Mitarbeiter* 6A ■ **44**
stake *Anteil* 12A ■ **94**
stallholder *Standinhaber(in)* 13A ■ **102**
to stand out *sich auszeichnen* 8B ■ **63**
to stand to do sth *wohl etwas tun* 14.6 ■ **114**
standing order *Dauerauftrag* 4A ■ **28**
staple foods *Grundnahrungsmittel* 1 Info ■ **9**
start: to make a start *anfangen* 8 UPh ■ **62**
start-up *neugegründetes Unternehmen* 1B ■ **10**
state-of-the-art *modernst, allerneuest* 5A ■ **36**
state-owned bank *öffentlich-rechtliche Bank* 3A ■ **21**
statistics *Statistik* 1 Gr ■ **12**
statutory *gesetzlich (vorgeschrieben)* 11A ■ **87**
statutory goal *gesetzlich verankertes Ziel* 13B ■ **106**
steady *stetig* 6.1 ■ **44**
steel plant *Stahlwerk* 10.7 ■ **81**
stench *Gestank* 15.5 ■ **121**
to step down *zurücktreten* 12.10 ■ **100**
stevedore *Schauermann; Verladegesellschaft* 10B ■ **82**
to stick by *festhalten an* 12B ■ **98**
to stipulate *vertraglich vereinbaren/festlegen; fordern, verlangen* 11A ■ **87**
stock *Aktie* 12B ■ **98**
stock exchange *Börse* 12A ■ **94**
stock in hand *Warenlager, Warenbestand* 12.6 ■ **98**
stock level *Lagerbestand* 5B ■ **38**
stock management *Bestandsverwaltung, Lagerhaltung* 10A ■ **78**
stock market *(Aktien)Börse* 13A ■ **102**
stockbroker *Börsenmakler(in)* 13A ■ **102**

T

topsy-turvy *auf den Kopf gestellt* 15B ▪ **120**
tour operator *Reiseveranstalter* 3A ▪ **21**
to tow *abschleppen* 11.2 ▪ **88**
toxic *giftig* 10.13 ▪ **84**
toxin *Giftstoff* 15B ▪ **120**
track: on track *auf Kurs* 2B ▪ **16; to keep track of** *nachhalten, überwachen* 4A ▪ **28**
tracking and tracing *Sendungsverfolgung* 10A ▪ **78**
trade barrier *Handelsschranke* 9.3 ▪ **70**
trade fair *Handelsmesse, Fachmesse* 5 ▪ **35**
trade journal *Fachzeitschrift* 5 ▪ **35**
trade pattern *Außenhandelsstruktur* 9.3 ▪ **70**
trade ties *Handelsbeziehungen* 9 ▪ **68**
trademark *Markenname* 8B ▪ **64**
trading partner *Handelspartner* 2.10 ▪ **19**
trading room *Börsensaal* 13A ▪ **103**
trainee *Auszubildende(r)* 6.5 ▪ **46**
traineeship *Ausbildungsplatz* 5.7 ▪ **39**
trainers *Turnschuhe* 8B ▪ **63**
training course *Ausbildungskurs* 6B ▪ **47**
trainload *Zugladung* 10 Info ▪ **84**
tramp *Trampschiff* 10 Info ▪ **84**
transaction *Bankauftrag* 4A ▪ **28**
transaction fee *Bearbeitungsgebühr* 1B ▪ **10**
transfer *Überweisung* 4A ▪ **27**
to transfer *übertragen* 2.1 ▪ **15**; *umladen* 10B ▪ **82**
transferable *übertragbar* 16.8 ▪ **132**
transformer *Transformator* 10 Info ▪ **84**
transit country *Transitland, Durchgangsland* 16A ▪ **125**
to translate *umsetzen* 10B ▪ **82**
transparency *Folie* 8 UPh ▪ **62**
transport *Transportgewerbe, Transportwirtschaft* 2A ▪ **14**
transport chain *Transportkette* 10B ▪ **82**
transport equipment *Transportausrüstung* 2.7 ▪ **17**
transport facility *Transportausrüstung, Transportgerät* 10.2 ▪ **79**
transport mode *Transportart, Beförderungsart* 10A ▪ **78**
transport volume *Transportaufkommen* 10B ▪ **82**
to transship *umladen* 10B ▪ **82**
transshipment *Umladung* 10.6 ▪ **80**
trash *Abfall, Müll* 15B ▪ **120**
trashing *Abfallproduktion* 15B ▪ **120**
travel agency *Reisebüro* 3B ▪ **23**
travel arrangements *Reiseplanung* 5B ▪ **38**
travel insurance *Reiseversicherung* 4.4 ▪ **29**
travel spending *Reiseausgaben* 3B ▪ **23**
to trawl *absuchen* 6B ▪ **47**
Treaty of Rome *römische Verträge* 16.3 ▪ **127**
treaty-based *auf Verträgen basierend* 16.12 ▪ **132**
tremendous *riesig, enorm* 15B ▪ **120**
tribe *Stamm* 1A ▪ **7**
tricky *schwierig* 1B ▪ **10**
troubled *in Schwierigkeiten befindlich* 12B ▪ **98**
truck *LKW* 10.5 ▪ **80**
truck and trailer *Zugmaschine und Hänger* 10 Info ▪ **84**
truck fleet *Lieferwagenflotte* 10.12 ▪ **83**
turkey *Truthahn* 7.10 ▪ **56**
to take a turn *eine Wendung nehmen* 16.3 ▪ **127**
turnaround time *Umschlagszeit, Verweildauer* 10B ▪ **82**
turnover *Umsatz* 7B ▪ **55**
TV presenter *Fernsehredakteur(in), Fernsehmoderator(in)* 1.3 ▪ **9**
twin *Zwilling* 7A ▪ **50**

U

ultimately *letztlich* 9A ▪ **69**
unalterable *unveränderbar* 6.1 ▪ **44**
to uncover *entdecken, aufdecken* 15A ▪ **118**
underlying rate of inflation *Kerninflationsrate* 13.12 ▪ **109**
underlying trend *Grundtendenz* 13 V ▪ **106**
to undermine *untergraben* 12B ▪ **98**
under-retailed: to be under-retailed *zu wenig Einzelhandelsgeschäfte haben* 7A ▪ **50**
to undertake *leisten* 14B ▪ **113**
underwriter *Versicherungsgeber(in)* 11A ▪ **87**
underwriting *(Risiko)Absicherung* 11A ▪ **87**
unemployment *Arbeitslosigkeit* 11A ▪ **87**
unemployment benefit *Arbeitslosengeld* 11.11 ▪ **92**
UNESCO (United Nations Educational, Scientific and Cultural Organization) 9.9 ▪ **74**
uniformly *einheitlich* 16.4 ▪ **128**
unilateral *einseitig* 9 Info ▪ **74**
unincorporated *nicht eingetragen* 12A ▪ **94**
uninsured *unversichert, ungedeckt* 11A ▪ **87**
uninsured motorist coverage *Deckung bei Unfällen mit nicht versicherten Autofahrern* 11A ▪ **87**
unique *einzigartig* 16.12 ▪ **132**
unit price *Preis pro Anteil, Anteilspreis* 13.6 ▪ **104**
unit trust *Investmentfonds* 13.4 ▪ **103**
unlikely *unwahrscheinlich* 12 Gr ▪ **100**
unlikely: to be unlikely to do sth *etwas wohl nicht tun* 1B ▪ **10**
unprecedented *beispiellos, ohnegleichen* 1A ▪ **8**
unsolicited application *Initiativ-, Blindbewerbung* 5.3 ▪ **37**
to upgrade *verbessern, modernisieren* 10B ▪ **82**
upmarket *hochwertig* 7.8 ▪ **55**
uptrend *Aufwärtstrend* 13.6 ▪ **104**
urban *städtisch* 2B ▪ **16**
urban clothing *Kleidung für die Stadt* 8B ▪ **63**
urbanized *verstädtert* 2A ▪ **14**
to use up *aufbrauchen, aufzehren* 12B ▪ **98**
utilities *Versorgungsunternehmen* 1.3 ▪ **9**
to utilize *ausnutzen* 3B ▪ **23**

V

vacancy *freies Zimmer* 3.5 ▪ **24**
vacancy *freie Stelle* 6.10 ▪ **48**
value-added service *Mehrwert schaffende Dienstleistung* 10B ▪ **82**
value-added tax (VAT) *Mehrwertsteuer (MwSt.)* 14A ▪ **110**
valued *wichtig* 6.5 ▪ **46**
varied *verschiedenartig* 1B ▪ **10**

German–English word list

Diese deutsch-englische Wortliste bezieht sich auf die Übsetzungssätze am Ende jeder Unit.

abfinden: sich abfinden mit to put up with
abgelaufen past
abheben to withdraw
Arbeitsmobilität labour/occupational mobility
auf Grund because of
ausführen to carry out, to execute
ausliefern to deliver
ausschütten to distribute, to pay
Außenwand outer wall
Auswirkung impact
Bankgebühr bank charge
Bargeld cash, currency (US)
bedauerlicherweise regrettably
befördern to transport
Befürchtung fear
Begriff term
Beitrittskandidat candidate for accession
Beitrittsverhandlungen negotiations for accession
benötigen to require, to need
berechnen to determine, to assess
berücksichtigen to consider
beschäftigen to employ
beschäftigen: sich beschäftigen mit to be working on
bestellen to order
betreffend concerned
beziehen: sich beziehen auf to refer to
Binnenverkehr domestic transport
Börsengeschehen price movements (in the stock market)
Busreise coach trip
der Kreislaufwirtschaft zuführen to recycle
die Beschäftigten staff, workforce
Dienstleistungssektor service sector
eigentlich strictly speaking, really
Einbruch burglary
eindecken: sich eindecken mit to cover one's requirements
einfliegen to fly in
eingehen to arrive
eingetreten incurred
einheitlicher Wirtschaftsraum single market
einschreiten to intervene
engagiert committed
Englischkenntnisse proficiency in English
entfallen auf to account for
erforderlich necessary
ergiebig big, rich
erholen: sich leicht erholen to show signs of recovery
erschweren to make difficult
Erstellung development
etwaig any, possible
Europäischer Gerichtshof European Court of Justice
Festsetzung determination
Finanzbehörde finance authority
flächenmäßig in terms of surface area
Fortschritte machen to make progress
freisetzen to release
fusionieren to merge
gefragt sein to be in demand
gehalten sein to be required
Geheimnummer PIN (personal identification number)
geltend machen to claim
Gesamtbeschäftigtenzahl total number of people employed, employment total
Geschäftsergebnis company results
Gewinnerwartung profit expectation
Gewinnwarnung profit warning
Größenvorteil economy of scale
großzügig generous
Guthaben credit balance
Handelsbilanzüberschuss (balance of) trade surplus
Handlung action
Haupteinnahmequelle main source of income/revenue
Hausratversicherung home contents insurance
heimischer Markt domestic market
herstellende Industrie manufacturing industry/sector
Herstellungsverfahren manufacturing/production process
heutzutage nowadays, today
Hinterbliebene(r) dependant
Hotelier hotelier, hotel owner/operator
Hotelunterkunft hotel accommodation
Immobilie property
Immobilienpreise property prices
in der Regel usually, as a rule
in Prozentzahlen in percentage terms
Industrie- und Handelskammer chamber of industry and commerce
Interneteinzelhandelsunternehmen internet retailer
Investitionsgüterpreise prices of capital goods
Investitionstätigkeit investment activity
jdm. raten to advise sb
Kapitalanleger investor
Kapitalbilanz balance on capital account
Kartellbehörde cartel authority
Kaufverhalten shopping pattern/habits
Kleinanleger small private investor
Komplementär general partner
Konsumgüter consumer goods
Kreditbeschaffung borrowing
Kursanstieg rise

kurzfristig short-lived
Lebensqualität quality of life
leitende(r) Angestellte(r) executive
Linienfrachtschiff cargo liner
Markenartikel branded product
Marktuntersuchung market survey
Marktwirtschaft market economy
Massenprodukt mass (market) product
Mehrwertsteueraufkommen VAT revenue
milliardenschwer multi-billion
Müllverbrennungssystem waste incineration system
mutwillige Zerstörung vandalism
nach unten korrigieren to revise down(ward)
Nachbarstadt neighbouring town
Nachfrage demand
Nahrungsmittelpreis food price
Niedriglohnland low-wage country
Normcontainer standard container
offen legen to disclose, to reveal
öffentliche Ausgaben public expenditure
ohnehin anyway
Pauschalreise package tour
Personalberatungsfirma recruitment consultancy
Personalknappheit staff shortage
Prozentpunkt percentage point
prüfen to check, to examine
rasante Entwicklung rapid rise/increase
ratsam advisable
Restmüll residual waste
Rohstoff raw material, commodity
Rohstoffexport commodity export(s)
Rohstoffpreise commodity prices
Sanierung restructuring
Sättigung saturation
Schadensfall loss
Schlange queue
Selbstdisziplin self-discipline
Senkung lowering, reduction
Sparguthaben savings
Sprecherin spokeswoman
Standortwahl choice of location
Stelle besetzen to fill a vacancy
Steuerquelle source of taxation
subventionieren to subsidize
tauschen to swap, to barter
Teilhaber partner
Terminbörse futures market
überschwemmen to flood
Überseesendung overseas consignment
Überseeverkehr overseas transport
übertragen to charge with
umfassend comprehensive
Umverteilung redistribution
Umweltauflagen environmental regulations
Umweltdinge environmental matters/issues
Umweltverschmutzer polluter
unbefriedigend unsatisfactory
unbeschränkt fully unlimited
unterbreiten to submit
Unternehmensbeteiligung interest, stake (in a company)
ursprünglich originally
veranlagen: sich gemeinsam veranlagen lassen to file a joint tax return
veräußern to sell, to dispose of
Verbindlichkeit liability
Verbraucher consumer
verbringen to take
Verkaufserfolg sales performance
Verkehrspolitik transport policy
verlassen: sich verlassen auf to rely on
vermutlich probably, likely, presumably
Verpackungsart type of packaging
verrechnen to set off against
Verrechnungsscheck crossed cheque/check
Versicherung abschließen to take out (an) insurance
Versicherungsvertrag insurance contract, policy
verspätet delayed
vertreiben to distribute
verzollen to declare
vorhersagen to predict
Vorstand board of executive directors
VVaG mutual insurance company
Weihnachtsgeschäft Christmas business/trade
weitgehend largely
weithin generally, widely
Werbungskosten job-related expenses
Wertsachen valuables
Wirtschaftsgüter capital goods
Zinssatz interest rate
zufolge according to
zurückgehen to go down, to decrease
zurückhalten: sich auffallend zurückhalten to show conspicuous restraint
zurzeit at present
zwanzigjähriges Bestehen twentieth anniversary

Acknowledgements

Grafiken
Oxford Designers & Illustrators, Oxford

Cartoons
Austin: S. 30; Roger Beale: S. 45, 67, 114, 122; Louis Hellman: S. 55; Tom Husband: S. 41, 46; MATT: S. 112; Pilbrow: S. 111; RGJ: S. 100; Bent Thompson: S. 113;

Fotos
Titel: COMSTOCK, Getty Images/Keith MacGregor, Corbis/Jean Miele;
Action Press, Hamburg: S. 20/Atlas Photography, S. 77/Krüger;
Argus, Hamburg: S. 84/T. Raupach/P. Frischmuth;
Advertising Archive, London: S. 59 (2);
Automobile Association, Basingstoke: S. 61;
Janet Chipps, London: S. 53 (2);
COMSTOCK, Luxemburg: S. 32, S. 35, S. 48, 53;
Corbis Stockmarket, Düsseldorf: S. 10/MugShots, S. 20/J. Feingersh, S. 43/M. Barley/J.L. Pelaez Inc./L. Lefkowitz/C. Savage, S. 68/L. Lefkowitz,
S. 83/C. Savage, S. 102/A. Schein;
Das Fotoarchiv, Essen: S. 7/J. Meyer, S. 53/J. Tack;
dpa-Bildarchiv, Berlin: S. 107/F. May, S. 109/Keene, S. 127/B. Thissen;
Getty Images, München: S. 19/P. Chesley, S. 26/L. Monneret, S. 77/M. Wagner/D. Hughes;
Greenpeace Fotoarchiv, Hamburg: S. 117/Hodson;
IFA-Bilderteam, Düsseldorf: S. 84/Kopetzky/Diaf/TPL/Disc, S. 93/Krämer, S. 121/Jochem;
The Image Bank, Berlin: S. 31/D. Hamilton, S. 82/G. Cralle;
Photo Affairs, Deißlingen: S. 84;
Picture Press, Hamburg: S. 7/Corbis, S. 14/M. St Maur Sheil, S. 16/R. Cummins, S. 31/P. Gould, S. 50/51/O. Franken;
Premium, Düsseldorf: S. 13/MacKay (2);
Stock Food, München: S. 57/J.-P. Westermann/H. Bischof;

Textquellen
S. 10: The Economist Newspaper Ltd, London (21.10.2000); S. 16: www.ci.las-vegas.nv.us textfile/1316.htm; S. 20/21: The Observer (20.2.2000); S. 23: Business Life (October 1999); S. 29: The Independent (26.8.2000); S. 31: The Observer (May/June 2000); S. 43–44: Business 2.0 (December 2000); S. 47: Newsweek (3.4.2000); S. 50–51: www.mallofamerica.com S. 53: FoodFile ; S. 55: Financial Times (12.6.2000); S. 60–61: Principles of Marketing, by Brassington and Pettitt, ©Pearson Education Ltd 1997, 2000, reprinted by permission of Pearson Education Ltd; S. 63–64: Financial Times (26.5.2000); S. 65: Interbrand's 2000 Survey; S. 69: Britain 2001 – The Official Yearbook of the United Kingdom; S. 89: Financial Times (23.1.2001); S. 98: Financial Times (19.4.2001); S. 113: BBC on Air (Spring/Summer 2002); S. 118: Financial Times (June 2000); S. 120: BBC on Air (November 2000); S. 123: The Guardian (21.2.2001); S. 131: Financial Times (9.3.2001); S. 128–129: Europaparlament http://europa.eu.int; S. 141: The Guardian (4. 7.2000), Times Newspaper Ltd, London (3.2.2002); S. 142: The Guardian (27.6.2000), Harvey Jones/Times Newspaper Ltd, London (5.11.2000), P&O Princess Cruises plc, 2000; S. 143: International Herald Tribune (17.5.2001), The Scotsman (7.2.2002), The Guardian (12.5.2000); S. 144: Schweizer Touristik (November 2001), Süddeutsche Zeitung, Sylvia Englert (2./3.2.2002), Conference and Incentive Management 1/2000; S. 145: Frankfurter Allgemeine Zeitung (2.2.2002), Nachrichten-börse Deutsche Post (Juli 2001); S. 146: Westdeutsche Allgemeine Zeitung, Frankfurter Allgemeine Zeitung (26.2.2002);

Danksagung
Wir danken folgenden Firmen für die Bereitstellung von Bildmaterial:
S.9: British Petroleum, IBM, McDonald's, Volkswagen AG;
S. 59: NOKIA Mobile Phones Ltd
S. 71: Airbus Deutschland GmbH, Hamburg